TWICE
AROUND THE
BASES

◆

TWICE
AROUND THE
BASES

*The Thinking Fan's Inside
Look at Baseball*

KEVIN KENNEDY
WITH BILL GUTMAN

WILLIAM MORROW
An Imprint of HarperCollinsPublishers

HarperCollins books may be purchased for educational, business, or sales promotional use. For information please write: Special Markets Department, HarperCollins Publishers, 10 East 53rd Street, New York, NY 10022.

FIRST EDITION

Designed by Renato Stanisic

Printed on acid-free paper

Library of Congress Cataloging-in-Publication Data

Kennedy, Kevin, 1954–
  Twice around the bases: the thinking fan's inside look at baseball / Kevin Kennedy with Bill Gutman.— 1st ed.
     p. cm.
  ISBN 0-06-073463-9
1. Baseball. I. Gutman, Bill. II. Title.

  GV867.K46 2005
  796.357—dc22

05 06 07 08 09 DIX/RRD 10 9 8 7 6 5 4 3 2 1

To my gorgeous mother-in-law and sister-in-law, Minx and Cynthia, thank you for all the years of support and encouragement. And to my beautiful wife, Cathy, a special thanks for your caring support and love.

Contents

Foreword
BY ROGER CLEMENS

Playing for Kevin Kennedy was a totally enjoyable experience. It was apparent immediately that he knew the game, was extremely intense and thorough in his preparation, and wanted to win. To me he'll always be "the Skipper" and when I see him today I still call him Skip. That's more than just a nickname for a former manager. It's a real mark of respect, something he fully earned when he was at the helm of the Red Sox in 1995 and 1996.

Kevin was always extremely precise in the way he explained the finer points of the game and wasn't hesitant about telling the team how he wanted things done. You always knew just where you stood, as well as where he stood. At the same time, he always kept everyone focused and ready to play, yet would listen to his veteran players and was always straight with them. I was always completely honest with him in return and I think he appreciated that. He also had the ability to recognize when guys were starting to tighten up and knew the importance of getting them to relax and enjoy the game more if they wanted to win. That was one of his strengths, his ability to understand the various personalities on a twenty-five-man roster and to know the capabilities of each player. Because of that, he would put each guy in a role that would give him the chance to succeed.

I always enjoyed watching Kevin manage as well as listening to him during a game. A lot of guys like to sit at the far end of the bench, but I always sat closer to Kevin so I could hear the situational points he would make during each game as well as the comments he would pass on to us between innings. There were always these little tidbits that you could learn from that would help you sometime down the road. In other words he had a ton of baseball knowledge and you could absorb a great deal by listening to him closely.

He also cared deeply about his players. About thirty minutes before I was due to warm up for one of my final starts in 1996 he poked his head into the trainer's room. He knew I had a chance to tie Cy Young's Red Sox record for shutouts, and with the season winding down he felt this game with Detroit might be as good a chance as I'd have. He told me a story that he heard from Sandy Koufax years earlier, about how Maury Wills threw home in the ninth inning of a Dodgers blowout to cut off the run instead of going for the sure out at first. Maury told Sandy afterward he felt his pitcher deserved the shutout because he had to work so hard to win all those close games for the low-scoring Dodgers. Kevin then told me he would do the same thing, and if the situation called for it, would bring the infield in to cut off the run at home even though the book might dictate doing it otherwise. I was concentrating on a win, not a shutout, and when Kevin said that it meant a lot to me.

As the game went on I began thinking about the shutout and I remember peeking around a couple of times to see where the infield was. In addition to getting the shutout, that was also the game in which I tied my record of 20 strikeouts, so it was a pretty special night and Kevin's willingness to go against the book helped make it a little more special.

I can't talk about Kevin without touching on his intensity and desire to win. Sometimes, after a loss in which we played poorly, I knew we weren't going to eat because Kevin would come into the clubhouse and dump the spread all over the floor. He wouldn't do it when we played well and lost, but only if we had beaten ourselves and didn't play up to the level he expected from us. After dumping the food to get our full attention, he would let us know all about it, because he never wanted to give away a single game.

Now, of course, he's gone into broadcasting and I think what he's doing on radio and TV is great. He tries to bring many of the technical aspects of the game to his audience and gives them a better perspective about the things that are happening on the field. That's nice to hear. Many former players, managers, and coaches who make the switch to the broadcast booth tend to forget about their days on the field and just how difficult the game really is. I think that's because the game always looks easier from the stands or the booth. But Kevin has never forgotten his days as a player and manager, and he understands fully the speed at which the game is played and the skills needed to do it right. That's what separates him from so many of his peers.

I'll always have tremendous respect for him as one of my former managers. Managing a team at the major-league level is a difficult job and I've always felt that a good manager can figure in 20 to 25 wins a year with the proper strategies—positioning players, changing pitchers, calling particular plays at the right time. When you win your division by two or three games, you begin to realize just how important the manager is. A good manager not only has to put you in a position to succeed, but he has to do it for 162 games. That's something Kevin always did, day in and day out, and the reason I'll forever refer to him as Skip.

Introduction

I received a call from Tim Scanlan, ESPN's production coordinator for *Wednesday Night Baseball,* in January of 1997. The call came just three months after the Red Sox had let me go, so I was still dealing with losing my second managing job in the last four years and I wasn't sure what I wanted to do in terms of my career at that point. Tim, however, had remembered a game just before the All-Star break in 1996, when ESPN had me miked in the dugout. "If you can make those same observations on the air, that's great foresight," he told me.

I auditioned for ESPN with Charley Steiner, calling a taped game between the Rockies and the Padres, doing analysis during the last two innings. Coincidentally, two pitchers who came into the game late—Darren Holmes and Mike Muñoz—had pitched for me in the minors, so I was able to tell some stories about them. Knowing I had managed in the American League, the ESPN brass probably had me call a National League game to see if I knew the other league. I did, and I got the job.

I worked for ESPN for two years, the first year serving as an analyst on their late Wednesday night games as well as doing some studio work. In 1997, along with my television work I also broadcast the Sunday night games on radio, teaming with Charley Steiner, as well as the playoffs and World Series. Then in the winter of 1998, after being the runner-up to Davey Johnson for the Dodgers managing job, I decided that if I was going to make broadcasting a second career, I wanted to do it right. That meant being an all-around broadcaster and analyst, doing both TV and radio work, as well as hosting other types of sports shows.

About that same time I learned that the Fox network had some interest in me. They finally ended up offering me a package to do *Fox Sports News,* which was similar to *SportsCenter,* and I signed a two-year deal that allowed me to work out of my hometown of Los Angeles. I joined Fox in 1999 and have been there ever since. During this time I have approached broadcasting with the same drive and intensity that characterized my entire baseball career. I've also branched out and done work with many other sports and sports celebrities on Fox sports radio on a national basis year-round. *GameTime* has also given me the opportunity to talk with a variety of people, including actors and other nonsports celebrities. I've also been able to do a similar thing on television via Fox's *Best Damn Sports Show Period.*

People often see me on the Fox *Game of the Week* pregame show and ask how I got there. I've always felt it's the result of all the things that happened to me in baseball, all my experiences from playing in the minor leagues and in winter ball, then managing in the minors, Latin America, and finally the majors. By dealing with a variety of different personalities all those years I'm now comfortable interviewing people from all walks of life. I also listened carefully and learned from guys like Jon Miller, Chris Berman, Charley Steiner, and Vin Scully, from former players like Joe Morgan and Tim McCarver, and from all the other professionals with whom I've had contact. I not only wanted to learn how to do it, I wanted to learn how to do it right.

So I never really looked at broadcasting as a stop-gap job. Being a former manager, I know how success can come and then go away just as quickly. But right now, I look at being behind the mike as a second career. Good managing jobs are hard to come by, but so are good jobs as lead analysts. There are a lot of people out there who would love to have my job now, so I don't plan my life around waiting for another managing job. I have a great job now and have the same kind of passion for it that I had when managing.

Has broadcasting changed the way I look at managing? No, not really. I always felt I knew how to win as a manager, and as a broadcaster I have been able to see the way other managers run their ball clubs. I agree with some, disagree with others, but always remain aware of where I am. The game looks easier when you're sitting up in the booth, and it's always very easy to criticize, almost too easy. The trick in broadcasting is to explain *how* and *why*. I don't just tell the audience that someone threw a ball away, I try to tell them how and why he threw it away. I've also critiqued other broadcasters who don't explain why. If you're going to say that a guy is no good, you'd better be damned ready to back that up by explaining why he's no good.

Now I've reached the point where I really enjoy doing the sitdowns, the extended one-on-one interviews. My feeling is that because I've been there and done that, and understand the athletes' world, they'll open up to me in a candid and different way. Having been a broadcaster for some eight years now, I appreciate the talent of the players even more. As a manager, you deal with your own team and your own players, but now I get to see and talk with players from all teams, and I'm able to break down their skills on a consistent basis. For example, I've now seen enough of a top hitter like Albert Pujols up close to break down his swing completely, from the time he loads up to when he follows through. I couldn't do that while managing in the American League. As a broadcaster, I see the game from another perspective and have come to appreciate great talent even more.

In the following pages I'll be talking about my baseball life before broadcasting, touching on a number of areas of the game, things I have learned and experienced over my four-decade involvement with the national pastime. I'll discuss how baseball players and teams have always tried to get an *edge,* in ways both ethical and otherwise, finally leading up to today's controversy involving performance-enhancing drugs. I'll also tell you about how playing and managing in the Latin American winter leagues is as much a culture clash as it is a chance to gain valuable baseball experience.

You'll also learn about my four years behind the bench, managing in both Texas and Boston, and how a good ol' boys' network often dictates hirings and firings. You'll discover the importance of working with people you know and trust. Otherwise, you'll find yourself on a managing merry-go-round, one I decided to get off once my tenure in Boston ended. And I'll also talk about the great players I've seen through the years, picking the best hitters and pitchers, and the most complete players, and taking you back to revisit the greatest baseball games I've either witnessed, played in, or managed.

Broadcasting is, in a sense, my second trip around the bases. I may be on the outside looking in, but I'm still part of a game I have always loved and respected. Baseball will always endure and continue to turn out great players in the same traditions that began more than a hundred years ago. All of us who play, coach, manage, broadcast, or just watch love baseball for what it has been, what it is, and what it will continue to be in the future.

Author's Note

As this book went to press, baseball's steroid scandal continued to make headlines on the nation's sports pages and talk shows. I have certainly expressed my feelings about performance-enhancing drugs and how their use has put many of the home run feats and records set since 1998 under possible suspicion. At the same time, I have spoken about my personal relationships with a number of players who now may be looked upon differently, especially Jose Canseco, and talked about some of the reasons they, and other stars, are such outstanding hitters.

Obviously, I cannot qualify every positive comment with the caveat that possible steroid use might have played a part because I simply don't know. With the admissions by Canseco and the late Ken Caminiti, and the stories coming out of the BALCO investigation, there is no longer the slightest doubt that a number of major-league players have been using these substances in an attempt to improve their performance. But this book is not about speculating on who did and who didn't. As a manager and now as a broadcaster, I never witnessed any player in the act of using performance-enhancing drugs.

Therefore, most of my observations and comments are based on my personal interactions with these players and what I saw them accomplish on the playing field. A player's batting style and technique is what it is, as well as the starting point for anything he accomplishes as a hitter. So in most cases, I'm going by what I have personally seen, and any comments about players using performance-enhancing substances are based on what I have learned and been told, as well as the result of what has already been made public in the media.

TWICE
AROUND THE
BASES

◆

CHAPTER ONE

◆

Getting the Edge, Any Way They Can

Suppose the team has played twenty days in a row. The players are tired and the pitching staff is thin. A couple of guys have tender hamstrings. What the home team could really use is a rainout, giving everyone a day off. According to the rules of Major League Baseball the manager of the home team has the right to call a game right up to start time if he feels the field is not in playing condition. If it rains early in the day all they have to do is leave the field uncovered and even if the rain stops, it might be too wet to play. They've got their rainout and another way to give the team an edge.

It's no secret that getting the edge has always been a way of life in baseball. If a player or a team can find even the smallest advantage, a little something that might help them win, they'll usually use it. Ty Cobb's reputation for sharpening his spikes and coming into a base high and hard probably led to more than one infielder backing off just enough to let him slide in safely. Whether Cobb spiked the infielder or not didn't matter. The perception that he would use his spikes as a weapon gave him a decided edge on the base paths.

Being a fan first and then a player, I learned very quickly that things in baseball were not always what they seemed to be. I remember being shocked in the early 1960s when I saw my favorite player, Maury Wills, smoking a cigarette in the runway of the dugout between innings. It wasn't until years later that I learned he smoked because it relaxed him, allowing him to play better. Right or wrong, players always have a reason for most everything they do.

I learned firsthand about getting the edge a few months before the Orioles made me an eighth-round draft pick in 1976. I was a catcher out of San Diego State and coming off two great collegiate years, so I figured I'd be picked pretty high in the amateur draft. I knew the Orioles were interested because the local bird-dog scout who had first spotted me always told me when Ray Poitevint, Baltimore's Western Regional scouting supervisor, would be at the game. "Give me a couple of good throws today, Kevin," he'd say. "Poitevint's gonna be here."

Then one day he came up and asked me to fill out a scout card. It contained basic information—birth date, height, weight, and whether I was a right-handed or left-handed hitter and thrower. After I filled out the card, the scout looked at it and shook his head. "Uh-uh," he said. "Gonna change this five to a nine."

I didn't know what he was talking about. I was born on May 26, 1954, and had written "5/26" on the scout card. By making the 5 a 9, he was changing my birthday, making me four months younger. At first I couldn't understand why it was important, but he was quick to tell me.

"Think about it, Kevin," he said. "The draft is on June 4. It looks a lot better if you're a twenty-one-year-old senior than a twenty-two-year-old senior. It might even mean being drafted higher."

Talk about a small edge. At the time it was an almost meaningless move to me. Yet I would learn over the years that it did mean something—valid or not—because there was such an emphasis on getting not only the most talented, but also the youngest, kids possible into the organization. So I went in and negotiated as a twenty-one-year-old. In fact, my very first baseball card had my birth date listed as September 26, before it was finally corrected.

Age is just one of many ways players, teams, managers, scouts—everyone involved in baseball—try to get that little extra edge that will help them succeed and win, even though the rationale behind these decisions doesn't always make sense. Let's face it, a great player who comes up to the majors at twenty-five will produce more in a shorter time than a mediocre player who makes his big-league debut at nineteen or twenty. While it doesn't take a genius to understand that, most teams still look for youth. That's why so many Latin American players coming in have changed their ages over the years. It's much easier to change or create a new birth certificate in a third world country, where records are not kept so closely. However, 9/11 has changed all that.

Some Latin players who don't get their big-league shot until a bit later in life feel they have a better chance to get a real look and sign a long-term contract if they appear to be three, four, maybe even five years younger than they actually are. Pitcher Ramon Ortiz was born in 1973, but when he was first signed by the Angels, the club thought he was two years younger. When Orlando Hernandez, "El Duque," defected from Cuba and joined the Yankees several years ago, everyone knew he was older than he claimed to be. The Yankees always listed his birth date as October 11, 1969, while the Baseball Reference Web site has it as October 11, 1965. Most feel this second date is closer to being the correct one. Either way, the Yankees had done their homework. They knew how he could throw, and he has proved to be a great big-game pitcher.

Advantages are gained in other ways, too. A few years ago both the Dodgers and Yankees offered more money to Miguel Cabrera, who was from Venezuela, but he signed with the Florida Marlins instead. It turned out that someone from the Florida organization had been good to his family and that had impressed him. There's that edge again.

Scouts will often go in and befriend families and kids even before they can sign at sixteen, the minimum age. In fact, they're now watching kids from the Latin countries at thirteen, fourteen, and fifteen because some of them are already showing so much promise. Often the scouts move very quickly because the competition for the best Latin players has become so intense. Adrian Beltre was just fifteen when he signed with the Dodgers. The organization might not have known it at the time, but apparently someone went to him and said that if he could produce a birth certificate that said he was sixteen, the club would sign him. Presto!

When Ichiro Suzuki announced that he wanted to come to the

United States, teams had to bid for the rights to negotiate with him, paying money to his Japanese team. That's because he had played just nine years in Japan, and it takes ten to become a free agent. The Mariners wound up offering more than anyone else, in effect paying for the right to be the first team to try to sign him. The bid was in the $13 million range. Yet when both Matsuis (no relation) decided to come over, Hideki in 2003 and Kaz in 2004, they were able to call their own shots and were free to negotiate with any team. That's because both had played ten years, and their contracts with their Japanese teams were up and they were free agents.

Many of these foreign players want to show their stuff immediately, and that usually means signing with a high-profile, big-market team that wins. (Can you spell Y-A-N-K-E-E-S?) Therefore, a select number of teams have a huge edge in signing the best foreign players, a situation that sticks in the craw of the other teams. When Jose Contreras defected from Cuba and subsequently signed with the Yanks, Boston's Larry Lucchino was so upset that he dubbed George Steinbrenner's team "the Evil Empire." But Contreras, like so many foreign players, knew about the Yanks' mystique and thus wanted to play in New York.

Unless the rules change, these top foreign players will likely continue to pursue the most successful big-market major-league teams. Not only do these clubs give the players a better chance to win and showcase their talents, but they are able to offer more money as well. Incidentally, both Contreras and Orlando Hernandez were both free agents because they didn't come to the United States after defecting. They went to other Latin American countries and established residence. Had they come to, say, Florida, they would have been subject to the first-year draft, had no choice in deciding which team to sign with, and made considerably less money.

Like I said, a guy starting out at twenty-three or twenty-four can always have a great career, but the question How old is he? is still asked as soon as a new player comes up, especially at the lower levels. If a kid who is eighteen has the same ability as a guy who's twenty-one, the team's going to keep the eighteen-year-old. Youth is definitely viewed as an edge, but it shouldn't be an absolute.

Tobacco, Booze, Greenies, and the Rest

Baseball players have always been known for chewing, spitting, and drinking. Whether it's gum, sunflower seeds, tobacco, coffee, Gatorade, water, or beer, ballplayers have always been associated with these things, which are often used to help players relax, stay cool, and even to escape. These substances are used by players trying to perform better on the field and hoping to find a competitive advantage.

When I spotted Maury Wills lighting up cigarettes in the runway of the Dodger dugout between innings, I began to understand why players use a variety of substances as part of their overall baseball lifestyle. Wills smoked during the game to relax, but whether it's perception or hard fact, almost everything a player does is geared to giving him an edge, no matter how small or slight it might seem or really be.

When I played at San Diego State in the 1970s there were already players chewing tobacco. Some guys said it relaxed them; but others claimed it gave them a little buzz and acted as a pick-me-up. When you first try it—whether chewing a wad or just putting some smokeless tobacco between the cheek and gum—it does give you a buzz. Some guys who used it said they didn't feel the pressure as much. Whether it's tobacco, gum, or sunflower seeds, players use these things to relax. As for whether it's addictive or not, that's another story. By now, certainly, every player should know the potential dangers of chewing tobacco.

I never chewed tobacco, maybe because the one time I tried it was a horrible experience. It happened in 1976 when I was promoted from rookie league up to Double-A after just a few weeks. Blake Doyle, twin brother of former major leaguer Brian Doyle, was my teammate on the Charlotte Orioles, and one day when we were waiting out a rain delay he offered me a pouch of chewing tobacco. I figured why not, let's see what this is all about. Besides, the way it was raining it didn't look like we had any chance of continuing the game. So I tried a full wad. Within ten minutes I was dizzy and sick to my stomach. I'll never forget what a lousy feeling it was. Unfortunately, that isn't the end of the story. The guys really set me up. They knew the vagaries of the weather and field conditions there, and sure enough, the rain stopped shortly afterward. The field dried almost instantly and within a half hour we were playing again. I had to catch the rest of the game with that sick feeling in my stomach, and I never chewed tobacco again. While setting me up for a typical baseball joke, Blake and the boys actually did me a big favor.

But chewing and smoking are just the tip of the iceberg, small ways for players to relax and hopefully play better. There's much more. From rookie ball right through Triple-A I often heard players talk about "red juice." Though I'm not sure if it was the same thing, I once took a vitamin B_{12} shot that was red in color. The purpose was to help give a boost to those guys who were run-down and fatigued during the second half of the season. The baseball season is a marathon, and in the minors you play virtually every day with little or no time off. Oddly enough, the one time I took the shot, I didn't feel any different, so that was the last time.

"Greenies" were a different story. I first began hearing about them in Triple-A. It seemed that the higher you went in the minor-league system, the more things you were offered to help you improve your performance. Greenies, better known as amphetamines or uppers, were supposed to give you the energy to get through the long season. In 1978 I was playing for the Rochester Red Wings, a Triple-A team in the Orioles organization, and we had a veteran player with us then, a guy who swung between the majors and Triple-A. He was a real seasoned pro, especially in our eyes. I remember it being a rainy year on the East Coast and we were losing a lot of games to the weather. One day, just after another game was canceled, this guy came up to me, obviously pissed off. "Hell," he said. "I already took my greenie and we're rained out."

Why was he upset? Simple. With greenies, guys were always trying to time it just right, and the rain sometimes made it tough. "If I take my greenie too early and we're rained out, I'll be up all night," guys would say. "Got to be sure we'll play before I take it." That's why even this veteran player was annoyed. He knew he'd have a rough time sleeping that night.

Most players felt the greenies helped them get through the dog days late in the season when everyone was usually dragging. Obviously, taking these pills can lead to a dependency, but back then this possibility wasn't something that was talked about. You knew who took them and who didn't, but no one made it a clubhouse topic. I don't think the baseball establishment was too concerned with greenies at that time, because they certainly didn't do anything about it. Even today, with the current drug policy, greenies, or amphetamines, are not included on the testing list. But they should be.

Down in winter ball, trainers would sometimes spike the coffee with another amphetamine. If the team was performing poorly, the coffee would suddenly take on a slightly different taste. Baseball was a big gambling sport down in Latin America in the 1970s, as it still is today, and some of the trainers were definitely not *trainers,* if you get my drift. Everyone always drank the coffee from little plastic cups, and once in a while someone would take a sip and say, "Uh-oh, the coffee's spiked tonight." In fact, I also remember hearing that some of the local players, even some of the local coaches, were occasionally the guilty parties, adding something to the coffee to wake up the team. There were probably more than a few bucks, or pesos, riding on the outcome of the game that night.

Players also often drink straight coffee during games, again to give them a little caffeine boost. In fact, I used to drink it during games as a manager. Does it give you an edge? Probably not, but sometimes all it takes is for you to think it does. If you're convinced coffee gives you an edge and makes you a little more alert, then it just might.

Not surprisingly, Major League Baseball has always been more concerned with cocaine and marijuana use. Many players, however, began using these drugs for the same reason they chewed tobacco or took greenies. When I got to the Dodgers' Triple-A team at Albuquerque in 1982, some of the pitchers were already talking about Steve Howe, who had been with the parent club since 1980. Howe's problems with cocaine are now well documented, but it was obvious he had a problem even back then, and I was told he would snort cocaine in the bullpen before entering the game in the ninth inning, saying later that it made him feel he could conquer anything.

In the majors back then there were other guys actually doing coke during games. Even though most minor leaguers couldn't afford it then, because coke had become so fashionable as a designer drug of choice at that time, guys were getting caught up in it. It made them fearless, but this false bravado was in no way going to make them better ballplayers. In fact, it would eventually destroy careers. It came close to doing that to Steve Howe, though he was given a number of second chances. Without cocaine, he might have become the best closer of the 1980s.

In the minors, we used to have meetings about coke. Sometimes FBI agents would come in to talk with us, reminding everyone that coke was an illegal drug. They also warned us about consorting with the kind of shady characters who might try to set us up. Some of these undesirable people were well aware that top minor leaguers were possibly on the verge of making a lot of money, so what better than to get them hooked early.

Maybe it was because they were located in Los Angeles, but the Dodgers were always a very proactive organization when it came to drugs. They even used scare tactics at some of the minor-league meetings, gathering a couple hundred young players in a big auditorium every spring and bringing in guys to warn us about various dangers and potential pitfalls. Sometimes they would have people there who had done illegal drugs or gambled, and maybe trashed their careers. It was a strange era in some ways, but I think these meetings helped. They were all-encompassing, and if the young players were receptive to getting the message, they would respond to it.

It also helped that you could drug-test in the minor leagues then, though not in the majors. When I managed in the minors from 1984 to 1991, we did a lot of drug testing. If guys tested positive, whether for marijuana or cocaine, the Dodgers would get them counseling. If a player refused or didn't want help, then he was released.

Marijuana was, of course, a separate problem. I had a roommate back in 1979, when I was still playing, who always smoked a couple of joints before we left for the ballpark. Because I wasn't into that at all, I asked for another roommate. The guy hit around .350 at Albuquerque one year, actually led the league in hitting, but a year later he hit about .250 and was missing a lot of routine ground balls at first. By this time he was playing high all the time, and the results were obvious.

I've also known guys who had a couple of beers before games and even one big-league manager in a tough city who used to drink a six-pack before his team took the field. The clubhouse man said he used to see him firing them down, and the pitchers could smell it on his breath when he went out to the mound.

Beer has always been an accepted part of the game. Players drink. I'd sometimes have a beer after a game, but never before. I remember when I was at Triple-A Rochester, there was always a full keg of Genesee Cream Ale or Miller Genuine Draft in the clubhouse after games. Both were team sponsors, and we used to sit and drink a few beers while talking baseball. It was almost a ritual, and because we were talking baseball we learned from each other. It's no secret that there has always been a degree of alcoholism among ballplayers, just as there is in the rest of society. Drinking has been part of sports for a long time. It depends on the individual whether he will allow it ultimately to hurt his performance and his game. But no way, however you spell it out, will alcohol or drugs give a player an edge of any kind in the long run.

Steroids and Performance-Enhancing Drugs

Steroids and similar performance-enhancing drugs are *the* big story in baseball right now. President Bush mentioned steroids in his 2004 State of the Union address, asking all sports to take steps to eliminate them and individual athletes to stop using them. Unlike alcohol, marijuana, and cocaine, anabolic steroids *can* give a player a definite physical edge. I've had players tell me that steroids make them feel like King Kong, that they can lift a thousand pounds.

Steroids, by their very nature, build muscle mass. I think that's one reason some players are hurt all the time. Though they certainly become stronger, they sometimes develop too much muscle mass for their body structure, causing the ligaments and tendons to break down, or muscles to pull. A number of doctors, including one in Texas in the 1990s, have talked about this with me, linking steroids with injuries such as complete muscle tears and also equating an increase in injuries to steroid use. Unfortunately, that isn't stopping athletes, not when sports in general is throwing around enormous amounts of money, offering a chance for young guys to set themselves up financially for life. Many players will do almost anything to find that kind of security.

Young players think they're going to live forever. They don't even think about becoming fifty or sixty years old. *Nothing is going to happen to me* is their prevalent way of looking at life. The young player today knows he has the opportunity to compete, win a job, get the big $60 million, five-year contract, then retire in his late thirties and have security for the rest of his life. It's no secret that steroids can give a hitter more power simply because they make him stronger. Steroids can also give a player a mental edge, letting him feel as if he can hit any pitch thrown to him, and they are known to speed up recovery time, allowing older athletes to work out more and bounce back quickly from many of the aches and pains associated with aging.

Jose Canseco told me just a couple of years ago that he took steroids when he came up in the late 1980s, and he also intimated that no one who suspected him of using steroids discouraged him from introducing other players to the most effective ways of using them. Ken Caminiti, before dying of a drug overdose at the age of forty-one, admitted publicly that longtime steroid use had ruined his life. Among other things, Caminiti said his continual use of steroids made him impotent. Studies have also shown that the use of steroids can lead to heart and liver damage, strokes, elevated cholesterol levels, and mood swings and aggressive behavior.

Canseco and Caminiti have been the most vocal and outspoken former players to talk about widespread steroid use even though a lot of people don't believe them. But looking around the league you sometimes have to wonder. If you check out tapes of games just fifteen years ago, the players on a whole were thinner and smaller, not as thick and sculpted. That's a fact.

After the 2003 season, a federal grand jury began investigating a West Coast–based company called the Bay Area Laboratory Co-Operative, BALCO for short. It was suspected of dispensing performance-enhancing drugs to athletes. Targets of the grand jury probe were BALCO founder Victor Conte and Greg Anderson, who was Barry Bonds's personal trainer. Several baseball stars, including Bonds and the Yankees' Jason Giambi and Gary Sheffield, were called to testify. None of the players publicly admitted the use of steroids, but suspicion continued to grow among baseball people.

At the start of the 2004 season, a number of players, including the Yanks' Giambi, were noticeably smaller. Then, after the season ended, some of the grand jury testimony was leaked to the *San Francisco Chronicle,* which published parts of the transcripts. In the story, Giambi allegedly told the grand jury about his long-term steroid use, detailing the different substances he had taken. Both Bonds and Sheffield said they had used substances called the "Cream" and the "Clear," but said they did not know these substances contained steroids. Both said they stopped immediately when they learned their true nature. Giambi was coming off a terrible season in which he was injured and ill, admitting to a benign tumor at one point but not revealing its location. Many suspected his problems were linked to long-term steroid use. Both Bonds and Sheffield had outstanding years. Bonds, of course, won the NL batting title, hit his 700th homer, and set a number of records, including winning his seventh MVP award.

The grand jury admissions, however, set off a firestorm of protest. Senator John McCain and President Bush again demanded that baseball get tougher with its testing program and punishments. Commissioner Bud Selig also called for the elimination of these performance-enhancing drugs from the game. And many fans are now looking at all the home run records set since 1998, when Mark McGwire erupted for 70 and Sammy Sosa hit 66, with renewed suspicion, pointing to the older sluggers from Babe Ruth to Roger Maris as guys who didn't need help to set their records. Others are calling the so-called steroid scandal baseball's biggest black eye since the Black Sox scandal of 1919.

Until recently, the Players' Association had always fought against random drug testing, and thus provisions for testing were never negotiated into the basic labor agreement. The union fought it and won. Now, for the good and the future of the game, both sides have had to make concessions. I think the charges made by Canseco and Caminiti helped force the union's hand somewhat, and the revelations coming out of the BALCO investigation may finally have pushed things over the top. I know that many players who have never touched steroids or other substances don't feel that it's fair that some are finding an advantage by taking them and reaping the benefits of their performance enhancement. If more of these "clean" players begin to stand up, and I believe they are beginning to do just that, there will be even more pressure to clean up the sport.

By 2004, players were subject to two unannounced tests for steroid use per year conducted by the commissioner's office, but this has now been upgraded, and random testing can now occur at any time and be repeated any number of times during the year, and in the off-season as well. The minor leagues have always had a much tougher drug policy, and it's time to bring this kind of policy to the majors. Penalties for violators must also be more severe. A slap on the wrist doesn't do the trick, nor does a minuscule fine for players who are multimillionaires. Only significant suspensions without pay will make players think twice about trying to cheat or beat the testing system.

Why must these performance-enhancing substances be eliminated? To put it in a nutshell, steroids threaten the integrity of the game. Their use compromises what takes place on the field, and they simply have no place in the sport.

As a manager, any kind of drug or steroid use is going to affect my club, its discipline, as well as the organization as a whole. Players are all trying to do well, trying to get to the big leagues. They're all looking for an edge, and as a manager, you're looking for an edge too. You want your team to do well. When I managed in the minors I was no different from the players in one way. I also wanted to be in the major leagues. I took great pride in what I was doing, and my edge was learning as much as I possibly could and then putting the best team I had out on the field every day. Players should look at their game like this as well. Take pride in what you do. Learn, train, practice, and become better—but do it the right way.

Some Other Tricks

There are some on-field tricks that players have used for years trying to gain that little bit of advantage that will help them win. And on occasion, other people in the organization are involved. I first saw it happen in rookie ball at Bluefield, West Virginia, when I was starting out in the Orioles organization. We had a young pitcher named Tim Kelly who had been the closer at LaVerne College in Los Angeles. Tim didn't throw real hard; he had a little fastball and a slider, but not a hellava lot of *stuff*. He was a nondrafted free agent, a good guy, but in reality what they called a nonprospect. The organization probably knew he would never advance beyond A ball. To keep him around a bit longer, one of the first things the coaches did was teach him how to throw a spitball. Here we were, in the late 1970s, and the coaches were teaching a pitch that had been illegal since 1920. Of course, it was no secret that some big-league pitchers still threw it in order to get an edge, so in retrospect, maybe it shouldn't have come as a total surprise.

Gaylord Perry, who was still in the majors then, let everyone know for years that the spitter was alive and well. Gaylord wasn't caught very often, but his hands were everywhere before he threw—on his face, his uniform, around his mouth, under the bill of his cap—and that got hitters to thinking. Was he loading up? As soon as a hitter began thinking about it, Gaylord had an edge. Just for the record, one way the spitter is thrown is by putting the first two fingers on the white of the ball with the seam in between. The saliva causes the fingers to slip off the white of the ball as the delivery is made.

The funny thing was that after Tim learned it, all the guys wanted to try it. We all tried to throw the spitball, and damned if it didn't really move. Don't get me wrong, this wasn't something they taught all young pitchers, but I think they felt Tim could go a little further in the organization if he could load up—and he stayed around about a year and a half because of it.

Despite the fact that it hadn't been a legal pitch for decades there were still some real techniques for getting away with using the spitter. I've seen pitchers who would wipe a layer of Vaseline on their faces, allowing it to mix with their perspiration. Then they would wipe their face with their two fingers, but when they went to wipe their hand on their pant leg, supposedly to dry the fingers, they would swipe the pant leg with their thumb and let the two fingers glide above it. So they were loaded and ready. Another trick was for the pitcher to tell the ump he wanted a new ball. When he threw the old one in, he lobbed it high to his catcher. Everyone always watches the ball, so the pitcher went to his mouth as soon as he lobbed the ball. By the time he got the new ball, his fingers were already wet. So today, if you hear that the spitter is long gone, don't believe it. Someone, somewhere, is teaching it; and someone, somewhere, is throwing it to hitters.

The knuckleball, of course, is a legal pitch and a perplexing one. Not everyone can throw it, and not everyone who can throw it well can control it. Those who can do both often have long, successful careers, because the pitch puts little strain on the arm. But good knuckleball pitchers are few and far between, attesting to the difficulty in mastering this pitch. Hoyt Wilhelm stayed in the majors until his late forties throwing it. So did Phil Niekro, who won more than 300 games. Both are Hall of Famers. In the 2003 playoffs, Boston's Tim Wakefield had the good knuckler working and baffled the Yankees twice in the ALCS—that is, until Aaron Boone hit the walk-off series-winning home run off him in Game 7. That pitch apparently didn't dance.

When Tommy Lasorda was managing the Dodgers he told Charlie Hough flat out that he wasn't going to make the majors unless he learned the knuckleball. Hough took him at his word, mastered the pitch, and went on to a successful career. Tim Wakefield was a first baseman who wasn't going to make it as a position player. And like so many others, he started fooling around with the knuckler before games and suddenly found he had a good one. Not only did it change his career; it saved it.

Pitchers will look for any other kind of edge they can find, a fact of baseball life everyone has known about for years. Most of them are private about what they are doing, because they don't want too many people to know. Some like to put a small cut or scratch on the white of the ball. They can do this by taping a tack to their glove hand, and when they take the glove off to rub the ball up, they cut it. Others will simply have a tack poking through their glove from the inside so they can scratch the ball when they rub it in their glove. Pitchers have been caught with small pieces of sandpaper inside their gloves or under their hats. Kevin Gross of the Phillies was caught a number of years ago when he reached into his back pocket, and after he took his hand out, a piece of sandpaper fell to the ground. He was fined and suspended.

A cut or scuff will change the aerodynamics of the ball just enough to make it move differently. If a pitcher cuts or scratches the white of the ball on one side, the movement will be the opposite way of the scratch. Even a fastball will move more than it ordinarily does because the air catches the imperfection on the otherwise perfectly round ball. Hitters generally know very quickly when a guy is throwing a doctored ball. They've all seen time and again how a good curve, slider, cutter, or splitter reacts, so if the ball is doing something else, they know the pitcher is doing something that day that isn't exactly aboveboard.

I remember a pitcher I'd had on one of my teams in the minors pitching against us when I was managing Boston. He was with Texas then and he knew how to cut the ball. Luckily, I knew it too. I managed to get my hands on about three of the balls early in the game, and they were all cut the same way on the same side. I didn't go to the umpire. I simply held the balls up from the front of the dugout where he could see me. He got the message that he better stop cutting the ball or I would bust him.

Pitchers have also been known to use pine tar to get a better grip on the ball on hot, humid days. Sometimes the catcher will be the accomplice by putting pine tar on his shin guards, then dabbing a little on the ball when he returns it to the pitcher. I remember a hot night when Gaylord Perry was pitching in Texas. After each pitch he'd go to the rosin bag, perfectly legal. But Gaylord was bouncing the bag in his hand, palm up, and when he was ready to pitch he had a nice covering of rosin in his hand. Then when he released the pitch, a spray of rosin would fly into the air, just enough, he hoped, to distract the hitter. They started calling it the "puff" ball. Leave it to Gaylord to come up with something like that.

Umpires generally won't look for this stuff unless the opposing manager or another player brings it up. Then they will check the pitcher, and if they find a tack, or sandpaper, or pine tar, he's out of the game. Embarrassing to get caught? Maybe. But everyone knows about the edge, and that guys are going to try almost anything to get it. A guy who gets caught will just shrug it off, pay his fine and serve his suspension, and then get right back out there again.

As for bats, I guess everyone has heard about cork. If they hadn't, they did in the summer of 2003, when Sammy Sosa was caught using a corked bat. Yet there have always been conflicting arguments whether the corked bat creates more power or not, and just what kind of edge it might give a player. Again, I think the corked bat provides a mental advantage more than anything else.

Corking is a simple concept. A round hole is drilled into the top of the bat all the way down to the sweet spot. Most of the hole is then filled with cork, while a wood plug is glued back into the top to conceal the subterfuge. Corking began years ago because players thought the ball would spring faster off a corked bat. That simply isn't true. In reality, the cork makes the bat lighter by about an ounce or ounce and a half, so a player in effect brings the same size bat to the plate, one with the same density, only now it's slightly lighter and enables him to create more bat speed. Regardless, a corked bat is illegal. A player caught using a corked bat will have the bat confiscated and will be fined, suspended, or both.

Who knows why Sosa did it? He's one of the premier power hitters in the big leagues and a guy who generates tremendous bat speed on his own. At the time he was caught he was just coming off the disabled list and was in a slump. Like most hitters, he was fighting to regain his stroke and maybe looking for that little extra. Unfortunately, the embarrassment he suffered at being caught was probably a lot worse than the slump.

The physical quality of the bats, however, has given the modern player something of an edge, just as today's large gloves are a huge advantage over the small, pocketless mitts of yesteryear. Major leaguers have always been given the better wood, while the generic products go to the minor-league teams. That's why some players in the minors try things like baking their bats in ovens to make the wood harder, hoping to keep them from flaking, chipping, and splitting. It could mean an extra hit or two somewhere down the line. Guys also "bone" their bats. They do this in the majors as well. Though it sounds strange, boning is just that, getting a huge leg bone or a ham bone and rubbing it along the grain of the barrel of the bat. The process makes the wood harder and a bit more dense.

You'll sometimes see players boning their bats in the dugout between innings. Remember, ballplayers have always been superstitious. If they think boning the bat will help them hit, they are going to continue to do it. A player always wants to feel good about his equipment, and for a hitter, nothing is more important than his bat.

When I played, almost all bats were Louisville Sluggers, made by one company, and they were all made from ash. As a minor leaguer I was told that you always pick the bats with the widest grain. That indicated the tree was older and the wood would be harder and more dense. Thin-grained bats tend to chip and splinter more easily. When Ken Boyer was managing me at Rochester he came up to me one day, looked at my bats, and remarked that I must know someone in Louisville, because I had a group of bats with great wood. I just laughed because I knew I had gotten lucky. Minor leaguers rarely had a choice.

Now there are different companies involved, and Louisville Slugger no longer has the market cornered. Many players are using maple instead of ash. Some think maple is a denser, less porous wood and doesn't absorb as much moisture as ash. They feel that the maple bats last longer and that the ball jumps off the drier, harder bats faster and travels farther. Barry Bonds, for instance, has been using a thirty-ounce maple Sam Bat made by a Canadian company. Players will go after the best bats, those they think will enable them to hit the ball harder and farther. That's why they will always listen when a sales rep from a new company comes along, and they'll give the new lumber a try. Why not? A different bat may lead to a hitting streak, and there isn't a player alive who doesn't want an edge like that.

Root, Root, Root for the Home Team

Is there such a thing as a home-field advantage in baseball? Definitely. Maybe it's the cheering crowds that get the adrenaline flowing, or simply the familiarity with the nooks and crannies of the outfield wall, or with the amount of running room in foul territory beyond first and third. Likewise, pitchers are more comfortable on the mound at home because they pitch there so often. Everyone simply enjoys playing in familiar surroundings.

The home team can sometimes do a little extra to give its players an edge. I first became aware of it in the 1960s, and had it confirmed in later years when I got to know players from the Dodger and Giant teams of that era.

When Maury Wills brought the stolen base back as a major offensive weapon in the early 1960s, some clubs decided they had to find new ways to slow him down. The Giants had a couple of tricks thanks to an astute grounds crew. Whenever the Dodgers came to town they used to overwater the area around first base, making the dirt very soft. As a result, Wills couldn't get the same push when he started for second, the soft dirt slowing him just enough to give the catcher a better chance of throwing him out.

They also watered heavily around home plate, softening the dirt there as well. Wills was again the reason. Maury hit a lot of Baltimore chops, and when they would bounce high on hard dirt, he'd beat them out. Softening the dirt meant the ball wouldn't bounce as high, and there was a better chance to nail him at first. Conversely, the Dodgers kept their field rock hard, both around first and around home plate, giving Wills every bit of an edge they possibly could.

Other teams would also try to find ways to slow or stop Wills. When he took a lead off first, some pitchers would throw over a number of times and the first basemen would try dropping to a knee and blocking the bag. That way, there was a chance the diving Wills couldn't get back or might even jam his hands in the process. Maury countered by going in feetfirst a couple of times. Because the first basemen didn't want to be spiked, they soon stopped the one-knee routine.

A good grounds crew has always played a part in giving the home team an edge. Whitey Herzog's St. Louis Cardinals teams in the 1980s had an abundance of speed. To help them out, the grounds crew had both the first- and third-base lines slanted in slightly, so that bunts down the line would probably stay fair instead of rolling foul.

Teams with slow outfielders might let the grass grow a little higher so balls hit in the gaps will slow down, allowing the outfielders to cut them off. Conversely, teams with a lot of singles hitters might keep the infield grass very short so ground balls move a little faster and have a greater chance of getting through for hits. Unless something is extremely overt, there is no way a visiting team can complain about this kind of home-field maneuvering. A good grounds crew is like a tenth man, and can enable the home team to win a handful of games during the season.

Ball clubs can also gain an edge by acquiring players whose talents mesh with the idiosyncrasies of their particular stadiums. Most clubs playing on artificial turf, for example, will try to build a speed team to take advantage of the ball moving so much faster on the turf than it would on grass. In fact, Whitey Herzog did the same thing in Kansas City before taking over at St. Louis in 1980. His late-seventies Royals teams were built for speed with the likes of Willie Wilson, Amos Otis, Frank White, and Freddie Patek.

When teams with speed came into Fenway while I was managing in 1995 and 1996, we took a page out of the old Giants' book. We kept the area around home plate soft, just something that might slow their speedsters down enough to make a difference. If you don't want to wet the field, you can also spike the ground around home plate and chop it up so the dirt isn't packed hard. This is just another way of slowing a fast team down just a hair.

If you look around the league, you'll see a number of teams that continue to set their rosters to get an edge in their home parks. Yankee Stadium has always been known for that short porch in right field. The House That Ruth Built. It's perfect for left-handed sluggers, and the Yankees have had a parade of them—from Ruth and Gehrig, to Mantle and Maris, to Mattingly and O'Neill, to Jason Giambi and Hideki Matsui today. Mantle, of course, was a switch-hitter. There are always a couple of bangers who can take advantage of that short porch in right. The Yanks would be nuts to field a team of right-handed hitters with the dimensions of that stadium.

Conversely, Dodger Stadium has always been a pitchers' ballpark. It's a big park to begin with, to the point that they moved home plate out a few years ago to shrink the dimensions. The other factor is that the air gets very heavy at Chavez Ravine at night. There are mountains all around the stadium, and the ball simply doesn't carry well after dark. Not surprisingly, pitchers love working in night games there, and in their heyday, the Dodgers were always known for their great pitching staffs.

Colorado, with the light mountain air, has always been a great place for hitters. The team started out that way with Andres Galarraga, Larry Walker, Dante Bichette, and Vinny Castilla as the original Blake Street Bombers. Then about three or four years ago they suddenly found themselves with a speed team, with guys like Juan Pierre and Tommy Goodwin. It didn't work, and in 2003 they went back to fielding a team of sluggers. They traded Pierre, one of the fastest players in the game, to Florida for Preston Wilson, then added Jeromy Burnitz and brought back Castilla. When you play half your games in that mile-high atmosphere, you'd better have the Blake Street Bombers in your lineup. It doesn't make sense to field a speed team, not the way the ball jumps off the bats. You get an edge by playing to the strengths of your ballpark.

Stealing Signs

While some of the ways of getting an edge are downright illegal—the spitball, steroid use—and others are a bit unethical—doctoring the field, *creating* a rainout—there are also many ways in which old-fashioned smart baseball can give both players and teams the edge. Good preparation is just one of them. The players who work the hardest, prepare themselves the best, will always have a leg up on success. A couple of quick examples.

Sandy Koufax and I worked together within the Dodger organization for nearly ten years. One of the things Sandy liked talking about was pitching to the elements, and being aware of the conditions in each ballpark. If the wind was blowing out to left in Wrigley Field, the pitcher had better make damned sure to keep the ball down and away to certain hitters. Some players today have their own ways of preparing. Shawn Green, now with the Diamondbacks, keeps a log on every pitch that is thrown to him, while Curt Schilling takes videos of hitters and studies them before he goes to the mound. It may be time-consuming, but it's well worth it if it makes them just a little bit better.

Some pitchers—even great ones—have reputations as head-hunters and want it that way. Bob Gibson and Don Drysdale were two from my early years, and Pedro Martinez and Roger Clemens are a couple of contemporary hurlers who don't hesitate to come inside. Are they trying to hit you? That's something you'll never know, but just the fact that you don't know when they are going to unleash one up and in gives them an edge. The hitters aren't quite so loose. Koufax always told me that you have to throw inside to be able to pitch outside. Down and away is the pitcher's part of the plate. That's his home. But if guys start hanging over the plate to take the outside corner away, that's when a pitcher has to be ready to come inside, just to keep the hitter honest. The way Koufax put it is, *You throw inside, but you don't live inside.* This is the real meaning of the *purpose* pitch. The pitcher is sending a message: Don't come into my territory. Low and away is my part of the plate.

In today's game, hitters are wearing protective gear that didn't exist in the past—wrist pads, thick elbow pads, small shin guards. As a consequence, they don't have quite the same fear they once did, and they also know that if a pitcher comes inside too often, he can be bounced from the game. The great pitchers, however, won't be intimidated. In order to survive and excel in the big leagues, they have to be able to use both sides of the plate.

Another great way to get an edge is to steal signs. It's both a skill to conceal signs and a skill to be able to steal them. That's all part of the mental game that everyone is always playing, or at least should be playing. A few years ago there was a flap when someone came out with a story that said the New York Giants of 1951 were stealing signs by having someone with binoculars or a telescope watching the catcher from the center-field clubhouse at the old Polo Grounds. It shouldn't be a shock. Teams have been looking for that kind of edge for years, and while a telescope in the clubhouse isn't exactly written into the rules, there are plenty of ways to get signs by simply watching carefully and knowing the game and the players.

Baseball certainly has a lineage, and those coming into the game are wise if they find some great veteran minds to learn from. When I was in the Dodger organization I learned a great deal about both giving and stealing signs from Joe Amalfitano, who was still coaching then. He learned much of what he knew from a master, Leo Durocher, who, incidentally, was the manager of that 1951 Giants team. Leo, of course, would do anything to get an edge, so I guess a telescope in the clubhouse wasn't that far-fetched.

Because I was a catcher as a player, signs were always extremely important to me. And because catchers direct so much of the game, I began watching opposing catchers, and I found early on that you could get an edge by noting not only the way they gave signs, but also the way they set up behind the plate. As a catcher, I always set up the same way behind the plate and didn't move too soon. But not all catchers do that.

For example, if a catcher sets up with his tail section up high, then you know he's expecting a breaking ball or something that might bounce. Catchers have a tendency to get up on the balls of their feet with their tails a little higher if they are anticipating making a quick move to block the ball, especially with men on base. If they set up with their tail low, then it's almost always a fastball. I learned as a catcher early on always to set up the same way and never telegraph what move I might make too soon. Knowing that, I could watch other catchers and sometimes get the signs just from the way they set up.

If a catcher sets up inside way too soon on a right-handed batter with a right-handed pitcher on the mound, then you can be 95 percent certain a fastball is coming. It may be a two-seam sinker or a four-seam power fastball, but it's definitely going to be something hard. Same thing for lefty-lefty. Only a handful of right-handed pitchers can throw a slider inside to a right-handed batter, and it's rare for a righty to throw an overhand curve inside, because that pitch is designed to go down and away. Hang one inside and you'll be turning your head to watch the ball sail into the stands. Again, the same applies for a lefty-lefty matchup. Leo Mazzone, the pitching coach of the Braves, will sometimes call for a changeup inside to fool hitters. The idea is to get them to jump at the ball and either pull it foul or pop it up. So there is always someone who can break the pattern and fool you no matter what you expect will happen. But again, if you make a mistake and the changeup is too far out over the plate, the head goes back on the outfield swivel to watch the ball sail. It's a part of the mental game.

There are certainly unwritten rules, such as the hitter not looking back to see where the catcher is setting up. But if the catcher sets up too soon and gives away the pitch, there's no rule against someone else giving a sign to the hitter so that he knows what to expect. Some hitters don't want the signs. They would rather wait, see the pitch, and react. Others, like Rafael Palmeiro, are always looking for a fastball. Many pitchers over the past decade have tried to sneak a heater past Raffy on different counts, but he was always ready, as his 500-plus homers attest. When I managed against him later, I would always tell my pitchers, "Don't you dare try to sneak a fastball past him and think you'll fool him."

Still others love to receive the signs. Jose Canseco always loved to have them, and Will Clark was another who thrived on getting signs. Clark, in fact, was something of a throwback. He played for me in Texas in '94 and learned to read the catcher's sequence quickly and could get the signs when he was on second base. Then he would relay them to the hitter.

Relaying signs can be done in several ways. If a guy leads off second by stepping out with his right leg, it can mean a fastball is coming. If he crosses over, using his left leg to step across his right, that can indicate a breaking ball. If the runner can't get the precise pitch, he can sometimes get its location and also relay it visually. If the runner on second moves the right leg off the bag first, it tells the hitter that the catcher is setting up on the third-base side of the plate; the left leg first indicates the first-base side. That way, either a right-handed or a left-handed hitter will know the location of the pitch. Still another way to indicate a pitch—and this can be done from the dugout—is to encourage the player by using his name or number. If you say, for example, "Come on, Joe, get hold of one," it means fastball. If you holler, "Come on, Thirty-three, get hold of one," you're telling him a breaking ball is on the way.

I used to teach my guys to look for the *indicator* in the catcher's sequence. For example, *first sign indicator* is very basic and still used today. If the indicator is one finger, the next sign after the one is flashed is the pitch he should throw. If it's two fingers, the pitcher waits to see the two to get the sign next. Some catchers use other types of sequences with different indicators, so it's up to one of the players on base to spot it early in the game and give his team an edge.

Some catchers are better than others at disguising signs or waiting until the last possible second to make a move. Pat Borders of Toronto was one of the best at not giving his signs away. He never moved before the pitch was thrown, and that's one of the secrets. But while Borders concealed his signs, his Toronto team in the mid-nineties was very good at stealing them from other ball clubs. I remember one game at Toronto when they were stealing every one of our signs. Every one. Now that's an edge. Once I realized this, I had a meeting with my catcher, Pudge Rodriguez, and all the infielders. We quickly changed the signs.

I told everyone to forget about the usual one-two-two finger sequences, all of them. For the rest of the game, they would mean nothing. Pudge would keep flashing the finger sequences, but only as a decoy. Pudge gave signs that day with the placement of his glove before each pitch. He would place it inside or outside his shin guard. How he held the glove, whether he closed or opened it, indicated the pitch he wanted. I remember we won the game with Rick Helling taking a shutout into the eighth or ninth. So we fooled them for one day. If we did the same thing the next day, they probably would have picked up on it. But that's the mental game, and if you do it well, you'll get an edge.

I've never forgotten a game I was managing years ago at Albuquerque. We were playing Colorado Springs, the Indians' Triple-A club. Many managers and pitching coaches will call the pitches from the dugout, relaying them to the catcher. I was coaching third that day, as managers usually do in Triple-A, and the Colorado Springs pitching coach was in my direct line of vision giving signs to the catcher. I watched him for a couple of innings, learned his sequence, and from that point on, I knew nearly every pitch they were going to throw before the pitcher did. I alerted my hitters to watch me because if I had time to relay the signs, I would in a crucial situation. Late in the game we had the bases loaded with Mike Huff up (Mike went on to play for the Dodgers, White Sox, and Blue Jays). I caught the sign from their dugout and opened my hand with the palm up to let Huff know a changeup was coming. He sat on it and belted a grand slam home run. I can remember him coming around third and pointing at me, saying, "That was all you, Skip." I just nodded and answered, "But you executed it."

There are signs for everything. In potential double-steal situations the catcher will come out a few feet in front of home plate and signal what he is going to do. For example, if there are runners on first and third, and the man on first breaks for second, the catcher can just hold the ball, throw through to second, or make an arm fake and try to draw the runner on third far enough off the bag to nail him. I've always studied catchers in those situations. If a catcher's first movement is to his chest protector and then he glides his hand down, for example, it can indicate a throw through to second. If he touches his left elbow, then goes back to his chest, that could indicate he is going to try to nail the guy off third. Sometimes catchers will use first and last touch so that the sequence is more difficult to read. Then, the only signs that mean anything are the first and last.

When I was Felipe Alou's bench coach at Montreal in 1992 we were losing to the Cubs one day, 1–0, in the eighth inning. We had Marquis Grissom on first and Delino DeShields on third. Darrin Fletcher was at the plate with two outs. I saw the catcher come out in front of the plate and give the sign. He signaled for a throw through. Once the pitcher got two strikes on Fletcher the catcher came out again. Because he had come out a second time I knew he was changing the sign, and now he wouldn't throw through, but only make an arm fake. Managers tend to get defensive and with two strikes don't want to risk an errant throw. That's when I told Felipe that the catcher had changed the sign and that Grissom could walk into second because the catcher was only going to arm-fake.

"Are you sure?" Felipe asked.

"Yes," I said. "Trust me."

He was right to be concerned, because if Grissom was thrown out the game would be over. However, I was 100 percent sure because two things had alerted me. One, I had picked up the signs early in the game. And second, he had come back out after two strikes. The only reason to do that would be to change the sign. Felipe trusted me. With two strikes, he sent Grissom toward second. The pitch was a ball and the catcher just arm-faked, allowing Grissom to steal the base standing up. On the next pitch Fletcher hit a little bloop single to center, both runners scored, and we won it, 2–1. Everyone was congratulating me after the game and asking, "Kevin, how did you know that?"

You know it because you study. You watch everything and everyone. You study catchers and look for patterns. You try to learn the tendencies of every team you play, every player you go up against, every opposing manager, and you steal signs if you can. By learning these kinds of things as a manager, you have a real edge, an edge that I can safely say helped us win several games a year wherever I managed.

Many people say that baseball is a simple game—pitching the ball, hitting the ball, catching the ball, and throwing the ball. But it's really a lot more than that. The mental game is a separate battle that has been going on for a long time. To me, it's one of the great ways to get an edge, by outthinking and outfoxing an opponent. The distressing thing is that some players cross the line to try to get an edge. This simply isn't necessary. In my mind, there are too many other ways to gain an advantage today without having to resort to crossing the line. Unfortunately, there will always be temptations, especially with $60 million contracts dangling in the air and players looking to sign on the dotted line.

CHAPTER TWO

Cheap in the Wrong Place— Player Development

A lot of older scouts have lost their jobs over the years. These guys are trained to find baseball players, and when they are fired or released, they don't have benefits and often can't get another job. They are men who have dedicated their whole lives to the game, and in the end they often wind up with nothing.

Developing players who go on to become productive major leaguers has always been one of the open secrets of a successful organization. That means finding talented players, evaluating them correctly, teaching them, and introducing them to the big leagues in the right way and at the right time. If an organization is capable of acquiring and developing players in this manner, chances are it will be able to put a competitive team on the field, even in this day and age of big-versus small-revenue ball clubs.

There is a problem, however, one that I've seen coming for quite some time. The problem, in plain language, is that in this era of huge salaries when money is often tossed around like rain, falling almost everywhere, it's not falling hard enough in one important place. Teams often pinch pennies in the areas of scouting and teaching, especially in the low minors, where marginal players used to become serviceable major leaguers, and good players were developed into stars.

But that can't be done if a team doesn't keep veteran scouts out in the field and the best people in key teaching spots. Some teams still get it, and others are now showing signs of realizing that being cheap in the wrong place can only hurt in the long run.

Doing things the right way was something I learned when I was drafted by the Orioles. The team's farm director was Clyde Klutz, a former catcher. And Jim Schaffer, my Double-A manager, had also played in the big leagues. At Triple-A Joe Altobelli was the manager; he had also managed in the majors and was another veteran baseball man with a world of experience. There was a whole group of good people in the organization at the same time, all old-school, and all strong instructors. Earl Weaver, of course, was the Orioles manager then, and a number of guys on his coaching staff—Jim Frey, Frank Robinson, Cal Ripken Sr., Billy Hunter, George Bamberger, and later on Ray Miller—went on to become major-league managers. Robinson, of course, had managed briefly before, having been the first African American to skipper a big-league team when he became player-manager of the Cleveland Indians.

When I moved on and began managing in the Dodgers minor-league organization, I was introduced to a blueprint of how player development should be handled, from top to bottom. They had a handbook that showed how the team wanted things done at every level. It described the kind of defense that the entire organization had to play, giving instructions for every conceivable situation, such as the outfield relays with the bases empty or with a combination of men on base, or what to do on a base hit to right or center in different situations. That way, the entire organization was on the same wavelength, and it ensured that the same things would be taught at every level, so one manager wouldn't have to contradict what the guy below him had taught.

This thorough handbook made such an impression on me that when I left the organization and become the farm director of the Montreal Expos in 1992, I incorporated the exact same concepts and system there, and did it again later in my career when I managed in Texas and Boston.

The Dodgers also had periodic organizational meetings with

everyone from scouts to player-development personnel at every level. We all got to know each other, discussing baseball philosophy, the types of players we were looking for, and the direction in which the entire organization was moving. All the managers had the opportunity to speak, reviewing their clubs from the previous season and separating the prospects from the nonprospects. Even when I was managing for the Dodgers in the minors, I did other things. At the organizational meeting I would give catching demonstrations— showing the proper techniques, footwork, and the correct way to give signs—for the other managers who had not been catchers. Then an infield instructor would take over and demonstrate different techniques suited to those positions. Everyone took turns teaching his specialty, and all of us learned the proper way to do things.

Al Campanis was the Dodgers' general manager then, and he wanted every manager in the organization to be able to teach players at each position what to do in every situation. He might single me out at the meeting and say, "Okay, Kevin, diagram and explain our bunt defensive plays with runners on first and second, and nobody out." At that time, we had four different defensive plays for that situation, and I had to teach what every player involved on that specific play should do. Then he might call out Terry Collins, another minor-league skipper, and say, "Okay, Terry, runners at first and second, one out, ninth inning with the tying run on second, slow ground ball between first and second to right field. Who's the cutoff man?" This was important because the cutoff man changes if it's a sharp ground ball base hit as opposed to a slow grounder, where the first or second baseman, or both, might dive for the ball. In that case, the pitcher becomes the cutoff man. If it's a sharp grounder or line drive, the first baseman becomes the cutoff man and the pitcher backs up home plate. In other words, Campanis was creating a specific situation and letting everyone know just how he wanted us to deal with it. That way, every person was on the same page and would be teaching the same things to his individual team when we broke for the season.

In fact, when I asked Maury Wills on one of my radio shows just how he learned to steal bases, all the credit went right back to Al Campanis. Maury said that when he was in the minor leagues, Campanis used to give everyone lectures on base stealing. He would even get out on the field in those days and actually demonstrate techniques. Maury also learned how to read the pitchers' moves and get a good jump off the bag. Learning how to utilize his speed and quickness allowed Maury finally to get to the majors after some eight years in the minors, and he went on to become not only the Dodgers' offensive catalyst during his career, but also a base-stealing record setter and National League Most Valuable Player in 1962. And he owes it all to Al Campanis.

Each manager in the Dodgers' minor-league system usually had two coaches with him, a hitting and pitching coach, something almost unheard of at that time. There were also roving pitching and hitting coaches who spent time with each team, such as Sandy Koufax, Maury Wills, Tommy Davis, Reggie Smith, Johnny Podres, Larry Sherry, Dave Wallace, Chico Fernandez, and Leo Posada. The organization had a good many Latin players then and always made sure they had a combination of English- and Spanish-speaking instructors. In effect, they had all the bases covered. Almost. At that time, the one thing I noticed they didn't have was a roving catching instructor. I felt this was an important, albeit missing, ingredient, so I went to Campanis and Bill Schweppe, the farm director, and asked for the job, and it was one I held for a number of years. The old joke with the Dodgers was that they had one instructor for every two players. Sometimes it really seemed that way, and it was a great way to run an organization and develop your players.

The Dodgers had a lot of name guys, but an organization doesn't necessarily need that if its instructors are good. What it must have is guys with passion who are willing to work. It also helps to have a combination of young and older instructors. The young coaches can go out and physically demonstrate skills and techniques, while the older guys can give everyone the benefit of the experience and knowledge they have accumulated over the years. When I served as the Dodgers' catching instructor, the great Roy Campanella was still an instructor with the organization. Campy, of course, was confined to a wheelchair as he had been since his tragic car accident in January 1958, but he was still full of enthusiasm for the game and had a world of wisdom from his years as a Hall of Fame catcher.

"My legs may not work, but my mind is strong," Campy often used to say. That's why we were such a good complement to each other. I could go out and do it, while Campy was great at telling players how to call a game. That's a perfect example of the balance I was talking about. In fact, when I initially joined the Dodgers organization and went to Albuquerque, the first person I saw was Sandy Koufax sitting on the bench. My immediate reaction was What the hell is he doing here? Then I found out he was a roving instructor, and soon after, I realized just how advanced the Dodgers were in terms of player development and why the organization had produced the unheard-of nine Rookies of the Year between 1979 and 1996.

When Peter O'Malley owned the ball club, his philosophy was to avoid the frenzy of signing free agents. He preferred to have the core of the team continue right up through the Dodger organization. It was a philosophy that stood for years but began changing way before O'Malley sold the ball club. In fact, it started with some bad free-agent signings in 1980. Then Al Campanis had to resign from his GM post at the outset of the 1987 season. Then a couple of years later longtime scouting director Ben Wade was forced out. Soon there was political infighting for these top positions, and more nonbaseball people began making the baseball decisions. If you have nonbaseball people, they must be supported by those with strong baseball backgrounds. In other words, if you haven't been in the game as a player at some level, it's very difficult, but not impossible, to evaluate talent. You simply cannot share another man's experience unless you've been through it.

Along these lines, Mark Shapiro, presently the general manager of the Cleveland Indians, has admitted that because he never played it's extremely helpful to have assistants such as former major-league pitcher Tim Belcher to help him evaluate talent and make trades. He isn't the only one. Many feel that the new wave of young general managers, like Boston's Theo Epstein and the Dodgers' Paul DePodesta, rely more on statistics than personal evaluation. While everyone uses stats, including field managers, they will never be the be-all and end-all of evaluation. Theo Epstein has had former professionals like Mike Port and Lee Thomas help him with player evaluation. DePodesta always has the venerable Tommy Lasorda close by as well.

In fact, after Al Campanis left the Dodgers in 1987, Fred Claire, a former newspaperman, became the general manager. Claire immediately turned to guys like Lasorda, Reggie Smith, Mel Didier, and Gary Sutherland to help him with personnel decisions. A good GM, whether he has played or not, will always get input from his big-league manager, his minor-league managers, and his scouts, as well as from the special adviser he always has on hand. So while the GM makes the final decision, he will have leaned on a number of people for advice before reaching his conclusions.

Experience always has to count for something in baseball. While statistics and computer analysis come in handy, this is not a computer game, but a very human game. I remember Curt Schilling saying that one of his coaches tried to give him some tips before he took the mound for Arizona in the seventh game of the 2001 World Series. He soon realized that someone who hasn't pitched a seventh game could not really tell him what that moment felt like. Being a baseball historian, Schilling mentioned that a guy like Sandy Koufax would be able to tell him because he had been there. When I heard that, I immediately connected it to Sandy because I had once heard him say the same thing, that no one can know what it's like to pitch a seventh game of the World Series . . . unless he has done it.

The Dodgers always emphasized scouting and player development. But slowly over the years things have changed, and teams have begun downsizing their scouting and development staffs. When you begin seeing things like first-class flights being switched to coach for the scouts and roving instructors, you know the handwriting is on the wall. It signals cost-cutting time, and while the organization might be saving money, in the long run it is hurting itself.

Scouts

Many organizations today underestimate the value of good veteran scouts. These men are the backbone of the game because without the players they provide, there would simply be no game. Active scouts watch games virtually every day, both in the United States and now in other countries of the world. They are trained to project and predict talent. When they see a fifteen- or sixteen-year-old in high school they have to project the kind of ballplayer he will turn out to be. How will his body fill out? What about his arm speed or bat speed? Can he be a better pitcher if his arm angle is altered, or can a kid be more of a power hitter if he's taught how to use his lower body? This is what they are up against every day as they seek out new players to recommend to their teams.

Players come and go, and it's the scouts who have to find the replacements. They watch amateur, high school, and college games, travel constantly, and rarely see their families. They have to look everywhere. For example, a scout named Mike Brito was the guy who found Fernando Valenzuela pitching deep inside Mexico. Mike heard about him from a local scout he knew and went to see him pitch in person. Without Mike, the Dodgers never would have found Fernando, who became such a big part of their team in the 1980s. Take away the scouts and there is no one else to do the groundwork.

Most longtime scouts have never had it easy. Many of them were minor-league players who eventually got a job within the organization. Not surprisingly, you just don't see superstar players retire and become scouts. The pay isn't good. They are on the road all the time, beating the bushes, living out of their cars or staying in small motels. It's not an easy life and there aren't a great many rewards, only the satisfaction of having one of their discoveries make it big.

While these scouts are working full-time, they have benefits from the ball club. But as teams cut back and new general managers come in, many of these long-term scouts are released, or the new GM wants his own guys to fill the slots. The scouts who are released are left on the street with no benefits and no pensions. In other words, everything stops. They're at the bottom of the baseball chain, and when teams get cheap in the wrong place, the scouts are often the first to go. Some of them are hired back part-time, but they lose all their benefits just the same. Just another little cost-cutting trick in baseball.

Fortunately, there are still a few of the old-timers around. George Genovese has more than sixty years in the game and is now with the Dodgers. Back when I was at Taft High School his name was already known by players all over the San Fernando Valley. He worked for

the Giants then and found some of the great stars of those San Francisco teams, including the likes of Bobby Bonds and George Foster. In
fact, he's helped put some sixty-odd players in the big leagues. That's
quite a legacy. George was once offered the Giants' managing job back
in the 1960s but turned it down because his heart was always in finding young players. The difference today is that even a great veteran
scout like George doesn't hold the same weight that he did in the old
days. That's because the system and the people have changed.

Teams today still have local scouts, more accurately called area
scouts. Once they spot a potential prospect they let the regional scouting supervisor know about him. He will cross-check the player and, if
he likes him a lot, go to the scouting director, who will then try to see
the guy who's projected as a top prospect. Because a team may be
drafting forty, fifty, or even sixty kids, the scouting director obviously
can't see everyone. That's why all the evaluators from the area scouts
on up have to know their business and be able to give accurate reports.
They don't want to let a prospect slip through the cracks, so the regional scout will try to see a prospect several times. What's been lost in
many cases today, however, is an organization's willingness in getting
to know a kid's background and his family situation. It's all part of
evaluating the type of player he can become.

I was still managing in the Dodger organization when I heard
that they had drafted a kid named Mike White out of Loudon, Tennessee. Carl Lowenstein, a longtime veteran scout, turned in the initial
report. He said that White had tremendous potential, and could hit,
run, and throw, so the raw talent was obviously there. The Dodgers'
top cross-checker—the decision maker—came to see White play, and
on that day the kid was walked three times. The fourth time he took
one swing and hit the ball four hundred feet with an aluminum bat.
The cross-checker put the okay stamp on him. Seeing just a single
swing of the bat, he said, This is our guy, our top pick.

But something was missing, something that Carl Lowenstein suspected. Carl knew that Mike White had never been out of Tennessee.
When he had to board a plane for the first time, Carl had to go with
him, and Lowenstein's years of experience told him what the organization would be facing. When you want to groom a kid to play at

Dodger Stadium in front of fifty thousand people, you've got to know everything about his makeup. If it's a Mark Prior, coming out of USC, you can be pretty sure he'll be ready for the big leagues if he has the talent. But a high school kid from Loudon, Tennessee, can be a different story, no matter how much talent he has.

Carl said that Mike White was a very reserved kid from a small town and he knew that we were going to have to get him acclimated. I had him in rookie ball in 1986 at Great Falls, Montana, and one of the first things he said to me was, "Kevin, I've never seen so many stoplights in one city." Knowing that Dodger Stadium held more people than the entire city of Great Falls, a light quickly went on in my head. The next year we were both at Bakersfield in the California League, Single-A, and this is when I began to recognize he was getting homesick.

Mike was a nice kid who had signed for about fifty thousand dollars, had a girlfriend back home, and had never been on the road before. Remember, the rookie-ball season lasts just two and half months and consists of only seventy games. The next year was his first full baseball season, beginning with spring training and going through instructional league. It was a period of nine months. One day we were on the road playing the Visalia Oaks in central California. When my coaches and I arrived at the ballpark we were told Mike was gone. His girlfriend had driven his car from Bakersfield to Visalia and picked him up, and the two of them had left. In effect, Mike had jumped the club. We heard that they were heading out to see the Grand Canyon. I think it was the pressure of trying to acclimate to becoming a pro, missing his girlfriend and wanting to get married, in addition to other stuff going on in his family. He eventually returned and we gave him another chance.

Here's where those intangibles come in. Those same years I had Mike White at Great Falls and Bakersfield, I also had our number two draft choice, Dave Hansen. Dave was from a high school around Los Angeles, a tough kid, and it was interesting to compare both players because the two of them are a perfect example of the things you have to know about your prospects ahead of time. There was no question that Mike White had more raw talent and power than Dave, and could run and throw better. Dave had a great swing and could hit, but he wasn't a great fielder and didn't have a ton of speed. On the other hand—and this is important—Dave was a fearless kid, and on top of that, he had an underlying confidence that he was going to make it to the big leagues. He wound up being a very serviceable major leaguer who is now recognized as one of the top pinch hitters of all time. Dave is a guy who made the most of his talent and overcame some of his limitations with grittiness, hard work, and the will to succeed.

As a manager, I was as tough with Mike White as I was with Dave Hansen. I was a disciplinarian and ran a tight ship. My job was to get these players ready for Los Angeles, not Great Falls or Bakersfield, so they had to learn and they had to acclimate. I think Mike White just had to adjust to too many things—the traveling, and being around players from different backgrounds and different areas of the country, as well as longtime baseball men who were not at all like him. I remember him even making it seem as if he had never heard much cursing before. But men are men. How was White going to feel if he was playing for Tommy Lasorda, whose choice of words around the team was always salty? I think he made it as far as Double-A, and I don't know what happened to him after that. But I always felt bad that I couldn't help him adjust and bring out his full talent.

If there were more scouts and better cross-checking, as well as the time for an organization to get to know each kid's family and evaluate his background and temperament, then there might be fewer mistakes such as drafting a player like Mike White. With number one draft picks getting a couple of million dollars just to sign today, it would benefit an organization to hold those mistakes to a minimum. By keeping veteran scouts who still have a passion for finding talent in the field, teams will always have a great resource for finding and evaluating new talent.

The Importance of Player Development

When I was a young player, I remember Ray Miller, the minor-league pitching coordinator of the Orioles, telling us that making the adjustment from amateur to professional baseball required at least a thousand plate appearances. The adjustments in technique that one had to make, however, were only part of the learning process. Going from two games a week in high school, to four in college, to playing every single day in the minors is yet another drastic change. Getting players mentally and physically ready to play a 162-game season is an essential part of preparing them for the big leagues. If this isn't done properly, some players might not reach their true potential or might be seriously injured along the way.

The fall Instructional League has always been a big part of player development. A team will send thirty-five or forty of its best young prospects who are close to advancing within the organization to either Arizona or Florida. All the minor-league instructors will be there, as well as some of the young managers in the system. The league runs from about September 20 until November 1, providing everyone with six weeks of intense instruction. I remember the Dodgers sending two full teams, about eighty players, with all their coordinators and coaches. Each team plays a thirty-five-game schedule, with the players coming mostly from rookie and Single-A ball, augmented by maybe a couple of players from Double-A, and even occasionally a Triple-A player who needs to improve a particular facet of his game.

In today's world sending everyone to the Instructional League can be very costly. Some teams don't want to spend the money that way anymore, and some, frankly, don't have it because so much is tied up in salaries. Teams that don't participate in the Instructional League will often hold minicamps a couple of weeks before spring training. They'll bring their prospects to these minicamps, but the level of instruction and competition just isn't the same. Again, it's a matter of being cheap in the wrong place. Some organizations, however, such as the Dodgers, take advantage of every opportunity and do both.

The Instructional League was where I taught Mike Piazza how to catch, as well as future big-league catchers Carlos Hernandez and Darrin Fletcher. Piazza was a first baseman when he was drafted, and it was Tommy Lasorda who had the idea of making him into a catcher. Since I was the roving major- and minor-league catching instructor, I began working directly with him, teaching him everything from calling a game to setting up properly, blocking pitches, giving signs, throwing, and blocking the plate. Mike could always hit, but he had to learn how to throw. I always felt Mike had enough arm strength to be a catcher, but lacked the proper technique. Watching him the last couple of years with the Mets, he seems to have gotten away from the basics, and his technique has deteriorated somewhat. He's now standing straight up, losing quickness with his feet, and not generating drive from his lower body. This causes him to throw with just his arm. He's also not in a position to throw before he receives the ball. This is all very correctable, and that's why constant evaluation and instruction are important at all levels, even the majors.

I spent two full years in the Instructional League, working on every phase of the game with Piazza. Without the benefit of the Instructional League, Mike might not have become a catcher, because there was no other way he could have received that kind of intense instruction.

There is normally less teaching at the big-league level, but with more players coming up at a younger age, you still need hands-on instruction in the majors, probably more so today than ever before. Mike Stanley was one of my catchers in Boston in 1996, a guy with twelve years' experience in the majors and a clutch hitter. He was always one of my favorite players, but I knew from managing against him that his throwing technique needed improvement. He wouldn't stay on top of the baseball and had a habit of bringing the ball up to his ear and pushing it. This resulted in a slow release, a loss of arm strength, and throws that would sail. What I did was take a bucket of balls, stand off to his right as he set up behind the plate, then underhand the ball to him low, just a few inches off the ground. He would have to barehand the ball with his hand on top and throw in one circular motion. This technique helped quicken his release and improved his consistency.

I would also break the great throwers down, always showing my catchers tapes of guys like Johnny Bench and Rick Dempsey. Neither of them cocked his arm, which causes the arm to pause and lose speed. They were quick with their feet, stayed on top of the ball, and threw in one quick motion. By teaching like this, you continue to develop players right up into the majors. But you need the right people to do it. Dave Wallace, for example, learned a great deal from Koufax over the years and is now a great pitching coach in his own right. Sandy used to mentor all the young pitching coaches in the Dodger organization, and Dave joined the organization as a coach after pitching a bit for the Toronto Blue Jays. Eventually Dave became the pitching coordinator for the Dodgers' minor-league organization, and in 2004 he was the pitching coach of the World Series–winning Boston Red Sox. Like I said, you learn from guys who have done it before you.

There's a rule of thumb that says a young pitcher needs between 600 and 750 innings in the minors and a young hitter needs from 1,000 to 1,500 at bats to be ready for the majors. In the old days, especially before expansion, players routinely stayed in the minors longer. Unless the player had the obvious talent of Mickey Mantle, Willie Mays, and a few others, he often toiled in the minors until his mid- to late twenties. These players got their innings and their at bats, and when they finally were promoted to the show they already knew the game.

Today, with more teams and the changing economic landscape, many players are rushed up early and have to get their seasoning on the job in the majors. That makes it even more important to have the right people watching. Rush a player who isn't ready and let him struggle, and you can easily sabotage a potentially great career. David Clyde is an example of rushing a career. He was a great high school pitcher in Texas and the Rangers needed a marquee player of some kind in 1973, so they brought the eighteen-year-old hometown product up with virtually no seasoning and against the advice of their scouts.

At the time, the move generated all kinds of publicity. David Clyde, it was predicted, was going to be the second coming of Lefty Grove and Sandy Koufax. Every time he pitched the Rangers knew there would be a sellout crowd. Well, it turned out to be a big mistake. Clyde didn't have great mechanics, nor did he have enough knowledge to pitch in the big leagues, and ultimately he hurt his arm. There's no telling how good a pitcher he might have become if he had been developed properly in the minors, but by being rushed he never had a chance to reach his potential. He was in the majors for parts of just five seasons, had an 18–33 record, and soon washed out of baseball.

If a pitcher is going to be brought up to get his seasoning in the majors, the team and its evaluators have to make sure he's ready—and not just physically ready to pitch. In 2003, the Tigers brought up a young right-hander named Jeremy Bonderman. He was just twenty years old and jumped directly from A ball.

Because the Tigers were not a good team in 2003 and thin on talent, they wanted to see what some of their best prospects could do. I remember talking to the Tigers' pitching coach, Bob Cluck, who said that Bonderman could handle it mentally, which is very important. But perhaps even more important was the fact that he had great mechanics. A young pitcher with the proper mechanics is less likely to hurt his arm. Because Bonderman didn't have many innings in the minors it was obvious he was going to take some beatings. That's what a young pitcher has to handle mentally. But Bob Cluck also said he had the best stuff of all their young pitchers in the minors, so they were willing to allow him to get his schooling with the big club.

Bonderman made 33 starts for the Tigers and did, indeed, take his lumps. He was 6–19 with a 5.56 earned run average and showed he still had a lot to learn, like keeping the ball down. But he also showed great promise, and because of his good mechanics, he did not encounter any arm problems. In 2004, Bonderman again made 33 starts, improved his record to 11–13, and lowered his ERA to 4.89. Opposing hitters batted just .242 against him as compared with .294 his rookie season. Once more his arm was fine, and he pitched his best games in the second half of the season. So the move to bring him up early may ultimately pay off. Still, it's something you would rarely have seen in days past.

In fact, when young pitchers came up years ago, even starters, they were often sent to the bullpen. Then they had to pitch well enough to crack the rotation. I remember the Dodgers doing that with Orel Hershiser and Dave Stewart. Both ultimately became outstanding starters, but they began their major-league careers coming out of the pen. Now a team often looks for the best arms and puts them right into the rotation. A team like Detroit, which was expected to lose 100 games in 2003, figured it might as well get its best kids up, see what they were made of, and teach them at the same time. If a kid can handle it both mentally and physically, why not? But again, to do this and avoid mistakes, you have to have very solid evaluators within your organization.

Another great example of the importance of developing sound mechanics early on can be found in two of the young pitching stars with the Chicago Cubs, Mark Prior and Kerry Wood. Both were great in 2003 and almost pitched the Cubbies into the World Series. Wood came up a few years earlier, a strikeout phenom with a great fastball and sharp curve. As good as he was, it was obvious that Kerry was stepping across his body pretty badly when he threw, and I remember saying to myself that this kid could very well hurt his elbow. Many times, organizations will leave their best prospects alone as long as they're having success. But poor technique must be corrected early or it will invariably lead to problems. This is all part of the proper development. Sure enough, Wood wound up having major reconstructive elbow surgery. Fortunately, he was young, and with today's advanced surgical techniques he was able to come all the way back. And he has finally begun to work on not throwing across his body.

Wood, who had the surgery several years ago, was 14–11 in 2003 with 266 strikeouts, but again had arm problems in 2004, finishing at 8–9. Correcting bad mechanics, however, is not just a matter of talent or stats. Some pitchers can be effective throwing across their bodies, but with mechanics like that they are going to break down. It's really a matter of longevity. Good mechanics give you a much better chance at staying healthy. Look at Roger Clemens. Most of his injuries—and there haven't been many—have been muscle strains in the legs or groin. His mechanics are excellent and he has rarely had an arm problem, even at the age of forty-two.

Let me explain exactly what I mean by throwing across the body. Right-handed pitchers like Wood have a natural stride in which their lead leg lands in the direction of the third-base on-deck circle. When a pitcher strides that way, he tends to land on his heel, which blocks out his hip, and this causes him to have trouble finishing the pitch. That results in all the pressure going to his upper body, specifically his elbow and shoulder. With this kind of throwing motion, a pitcher has a much greater chance of hurting himself over time. Rick Ankiel of the Cardinals was another young pitcher who, though successful in his first season, may have been rushed up too soon. He also stepped across his body terribly. After a great year in the minors he was brought up to the bigs. I remember seeing him pitch against the Brewers while doing a TV broadcast, and commenting on the air that his mechanics were not good and that there was a strong chance he would both hurt himself and have trouble consistently throwing strikes. Sure enough, he had control problems, then hurt his arm. He returned to the Cards briefly in 2003 and walked 25 hitters in 24 innings. In 2004, he had somewhat better mechanics, but still didn't pitch well, giving up 10 hits and 6 runs in just 10 innings of work. Mentally drained, in the spring of 2005 he decided to give up pitching and try to make it back to the majors as an outfielder.

There is a fairly simple way for a pitcher to correct his mechanics when he throws across his body. He can adjust by changing the position of his heel on the rubber. If a right-handed pitcher is stepping toward third when he strides, he should turn his heel on the rubber so that the toe is on the inside and the heel is out. The more he turns his toe in, the more difficult it is to stride toward third. The fact is that a lot of young pitchers are not taught how to set up on the rubber properly. That's the starting point and a very basic way to make corrections, since the back leg acts like a rudder on a ship, and can dictate the direction in which the front leg moves. Bob Gibson used the rubber almost like a starting block at a track meet. Good teachers and player-development people in the minors will spot and try to correct this problem quickly.

On the other side of the coin is a Mark Prior. He too came to the Cubs early as a phenom, a pitcher with not only good stuff, but great poise. He came out of the program at USC and was more than ready for the competition, the crowds, and the pressures of pitching in the bigs. But Prior brought something else as well, almost perfect mechanics. He uses his legs correctly and has good alignment with his feet, which produces the proper arm angle. He's had some minor arm problems, but with sound mechanics the chances of a major injury are much less. Prior was 18–6 in 2003, then was hampered by injuries and was just 6–4 in 2004. The trouble began with an injury to his Achilles tendon, and when you hurt your legs it can often affect your mechanics. Prior admitted as much when he said he tried to come back too soon, and with his mechanics altered, he suffered a minor arm injury.

Though the chance of injury isn't as great as it is with pitchers, hitters sometimes come to the majors with bad habits as well. When I was a young player I dove across the plate when I would stride, a habit I probably developed as a kid. When you're a diver, an inside pitch will tie you up. One of the better hitters in today's game, Luis Gonzalez of the Arizona Diamondbacks, is also a diver. Before he came to the Diamondbacks he had a closed stance and had trouble turning on an inside pitch. If you watch Luis hit now, he has a wide-open stance. A left-handed hitter, he waits for the pitch with his right foot almost pointing toward first. By opening up like that in the setup position, Gonzalez can still dive at the ball, but now the dive puts him in perfect hitting position, allowing him to get his hips through first, something he couldn't do before he opened his stance. No longer does his front foot step across his body. When he strides from an open stance, his two feet wind up perpendicular to the pitcher.

Incorrect hitting technique and bad pitching mechanics were all things that were corrected in the minors years ago, but aren't always caught today. It's a combination of rushing players up too quickly and not having enough instructors at the lower levels to correct these things early on. Cheap in the wrong place again. Years ago a young pitcher in the Dodgers organization would have the benefit of working with Sandy Koufax, Johnny Podres, Don Drysdale, Larry Sherry, Claude Osteen, Burt Hooton, and Ron Perranoski. The young hitters had equally gifted and experienced instructors. When kids are rushed to the big leagues today there just aren't enough quality instructors around. And you can only hope that the ones who are there are knowledgeable enough to spot problems before they hinder a kid's career.

By now you're probably wondering why these bad habits can't be corrected at the major-league level, where the best people supposedly reside. There's a good reason. At the major-league level you have to win. There's no time to take a young player, break him down, then build him up again, all while getting him the playing time needed to work on his mechanics or hitting technique. A hitting coach, for instance, can't spend a month working intensely with one or two young players. He's got to get all his hitters ready to contribute and help the team win. At the big-league level it's a money game, with winning the bottom line, and that's why the minor leagues are so important to the development of young players. That's the training ground, and that's where the best instructors are needed.

The job of an instructor is not only to spot, change, and alter bad habits, but also to know what it's going to take for a player to have longevity and maintain good habits. In addition, he has to be able to prepare a player mentally for what he will face in the big leagues. That's best not only for the player, but for the organization. Yet some continue to shy away from tinkering with a young player because he's so talented. That isn't the way to do it. A good instructor can make even the most talented young player better. When player-development people see a kid struggling, they should want to get involved. Obviously, there is a right way and a wrong way to handle each individual to get the most out of him. Do it wrong, and you can lose the kid for good.

There are some signs today that more organizations are waking up to the fact that they need solid, veteran people in developmental positions throughout the system. And some modern-day players like Robin Yount, Don Mattingly, and Paul Molitor are beginning to come back as coaches and instructors because they still have passion for the game. Mattingly, for example, is now the batting coach for the Yankees and works with young players in the spring.

One thing is certain, though: you can never allow statistical evaluation to completely replace the human element. Today the JUGS gun, for example, is used too often as a final authority when evaluating a young pitcher. Sure, a guy may throw 95 miles per hour, but does he have command and movement? Does he have a real instinct for pitching and for working hitters? Another guy might throw just 88 but do everything right. He's got ball movement, control, stamina, and the knowledge of how to pitch. Dismiss him because the gun doesn't register well over 90 and you might lose another Greg Maddux. So teams have to dig deep, and apply more scouts to determine a prospect's physical and mental makeup.

Some teams are beginning to see the light. Detroit, for all its problems the last few years, is now trying to get the pride back. The Tigers hired a former star, Alan Trammell, as their manager, and now have other former top players like Kirk Gibson and Lance Parrish working as instructors. Besides having been fine ballplayers, these guys were world champions and know what it takes to win. With a young team full of fine prospects, it makes perfect sense to bring guys like this back to help develop them. Prior to the 2004 season the Tigers brought in Pudge Rodriguez as a free agent. With his leadership, the team began to show improvement. They've already added veteran closer Troy Percival and power-hitting outfielder Magglio Ordonez for 2005, and seem to be blending their youngsters with a few seasoned veterans, a solid formula for success.

Some others who are on the right page include Billy Beane of the A's. He has a good feel for the game because he played at all levels, including a stint in the majors, and while he relies on stats to some degree he also has good baseball men around him. Kevin Towers, GM of the Padres, was a pitcher and shows a good feel for putting a club together within the limits of a budget. Sandy Johnson, now with the Mets, is another sharp baseball man. When he was with Arizona, he was instrumental in putting together the core group that won the World Series in 2001. But Sandy had a world of experience. He brought Juan Gonzalez, Pudge Rodriguez, and Sammy Sosa to Texas and the Alomars to San Diego, and trained Omar Minaya, who is now the general manager of the Mets. These are the kinds of guys who should be watching over an organization, supervising how its players are developing, and constantly evaluating talent in the event of trades and signings.

Brian Cashman, the GM of the Yankees, is an example of a guy who hasn't played, but still knows what is important when putting together a team. He allows his evaluators to have a great deal of influence over player moves and he's proud to admit it. He doesn't pretend, as some do, that he has all the answers. He listens to evaluators like Gene "Stick" Michael, who has had a lot of influence over personnel moves. I remember when I was on the road for my broadcasting work and I saw Gene in Chicago. I knew the Yankees had some interest in trying to deal for Sammy Sosa, and I told him I knew what he was there for.

Gene just looked at me and said, "Yeah, you know how it is."

Guys like that are always on the road, always looking at players. The good organizations never stop looking and never stop developing players. These franchises rely on their instructors as the lifeblood of their organizations because they understand that player development is essential to remaining consistently successful in an era of high roster turnover. It may even be worthwhile to pay the best instructors six figures a year to work in the low minors. While it may not be a glamorous job and these men won't ever enjoy a lot of notoriety, they will nevertheless be doing a job that is as important as any within the framework of a successful organization.

Bad Coaches Are Hurting the Game

The quality of coaching that young players are now receiving from Little League right up through college has been a concern of mine for some time. Baseball has taken some hits in the last few years, losing kids in the United States to other sports. You simply don't see as many kids playing baseball on the sandlots today as you did in the past. That's why coaching at the amateur levels becomes all the more important. It's the early part of player development before the pros step in. If youth coaches are contributing to kids losing their enthusiasm for baseball or leaving the sport to pursue other things, then, plain and simple, they are not doing their jobs the right way.

I had a coach in high school who had played in the Pirates organization, and because he had played professional baseball, he knew what it was all about. Don't get me wrong, he was tough. He didn't hesitate to embarrass you if you made a mistake, and he kicked guys off the team for being late. But we didn't run home to our parents whenever something went wrong. And while he may not have done everything the right way, he molded us into winners.

I've been teaching baseball privately on occasion around the Los Angeles area for the last five or six years, and just by listening to the kids that I work with, it sure seems as if a lot of coaches are giving them the wrong advice. I've heard at least five times that coaches at different amateur levels of the game are telling their kids that the swing they should be practicing and using is different from the swing hitters use in the pros. That's one of the clichés they like to use. I wish someone would tell me how and why it is different. It's not. A good swing is a good swing, and a proper swing is simply a proper swing. This is true at all levels. When I hear an amateur coach say, "He'll learn to swing like a pro when he turns pro," I have to wonder. How do you think Ken Griffey Jr. and Barry Bonds developed their trademark swings? They learned from their famous dads and by hanging around big-league ballparks from the time they were five years old. They were fortunate to have the right instruction at an early age. Not all kids are that fortunate.

Another piece of advice I hear is "Get your arm up, find your arm slot." But when the kid asks how he should do it, the coach will admit he doesn't know, repeating that the kid should just get his arm up. I've even heard coaches tell pitchers, "You don't use your legs to throw." Now that's sound advice. Just throw with your arm and see what happens. I even remember one coach at a high school in Los Angeles using an instructional manual from the 1950s. Some of the material was still applicable, but some of it wasn't. He was trying to paraphrase what the book was saying, but he didn't have a clue how to teach on his own.

Bad coaches at the amateur levels will sure as hell hinder the development of young players and sometimes destroy their passion for the game. Some aren't teaching the right things, and others are out to make a buck by teaching privately. There isn't much money in lower-level amateur coaching, so those involved have to be dedicated to it and have a passion for teaching and for the game.

When I first tried out at Taft High School in the tenth grade I was only five feet five inches tall. Not surprisingly, I was cut immediately. The coach said, "You're too small, kid." Fortunately, I'd had defensive skills from the time I was eight years old, and once I grew I made the team and wound up an all-city selection in Los Angeles as a senior. Kids who love the game have to persevere any way they can, especially if they don't have coaches to keep urging them on.

Even now, I still hear stories that amaze me. When I was working with a friend's son, who was a very good high school hitter, he told me that one of his early coaches instructed him to chop down on the ball—to swing in a downward arc. In reality, you want to swing through the baseball to create backspin, almost the same as a tennis player hitting the ball over the net. The ball is coming in on a downward trajectory, at a 5- to 7-degree angle from the pitcher's release point, and if you chop down, only one thing can happen: you'll pound the ball into the dirt and won't hit it squarely. A few speedy ground ball hitters, like Mickey Rivers and Maury Wills in the past, and Tommy Goodwin and Juan Pierre today, have been successful chopping down on the ball because their speed helps them create base hits. For the rest, especially hitters with pop, they have to swing through the ball, using their legs and hips to get their hands through and generate power, hopefully resulting in a line drive or home run. If a kid is taught any other way, he's being taught incorrectly.

I remember hearing a story about Reggie Smith, who was a great switch-hitter for the Red Sox, Cardinals, and Dodgers. Reggie's son was playing for a coach who kept telling him his swing was all wrong. He replied by telling the coach that he had learned his swing from his dad, then added that Henry Aaron had swung the bat that way and was baseball's all-time home run champion. You won't believe the coach's answer. He was completely serious when he said that Aaron made 755 mistake swings! This is what some of these coaches are telling kids, and it simply amazes me.

I've also heard these things firsthand. In talking with amateur, high school, and even collegiate coaches over a period of several years I was shocked at some of the things they told me. There are simply too many programs in which the coaches display a lack of a real understanding of the game and how to teach it. That's why many kids with talent today are seeking out private instruction and going to baseball academies.

So we're really talking about two different levels of player development, both of which must be upgraded if the game is to continue to find the best athletes and potentially the best players. If the amateur coaches don't do a better job, then many kids will leave the game before they have a chance to be drafted. Those who are fortunate enough to make it to the minors also need to be developed properly, and that means having both the top people and resources to get the job done. With all the money available in sports today, there has to be more than enough for player development, even if it means cutting back in some other areas. The game is only as good as its players, and every team in the majors should make it its responsibility to keep those players moving upward through a well-organized pipeline that develops them to their fullest potential.

CHAPTER THREE

◆

A Manager's Best Friend:
The Old Latin American Winter Leagues

The Latin American winter leagues were a great training ground for both players and managers. But the cultures were very different. In Venezuela we had two guards in the dugout with machine guns. Betting at games was heavy. After one game, the fans began shaking our van back and forth. Juan Berenguer, who pitched that day, said they were mad at him because he didn't strike out ten that night and a lot of people lost bets. It was scary because many of us were with our girlfriends and wives, and we all knew we were in danger.

There's no doubt in my mind that playing and/or managing in the Latin American winter leagues is a total baseball learning experience. The quality of baseball played in Mexico, Venezuela, Puerto Rico, and the Dominican Republic falls clearly between Triple-A and the big leagues. Unfortunately, because of the stipulations of today's long-term contracts, you don't find as many star players in winter ball as in the past. Certain teams forbid their Latin American stars from playing winter ball for fear of losing a player to injury. But Latin players have traditionally had a great deal of passion for playing in front of their countrymen. Competing in the winter also keeps these players in shape for the next season. Also, for young players on the verge of making it, winter ball is a great opportunity to get more at bats and playing experience, which can only improve their chances of reaching the bigs.

In the winter leagues, you're exposed to a change in culture and this includes fans who view baseball somewhat differently than in the States. Living and travel conditions are also quite different, and there is sometimes an element of danger that doesn't exist back home. Yet, it was an experience I wouldn't trade for any other, as I can say with complete certainty that the knowledge I gained playing and managing in Latin America was instrumental in helping me when I finally had my chance to manage in the majors.

My first direct experience with the winter leagues came in 1978. I had had a solid year at Rochester, my first full season in Triple-A, and got a call in late October to play that winter in Mexico. To be perfectly honest, my initial motivation was the money. I learned I'd be paid $2,000 a month if I stayed at a Holiday Inn about thirty miles from the ballpark, or $2,300 a month if I stayed in town. I decided to opt for the extra $300. The town was Guasave, about thirty miles from Los Mochis, where a rival team was located. There was still another team farther south in Culiacán. To get to Guasave, I had to fly to Tucson, then take a bus to a border town in Arizona called Nogalis, and then catch a train. The ride was like something out of *Butch Cassidy and the Sundance Kid,* almost a trip back in time. I thought the train would go directly to Guasave, but instead it went to Los Mochis, which was the last stop. Welcome to Mexico.

It was already 11:00 P.M. when I got there, and I didn't know where to go. I was sitting in the station with all kinds of luggage and looking more than a little bit lost. Next to me was a guy I had spoken with on the train who, while Chinese, spoke fluent Spanish. Thankfully, I spoke some Spanish, and I learned that he had settled in Mexico some twenty years earlier. When I explained my situation, he offered to give me a ride to Guasave, and for a good reason. He said in no uncertain terms that "it can be pretty dangerous around here late at night."

The town of Guasave was about the size of a football field. There was a little disco there, and I heard soon after arriving that a couple of years earlier an American minor leaguer was killed after hitting on a

Mexican girl at the club. Rule number one: You didn't mess around with local women while playing there. In fact, I remember getting a ride to the post office one day with two nineteen-year-old girls who said they were baseball fans. I just wanted to mail a letter to my fiancée back home, the only way I could communicate with her at the time. A policeman, who knew who I was because he was friends with the manager of the hotel, said, "Kevin, you shouldn't do that. You've got to be careful around here. I know why you wanted to go to the post office, but people around here may see it differently. Those girls were probably younger than nineteen. Take my advice and don't do it again." I think he was worried that I might be shot, so I never had anyone take me anywhere in Guasave again.

The potential dangers notwithstanding, playing in the winter league turned out to be a great learning experience. Because I stayed in the hotel so much of the time, I improved my Spanish by listening to the guy who worked the desk. My improved command of the language would help me later when I managed Latin players. The team was definitely a mixed bag. Besides naive young players like myself, there were some veterans on the roster who had been in the majors. Hal King, who played with several big-league teams in the late 1960s and early 1970s, was there, and so was George Brunet, who had some good years pitching with the Angels. In fact, George eventually married a Mexican girl and wound up pitching down there for years. Carlos Lopez, whom I met at spring training with the Orioles and who was already in the big leagues, also played on the team.

The next year I played in Venezuela for La Guaira, a port city near Caracas. The caliber of baseball was very strong, but the culture shock was daunting. This time, our accommodations were decent. We stayed out by the beach and were picked up by a van to take us to the ballpark. The team would rotate the roster, constantly adding or dropping players every few games, but there were always six to eight Americans on the roster at any one time. We had major leaguers like Clint Hurdle, who had set a Venezuelan League home run record there a year earlier before Bo Diaz eventually broke it. Mike Edwards, Danny Graham, Luis Sanchez, Buck Martinez, Roy Lee Jackson, U. L. Washington, Wayne Krenchicki, and Juan Berenguer also played that season. The roster was made up of a combination of big leaguers, Triple-A players, and native Latin players.

Caracas was our big rival. They had players like Manny Trillo, Ken Phelps, Dwayne Murphy, and Tony Armas. In fact, you could say the team had a big-league outfield—they were that good. The afore-mentioned Bo Diaz, who would play in the majors for more than a dozen years, was their catcher. The level of play was always great, but the culture made the adjustment difficult, beginning with a couple of guards carrying machine guns stationed in the dugout each night. Imagine that in Chicago, or Anaheim, or Kansas City.

I remember asking if the guards were necessary and being told they were there just in case any little problem arose. Little problem! Machine guns! Some potential problem solver. The games usually sold out, with the stadiums holding twenty-five thousand to thirty thousand fans. With that kind of crowd, I learned that a little prob-lem could turn into a big problem very quickly. The atmosphere was a lot like you see at soccer stadiums around the world as fans rooted with all kinds of fervor, and it didn't help that there was always heavy betting going on with sizable sums of money changing hands during the games. I think there were a couple of shootings in the stands that year, probably sparked by the emotion brought on by the gambling.

One night when we were leaving the stadium a bunch of fans sur-rounded our van and began shaking it back and forth. A few of us had our girlfriends and wives with us, so, needless to say, it was a frighten-ing situation. Juan Berenguer, who pitched that day, took the blame, saying that the fans were mad at him because he didn't strike out ten batters that night. He knew immediately those shaking the van had lost bets—maybe big bets—and were bent on doing real harm. This was no joke but fortunately it didn't go beyond the shaking. It was also an awakening to the real world of changing cultures and what was important to the people there. It made you appreciate all the more what you had at home.

It also wasn't surprising to have our van stopped and checked out by the military. Apparently, the government was worried about revo-lutionary activity in 1979 and they tended to stop vehicles that obviously contained foreigners. They would check our IDs and ask us what we were doing there and where we were going. Because they were all armed, it was very intimidating.

Our manager was Preston Gomez, who had already signed to take over the Cubs the following season. During a game right before the playoffs were set to begin, Preston went out to the mound to make a pitching change and someone threw a size-D battery at him. He went down as if he'd been shot, and when we got out to him, he was bleeding heavily and we could see that his eye was cut very badly. What came to my mind immediately was that the perpetrator was a disgruntled gambler who didn't want that pitching change made. Preston was so upset that he said he was going to leave, right then and there, and return to his home in Los Angeles. I remember most of the players going into the training room, seeing him on the table, and trying to convince him to stay, as we all had a great deal of respect for him as a manager. He was also something of a father figure, and we all felt we needed him to be there for the playoffs.

Preston was from Cuba and was still trying to get members of his family out of that country, and yet he couldn't believe the way some of the Venezuelan fans behaved. But in truth, similar things have happened in big-league stadiums, with fans throwing batteries and cell phones out on the field or at individual players. I saw it again in 2004 when Yankee fans began throwing baseballs on the field in Game 6 of the ALCS against Boston. People get passionate and emotional about their teams, and some always take it too far, but luckily not to the point where we need guards with machine guns in the dugouts. But who knows; when it gets to the point where drunken fans can run out on the field and begin beating a first-base coach, as happened to Kansas City's Tom Gamboa in Chicago in 2002, you wonder where it's all going to end.

Yet with all these surprising and potentially frightening events, there was still great competition on the field. During this time I had the opportunity to observe different players from other organizations, acquire an understanding of various cultures, work with several managers, and deal with people from a variety of backgrounds. Besides helping me as a player, those first two years in the winter leagues also provided me with experience that I carried over to when I managed in Latin America.

Heading South to Manage

My managing career began at Great Falls, Montana, in 1984, and I spent three years with the Dodgers' Pioneer League team there, in rookie ball. We had a tremendous season in 1985, going 54–16, breaking an all-time rookie league record, and finishing in first place, so I felt I was well on the way to establishing myself as a quality manager. The following spring, while I was also serving as the major- and minor-league roving catching instructor—rookie league didn't begin until June—Manny Mota came up to me one day and said: "Hey, Chief wants to know if you would manage in winter ball this year."

Chief, of course, was Al Campanis, the Dodgers' general manager, and when he spoke, you listened. I asked Mota where, and he told me Puerto Rico, explaining that the Dodgers had a new working agreement with the Santurce Cangrejeros, located in the San Juan area. I knew the Dodgers had a longtime agreement with Licey in the Domincan Republic and that Tommy Lasorda had managed there. Apparently they were branching out because they felt the winter leagues had real value, making this an offer I couldn't refuse.

When the Dodgers entered into an agreement with a Latin American winter-league team, it meant that the big-league club would supply the manager and one or two coaches, as well as a number of strong prospects from within the organization. Since the Dodgers had a reputation then for developing young prospects, most Latin clubs jumped at the chance to work with them. It was beneficial for both teams, and for winter baseball. I felt good heading down there because Luis Isaac, who was my third-base coach, told me he thought I was the first American to go directly from managing in rookie ball to managing in what the people in Latin America considered their big leagues. I was very proud and felt I was ready for the challenge.

I had an interesting team that year, including a number of Dodger prospects, with the most important one being center fielder Mike Devereaux. He was the guy on the fast track, whose immediate development was paramount to the parent club. Also on the team were players such as Sixto Lezcano, Ruben Sierra (following his first year in the majors), Juan Beniquez, Sandy Alomar Jr., Ivan DeJesus, Luis Aguayo, Jose Valentin, and Jose Lind. Dave Wallace, my pitching coach, was fluent in Spanish, and I could hold my own, so communication wasn't a problem. Other players in the league that year included Bernie Williams, who was very young and served mostly as a pinch runner, and Robbie Alomar, Juan Gonzalez, Edgar Martinez, and Bobby Bonilla.

Another player I remember well from back then was Ivan Calderon. Ivan was a native of Puerto Rico and was later murdered down there in December 2003. He was a rugged-looking guy who had some good years in the majors and could flat-out hit. He and I became friendly in Montreal in 1992, when I was bench coach under Felipe Alou. One night after a game in Philadelphia, Ivan and our hitting coach, Jay Ward, were having a couple of beers in Jay's hotel room. They invited me to join them, and we sat and talked baseball. After a while, Ivan stood up and said, "Guys, I gotta go." I liked Ivan and enjoyed talking hitting with him, so I said, "Hey, man, hang around a bit longer, why don't you."

He smiled and said, "Got to go. I have my wife on the sixth floor and my girlfriend on the fourth floor."

I said, "Are you crazy?" and he smiled again. When I read about him getting killed, I thought of that night in Philly right away.

I was just thirty-two years old and still learning the X's and O's of game situations when I took the helm in Puerto Rico. No one can learn everything overnight, and at the same time, the winter leagues always present young managers—or any first-time manager—with some inherent, built-in problems and situations whose solutions aren't necessarily found in the so-called book on managing. If you are able to handle these problems, learn, persevere, and still win, then you can say you've graduated from one of the greatest managing schools ever created.

Just what were some of the problems? For openers, the manager doesn't have the same kind of power he has in the minors, where the entire organization is behind him. Because of the many individuals he has to handle in the winter leagues and the fact that they aren't all from the same parent organization, the potential problems are multiplied. Some players have their own agendas, a few don't care much, and all the while you have to deal with personal animosities and a variety of egos.

The Dodgers sent Mike Devereaux to Puerto Rico because they wanted him groomed as their next center fielder, so he had to get playing time. That was very important to the organization. The incumbent center fielder was veteran Juan Beniquez, who had been in the majors since the early 1970s and played winter ball almost every year. Juan was a native of Puerto Rico and was expected to break the league's all-time hit record during that season. Now I had the unenviable job of telling him he wouldn't be starting. I had already heard he could be a problem, and that he sometimes didn't run hard on routine grounders and pop-ups. So it was a situation I knew had to be addressed immediately—and with some tact.

I called Juan in the first day to let him know that I was well aware that he was going for the hit record. I expressed the respect I had for him as a ballplayer, the solid big-league career he'd had, and his passion for the game, which led him to play winter ball almost every year. I told him he would get his at bats, see some time in the outfield, and serve as the designated hitter other times, and that we would work through the season together. I think he appreciated my honesty and the direct way I approached him. Our relationship quickly became one of mutual respect, and I never had a problem with Juan in the three years I managed him in winter ball.

Sixto Lezcano, another veteran player, had a habit of showing up late, or sometimes not at all. As a manager, you can't continue to allow this to happen, because rules and discipline must be the same for everyone. Finally, one day when he was late once again, I slotted him into the ninth spot in the batting order. He refused to play if he was going to bat last, saying that it would embarrass him in front of his fans. That was my opening. I told him he was embarrassing me, the coaches, and his teammates by showing up late consistently, and that he was showing no respect for any of us. That seemed to strike a chord, and after that run-in Sixto and I got along fine.

Orlando Sanchez, who had played with the Cards for a time, had been the Santurce first baseman for years. Larry See, one of the young Dodger prospects we brought down that year, was also a first baseman. Orlando knew that Larry had to get his playing time, but one day when we had a doubleheader, I started Larry in both games. That was too much for Orlando to take. As soon as the second game began, he left the dugout, got dressed, and went up to sit in the stands. What he didn't understand was that I was there to develop the Dodgers' prospects, and get them as many at bats as possible. We had had a couple of rainouts before the doubleheader and I felt Larry needed the work, but Orlando didn't see it that way. I talked to him after the game and explained why I had to get Larry See and the other Dodger prospects the majority of the at bats. At the same time, I told him I would try to keep the native players in the lineup as often as possible. After that, I found ways to get Orlando into the lineup more often, but still played Larry enough to accelerate his development.

There is another, related contradiction all managers face in winter ball. Whether it is Mexico, Venezuela, Puerto Rico, or the Dominican Republic, the ultimate goal for all the team is to win. That, in itself, isn't surprising. It's no different in the majors. These aren't developmental leagues. Yet part of the job of the manager is to help young prospects develop. That's the primary goal in the minors—development—and that's what the manager strives to do. Winning is secondary to getting your prospects to the big leagues, though it's still nice to win. In winter ball, however, the manager has to do both—develop his prospects *and* win. And believe me, there is always plenty of pressure to win, because the teams make a good deal of their money in the playoffs.

Ticket sales go up in the playoffs, and most games are sold out. Advertising revenues also increase. Sponsors have their businesses showcased on the outfield walls, and those prices can rise come playoff time. In addition, the Caribbean World Series is a huge event and teams get more money from television revenues. For these reasons, some of the owners of the winter-league teams couldn't care less about the prospects. They want to win, and on more than one occasion managers have been fired just a month into the season. So if I wasn't doing the job, I knew I could be fired too, and I didn't want that, for myself or for the Dodgers. Put all those ingredients into the pot and that's what made my first year in Puerto Rico the toughest of my managing career in the winter leagues.

In my second year there we had a great season and came within one game of going to the Caribbean World Series. Ruben Sierra dropped a routine fly ball in the sixth game against Mayagüez, forcing a seventh and deciding game, and that's how we lost it. Their team had stars such as Bobby Bonilla and Paul O'Neill, and was managed by my friend Jim Riggleman. Our team had many of the same players as the previous year but added Jay Bell to play shortstop. Jay really came into his own that year and led us into the playoffs.

My last year in Puerto Rico, 1988, was also a difficult one because we didn't get paid. Everyone is paid by the winter-league club, and the parent club's salary—in my case the Dodgers'—was separate. That's why a lot of guys play winter ball—for the extra money. But that year there were problems. Sometimes our checks were late. The veteran players were the first to take action, threatening to leave the team. We had four or five non-Dodger players from the States on the team, plus a number of native players, so the politics involved were very tricky. By the last game of the season it had become very ugly. Some players didn't want to play, but the team couldn't reach a unanimous decision. Some wound up staying, but others left, and I had to ask a couple of the coaches to play just to field a team. It was more of a farce than a real game, and shortly after the season ended the Dodgers terminated their working agreement with Santurce.

Fortunately, that didn't end my winter-league managing career. In 1989 the Dodgers asked me to manage the Licey Tigres in the Dominican Republic. The Tigres were located in Santo Domingo. The other team located there was the Escogido club, managed by Felipe Alou. That's how I got to know Felipe and came to have a great deal of respect for him.

At any rate, the two teams had a great rivalry. They had Sammy Sosa and Geronimo Berroa, among others, but my team was loaded as well. We had Dave Hansen, John Wetteland, Ramon Martinez, Pedro Astacio, Darrin Fletcher, and Felix Jose. The baseball was every bit the equivalent of the Puerto Rican League, as the talent was almost identical. There was, however, a difference in living conditions. The last couple of years in Puerto Rico I had stayed in a condo on the beach, overlooking the ocean. In the Dominican, I stayed in a hotel where accommodations weren't nearly as nice. The power was constantly going out and a generator had to be started. For American junk-food junkies, there wasn't even a Burger King to pop into after a game.

I also came to understand the abject poverty many of these players were surrounded by when they grew up. We were returning to Santo Domingo after one of our road trips and crossing over a bridge. Beneath the bridge were small, run-down shacks alongside the river. One of my coaches, Teddy Martinez, a Dominican who had played for the Dodgers at one time, pointed to one of the shacks.

"That's where Gilberto Reyes grew up," he said.

I had to look twice. Gilberto Reyes was the Dodgers' number one catching prospect at the time, a big kid with a powerful arm. He could throw guys out from his knees. Seeing the conditions under which a kid like that grew up helped me deal with different cultures when I was back in the States. I became more patient with certain players because I now had a better understanding of where they came from. Knowing that a guy like Reyes grew up in a shack on the riverbank allowed me to better understand why some players had different attitudes, and having a more complete understanding of Latin players was one of the reasons I got my first big-league managing job in Texas.

But seeing those shacks wasn't the only eye-opening incident from my time spent in the Dominican. Another time we were on the bus going to the opposite end of the island, about a three-hour ride. We were just outside the city going across that same bridge where the shacks were located. Suddenly there were a couple of teenagers in the road, flagging down the bus. The driver figured he'd better stop, and with good reason. Both boys were waving Uzis in the air. They jumped on the bus, and needless to say, when you're staring down at a couple of Uzis you begin to wonder what's going to happen next. I asked one of my Dominican coaches, but he didn't seem too concerned.

"Don't worry, don't worry," he repeated. "There's always a lot of revolutionary activity going on. These guys are probably just checking us out."

Fortunately, the kids spoke English. The coach told them we were the Licey Tigres, and then one of them recognized Ramon Martinez, Pedro's brother.

"Hey, Ramon," he said. "I'm a big fan. Okay, you guys go ahead. Win the game."

Then they jumped off. Thank God for baseball fans. I think if we had been a busload of tourists, we would have been robbed, and who knows if someone would have been hurt. I turned to Dave Wallace, my pitching coach, and asked him if he thought Fred Claire, who was then the Dodgers' GM, knew what we were going through down here. Dave just shook his head.

I shouldn't have been too surprised, because back then a lot of the players in the Dominican also carried guns. The bus would often pick up and drop off players along the way. Many of them still lived in depressed areas and they were worried about being robbed late at night. Games were often over at about 11:00 P.M., and when we were on the road we wouldn't get back until 2:00 or 3:00 in the morning. People knew ballplayers had money, and a lot of them wore gold chains, making them potential targets. One night we dropped Ramon Martinez off somewhere in Santo Domingo, and as he walked past to get off the bus, Dave Wallace smacked him on the side, as if to say way to go, and he hit a revolver, which was on his belt under his shirt. To be honest, carrying a gun made perfect sense to me.

Because of the difference in cultures, a manager sometimes had to deal with things in Latin America that would rarely or never occur in the States. One of my players in the Dominican was Felix Jose, who was just beginning his big-league career with the Oakland A's. He was slated to be my starting right fielder, and I had already heard rumors about how he hated managers who didn't play him. But I felt I could handle that situation by keeping an open dialogue with him. Plans changed about a week before the season opened when Felix was shot in the head during a robbery attempt. He was lucky. He tried to run from the robber, who then fired at him. Somehow, the bullet went around the back of his skull and didn't do any major damage. I re-member it being touted as a miracle story in the Dominican.

Later that winter, Felix rejoined the team. We were on our way back from a road game and guys were playing cards, talking, sleeping—all the things they do during a bus ride. I was sitting at the front of the bus when an argument started toward the rear. Juan Bell, whose brother George had a fine career with the Toronto Blue Jays, was sitting behind Felix. Apparently, he began tapping Felix on the head, teasing him. Felix told him to stop, saying he was tapping him in the place he'd been shot. Finally, Felix snapped and took a swing at Juan. The fight was broken up quickly, but when we arrived home, Juan jumped off the bus and vowed to get a gun, come back, and kill Felix. In the Dominican, this was nothing to laugh at.

Shortly after I awoke the next morning my phone rang. It was one of my coaches telling me that Juan was already at the ballpark, with a gun, and looking for Felix. Now it was serious. Simple teasing had turned into a potential life-and-death situation. We quickly got hold of George Bell, who was then retired, and he came out to the ballpark. George helped calm his brother down, and by the time Felix arrived the immediate threat had ended. But it still took some time to get the whole thing settled, even as both guys remained on the team. I've never forgotten the impact of that, how I felt about it, and what I learned about the culture in Latin America. As a manager, I had to watch everything and couldn't dismiss anything as trivial, no matter how slight it might seem at first.

We had a very good team that year and late in the season had a small lead over our archrival, Escogido. Ramon Martinez was pitch-ing a crucial game for us at their ballpark. We were ahead, 1–0, and tempers were running high. Ramon threw one close to Sammy Sosa and Sammy charged the mound. Fortunately, that scuffle was broken up with no harm done. It was still 1–0 with two outs in the bottom of the fifth, and Ramon was one out away from making it an official game. Suddenly, all the lights in the park went out! Total darkness, a complete power failure. The ballpark was packed and the fans just sat. Finally, after about two hours with no power, the game was called. I know they had generators there, but they never went on. Dave Wallace and I just looked at each other when it happened, wondering how the power had gone out at such a convenient time.

"Got to have been some major money on the game," Dave said. "I guess the wrong people thought they were going to lose big."

I just nodded. I had managed long enough down there to realize that the power outage was gambling related. The safest place for us that night was to remain in the dugout. Finally, after the game was called, we went to the clubhouse, where they put a small generator on and we were able to get dressed. We all knew that what had happened was more than an accident, more than a coincidence. It was all part of the way the culture viewed the game and how important gambling was. Seems odd, gambling and baseball. It's the biggest taboo in the States, has been since the days of the Black Sox and through the Pete Rose scandal, but you couldn't make stories like these up if you tried.

Managing in the winter leagues was an education in many ways. Among other things, it afforded me the opportunity to observe the talent in other organizations, and understand how it was evaluated compared to the Dodgers. Seeing a variety of players is also extremely helpful for future reference, especially if you wind up in a position where you are involved with trades and free-agent signings. By seeing so many players in Puerto Rico and the Dominican, I also learned how to pitch to certain players. I knew their idiosyncrasies. I was my own advance scout just by being in Latin America for those years. As it turned out, I got to the big leagues at about the same time many of the players I had managed and observed in the winter leagues did. So I already knew them well.

Sometimes, when you are with one organization for a long time, as I had been with the Dodgers, you know only one way to do things. But when you go out and watch how other players and other organizations operate, you take from them and learn, eventually applying everything to your own decision-making and evaluation skills. In other words, you are constantly filling the reservoir of your baseball mind. For example, I watched how Felipe Alou managed in winter ball. He liked to control the running game, and because I also liked to run I studied him. He had his pitchers throw to first often, and he'd pitch out occasionally. Felipe would also give the signals to his catcher, who would relay them to the pitcher.

Later, when I became Felipe's bench coach in Montreal, I watched again how he controlled not only the Expos' running game, but the opposition's as well. If you're a running manager, like Felipe and me, you don't want the other team running on you. Keeping them quiet on the bases is a high priority. Otherwise, you lose your advantage. But there are two sides to the coin. One time Felipe had Mark Gardner throw over to first five or six times before coming to the plate. Mark was struggling that day and wound up having a bad inning, and when he came off the mound he let Felipe know he wasn't happy. He felt that throwing to first so often was breaking his concentration on the hitter, which led him to make mistakes.

Gardner's outburst was emotional, but instead of getting in his face as some managers would have done, Felipe said, "Fine, we do it your way next time." He stopped signaling for throws to first, and the other team ran wild. While I understood Gardner's frustration, players have to trust their manager and have the confidence that he knows what's best for them and for the team. Gardner seemed to have learned his lesson because he went on to have a fine big-league career.

By studying other managers, you learn their tendencies. Maybe one manager likes to pitch out only on certain counts. Maybe another never pitches out on a 2-2 count. You try to learn on what counts they like to use the hit-and-run. You also try to get the signs from them by studying the dugout. Technically, this is something the advance scouts should do, but not all of them have the experience to do it well. I learned so much about this important part of managing in the winter leagues just by concentrating on the tendencies of both managers and players. A guy like Mark Whiten had a great arm, but because of his throwing motion it took him extra time to get rid of the ball, and that meant you could go from first to third on a base hit, a little tidbit I remembered when I got to the big leagues.

I managed against Jimmy Riggleman in Puerto Rico and noticed immediately that he was a defense-oriented guy. If he had the lead, Jimmy often put his defensive replacements in as early as the sixth inning. He made those changes earlier than any other manager I knew.

Later, I managed against him in Triple-A. It all helps. The more games you manage, the more you learn, and the more ammunition you have when you reach the big leagues. Because the caliber of baseball is so good in the winter leagues, you learn at a very high level.

For young American players, it's a great place not only to learn and improve, but to show their stuff. The Dodgers had a young third baseman named Jeff Hamilton who wound up playing in the World Series in 1988 at the age of twenty-four. Jeff was a big, strong kid with a ton of natural talent, but he always refused to go to winter ball. He had star written all over him . . . except for one thing. My feeling was he didn't have the drive to reach his full potential and always had other things on his mind. As it turned out, he really wanted to go back home to Michigan and open a fishery, which I was told he ultimately did. His career was relatively short. I always thought that playing winter ball might have opened his eyes to what he could be, and the experience might have helped give him some real passion for the game.

Dave Hansen, whom I've talked about before, was a guy who always looked forward to winter ball. He was fearless to begin with and he knew the experience could help him reach the big leagues. Playing in winter ball opened up everyone's eyes to what he could do. He finished second in the Dominican winter league in hitting in 1989, showed a beautiful, quick swing, and learned how to play third base. Before that, many evaluators weren't high on him, because his fielding was weak and he didn't run well. By playing in winter ball, Dave showed everyone that he could be a serviceable major leaguer, and while he never made a ton of money, he's had a solid career.

Kids today play baseball constantly throughout Latin America. If they don't have the proper equipment, they improvise. This is the way it used to be in the United States. In Latin America there are games going on everywhere, in the streets, on the sandlots, and around the many ballparks where their heroes play in the winter months. Kids are always on top of the outfield fences during batting practice. They all carry fishnets attached to long poles and try to scoop up the baseballs before the outfielders reach them. When they get a ball, they flip it to a friend beyond the fence, who takes off like a shot. That's how they often get their baseballs, shagging down foul balls or home runs, or using the fishnet. I remember throwing batting practice one day in the Dominican, and by the time we were finished, we had just four baseballs left. We had started with a couple of dozen but the kids swiped them left and right.

That's just another truth from winter ball, which gave me an invaluable baseball education, and an experience I wouldn't trade in a million years. If anyone has an opportunity to go to the winter leagues as a player or manager, he should take it and not even think about it twice.

Chapter Four

A Manager on the Job

I was always a proactive type of manager, an aggressive, make-things-happen type of manager—very intense and never content to sit back and wait for the three-run homer. My contention has always been that a manager can influence every game. That's why he's the manager. You can't have an orchestra without a conductor, and I've always hated hearing that all a manager with a good team has to do is fill out the lineup card and make an occasional pitching change.

A manager has to manage, and to do that he's got to get his foot in the door at the major-league level. Rule number one: He *must* take the first job that's offered him. He can't worry about big market/small market, winning team/losing team, a team with a big budget or one with no budget at all, or even a ball club that is in the process of cutting payroll. Whatever the circumstances, if you're offered your first big-league job it's a no-brainer—take it and take it fast. When I was hired by Texas in 1993 the team wanted new blood. They wanted a manager with a winning background who had come from a strong organization. The previous manager, Bobby Valentine, had been there eight years, and the Rangers wanted to change directions.

Most first-year managers don't come into high-expectation situations. No one thought the Kansas City Royals would turn into a contender in 2003 after losing 100 games the year before. When Tony Peña was interviewed for the manager's job prior to 2003, he had already done his homework and evaluated the talent within the organization. He told GM Allard Baird that the team wasn't that far away, that they had lost a lot of close games in 2002, many by two runs or less, and if they started doing the little things they could improve dramatically. Being a former catcher, Tony had a reputation for working well with pitchers, and because the Royals had a young team and a young staff it was a good fit. He made it all work to the tune of 84 wins and surprised everyone.

Unfortunately, there isn't always a big turnaround. In a sense, there is less pressure taking over a losing team because you're in a no-lose situation. If you win, you've done a great job. If you lose, well, it's expected. That's why when a Tony Peña unexpectedly wins, his stock rises. But it can also reverse itself. In 2004, the Royals had some key injuries early, the dynamics of the team changed, and they lost 104 games. Tony was the same manager, but suddenly he was on the hot seat. When Davey Lopes, a good baseball man, took over the Milwaukee Brewers some years ago, they gave him a three-year contract. He knew rebuilding would take longer than three years, and he was ultimately fired before the three years were up simply because the results on the field weren't up to the expectations of management. Adding insult to injury, a first-year manager usually does not make a lot of money, relatively speaking, and that makes it even easier to fire him. You can fire a guy making $500,000 a year without taking the same kind of hit as with a guy making $5 million.

I remember when Ken Boyer left Rochester in Triple-A (where I was playing then) to take over the St. Louis Cardinals in 1978. Ken had been a great third sacker for the Cards, so in essence, it was a dream job. He was going home. When he left, he said something I've never forgotten.

"I know I'm getting hired just so I can be fired," he remarked.

Strange thing to say before starting your first big-league managing job, and most guys don't want to admit it, but the reality is that getting canned is going to happen, sooner or later. Job security is not something you can count on. Still, you can't be fussy, because an offer to manage in the majors may not come again.

Of course, there are exceptions to every rule. Longtime Yankees coach and former player Willie Randolph made no secret of his desire to manage and interviewed with several teams over the course of a few years. He was on the brink of getting an offer to manage the Reds a couple of years ago, but he suddenly walked away. As I said, someone who wants to manage usually has to take that first job. But in Randolph's case it was something else. I was told by a prominent big-league manager that the Reds front office added a caveat to the package. Randolph was told that if he took the job he would have to fire coach Ken Griffey Sr. within a year. That's when Willie balked. He said the senior Griffey had been a teammate of his on the Yanks and he just couldn't agree to that. So he walked away and never got the formal offer.

Randolph was in a unique position though, because coaching for the Yanks he not only made a higher salary than most other coaches, but was virtually assured of major playoff or World Series money almost every year. He's not like the guys scratching their way through the minors and itching to manage in the bigs, so he's the exception, not the rule. In November of 2004, Willie finally reached his goal when the Mets named him their manager for 2005. Now he will get his chance. But unless he's successful immediately, he will find himself walking along the same precarious path as most other first-time skippers.

Handling the Modern Player

You can't walk into a new situation, look at a group of diverse players and personalities, and ask for respect. You have to earn it, and that comes with the way you treat people. As is the case with any leadership position, you need to create a situation where there is mutual respect. Once I was hired, I went about meeting my players individually and starting a relationship with each and every one of them.

I had just two main rules when I took over the Rangers in 1993: Be on time and Bust your tail. There is no excuse for being late. If stretching is at four o'clock, be there at four and be part of the team. If you run from home to first in 4.3 seconds, then I expect you to run 4.3 every time. I'm not going to demand a 4.0, but don't give me a 5.3, either.

You simply don't jog down the line just because you think you're a sure out. That's completely unacceptable. I also never try to embarrass guys. Showing the team up is an absolute no-no, and you let them know that from the start. It's all part of the respect I spoke about. But, on the other hand, if someone challenges you, you have to act on it immediately. As Whitey Herzog once said, Don't make so many rules that you can't enforce them. If you do, you'd better be damned well able to enforce each and every one of them, because once the players know they can break any rule, no matter how small, you're in trouble.

As a manager, I'm not in business to win a popularity contest. My job is to win games for the team and the organization. You always have to think team first. The label "player's manager" drives me crazy because many people think it means that the players tell the manager what to do. Not true. It simply means that you have great communication skills and can deal with the players as men. Dusty Baker, three times manager of the year, is a prime example of a players' manager. He's popular with his players, yet runs a tight ship. A perfect combination.

When I managed in the minors I was known as a tough guy, a disciplinarian, yet I still got along with all the players. In the big leagues, I always forged relationships of mutual respect with all the players, even the biggest stars. I learned early on that you had to get the star players to lead the rest of the team. The players also have to know that the manager has the backing of the front office, from the general manager to the owner. If the front office doesn't back the manager on matters of rules and discipline, then the inmates run the asylum. When that happens, players can help get a manager fired, and if a manager doesn't think this can happen, then he's not in the real world.

Terry Collins, who has been known to raise his voice at times, eventually lost his job in Anaheim because a number of star players couldn't come to terms with his style, and complaints by the players might also have had something to do with Jimy Williams getting fired when he was managing the Red Sox. This doesn't mean that Collins and Williams are bad managers, only that they didn't find a way for some of the players to come to terms with their style.

At Texas, I heard right away that there were a lot of cliques and players with entourages. Julio Franco was one of the veterans who had an entourage, and I knew I'd be tested by this situation eventually. So I stopped it before it became a problem. The clubhouse was for players only; friends had to stay outside. It wasn't fair to the guy in the next locker to have six or eight people he didn't know crowding around their buddy. As for cliques, I used an old trick that I learned from Red Adams, who was the Dodgers pitching coach when I was a young instructor in 1984.

One night during extended spring training in Florida my fiancée and I went to dinner with Red and the staff, and their significant others. Once we got to the restaurant, Red took over. He wouldn't let us sit next to our wives or girlfriends. "Nobody can sit alongside anyone they know," he said. That was Red's way of allowing everyone to get to know everybody else, and making sure no two people would just keep to themselves. It became an eight-person party. I decided to take this philosophy into the locker room.

I told everyone straight up that there would be no cliques, that we were a team. Then I assigned the lockers separating Latin players, whites, and African Americans. I also didn't want eight pitchers hanging together. It was a total mix and match. A player like Nolan Ryan, who had been there for so long, picked his own locker. I wasn't about to move him. And I didn't move guys like Rafael Palmeiro and Juan Gonzalez. But most of the players were assigned lockers away from their longtime buddies. It may seem insignificant, but it helped forge comaraderie. Without the cliques, the team came closer together and acted as a cohesive unit.

There are always going to be a few individual problems that will test a manager. Again, he has to act quickly and decisively, even if it involves a star player. If a player acts like a prima donna, you have to tell him straight out that the problem is his and if he can't correct it then you'll have to move him. Let him know it isn't about him or about you, but about the team. There may be guys worrying about their own at bats or earning certain incentives in their contracts, but the manager has to be worried about winning ball games and making sure his best nine players are on the field every game.

I always loved Julio Franco, a total professional hitter who is still a friend of mine. But my first year in Texas he was favoring a leg that he'd had surgery on a year or so before. He would warm up before games, and maybe twenty minutes before start time would complain that his leg was bothering him. Because he was already in the lineup, it was hard to make a last-minute change. Then, in some key situations, he wouldn't go from first to third when I knew he could, or wouldn't try to steal a base when the situation called for it. Finally, toward the middle of the season I called him in and told him the following.

"Juice"—his nickname—"it's come to a point where we can't put you in the lineup anymore. We're gonna put you on the DL and get you healthy. I know you can go from first to third, but you hold up. You've got to test it, got to let it go because this is affecting my ability to put the best team on the field. If your leg is really bothering you we've got to put you on the DL."

Julio was smart and he knew that once he came off the DL there was a chance he could be released. He was in the last year of his contract and he had been around long enough to know he had to show everyone he could still play. If he was released, his chances of signing a good free-agent contract would be greatly diminished. Still, that was one of our options, because I needed a player who could do these extra things on the bases. So I wanted him to know that if he couldn't play 100 percent, or wouldn't play 100 percent, he couldn't play for me. No more jogging down the line on a base hit. For Julio, the disabled list would have been the kiss of death. By the time he was healthy and returned, someone might have taken his job. Remember when Wally Pipp had a headache one day, it gave a young first sacker named Lou Gehrig a chance to play.

He thought a minute and then said, "No, Skipper, don't do that. I'll prove to you I can do it. I'll show you."

So I left him in the lineup and he played ninety of the next ninety-one games, hit well, as usual, but ran well, too. I never accused him of being lazy or faking an injury, and I think he appreciated that. He needed a wake-up call, and the thought of going on the DL or being released served that purpose.

I had a similar situation with Juan Gonzalez. It was late in the '93 season and we were trying to catch the White Sox for the division lead. Juan was having a great season, but he always had a tendency to get hurt, and sure enough, he pulled a hamstring. We gave him a rehab schedule but soon found out he wasn't keeping his appointments with Danny Wheat, the team trainer. That's when I called him in.

"Look, Juan," I said. "We've got to have you in the lineup. You've got to work to rehab the leg. But if I hear you're missing your rehab sessions again, I'm gonna have to take action."

We were up in Seattle when Danny Wheat called to tell me Juan hadn't shown up once more. This time I told the front-office people what I was going to do, and they backed me up and gave me their approval. I called Juan in again and this time told him just how it was.

"Juan, thanks for your 44 home runs and 100-plus RBIs, and the 130 games you played," I said, then added quickly, "but I've talked to you about missing rehab and you continue to do it. Go back to the hotel, grab your stuff, and head for home. You're suspended."

He got up, said "Okay, *me voy*," meaning "I am going" in Spanish, and walked out the door. Within seconds he was back, sat down, and apologized. He said he felt bad, that this wasn't what he was all about, and he would start making his rehab. I knew he was contrite. I liked Juan very much and I'm happy I didn't have to suspend him, but I would have if he hadn't changed. You have to do what's right for the team and the organization. If you can't do that, you're in the wrong job. Juan knew he was wrong and said he would do everything to get back, and he managed to play a little bit at the end.

With young players, you don't have to worry. They'll always listen because they want to stick in the big leagues. With a veteran like Juan, you have to handle it differently. If I had yelled and screamed at him about his rehab I would have lost him. If you have to talk to a player one-on-one to get him back on the field, you do it. But you have to do it firmly without allowing the player to dictate his terms to you. In other words, you have to back up your rules. In Boston, both Mo Vaughn and Troy O'Leary used to wear a number of earrings. I told them earrings weren't part of the Red Sox uniform, simple as that, and both players removed them without argument. It never became an issue. So if you treat your players with respect but let them know at the same time that you mean business, you normally won't have a problem.

Despite what some people seem to think, there *are* ways of handling the modern player, even if he is making millions more than you. The satisfaction comes when these players return and tell you how much you've helped them in their careers. When that happens, you know you've touched them in a positive way, and that's one of the best rewards a manager can have.

You're Hired!

Baseball is a 162-game marathon, and the manager who does the job the right way can wield a huge influence over many of those games, but he has to work pretty damned hard to put himself in that position. Many of the things that go with the job description have nothing to do with standing in the dugout, and it all begins for a manager as soon as he hears the words "You're hired!"

Those words may be music to a manager's ears, especially a guy getting his first job, but they also herald the beginning of the real work. I was hired by the Texas Rangers in late October of 1992, and I set out immediately to get ready for the 1993 season, which was still some six months away. You have to put in an unbelievable amount of time at the beginning—especially as a new hire—at least two months of seven-day weeks, long days in which to prepare to manage in the big leagues while fulfilling team and managerial obligations simultaneously. Besides having to meet your team and hire a coaching staff, you have a slew of media and promotional obligations to attend to.

The new manager has to deal with the media constantly. Everyone wants to interview you, talk to you about the team, about the changes you are going to make, the players you have, the players you might want—everything. The Rangers also believed in promoting the club locally and would send caravans out to many towns and cities around the state. The manager has to give speeches and appear at a variety of off-season events. I remember a Thanksgiving parade in November through downtown Dallas in which the manager and coaches sat in an open car wearing their Rangers uniforms. There was also a banquet tour and other promotional events that continued right up to spring training.

At the same time I was making all those appearances I had to hire a coaching staff. I think I got inquiries and messages from about seventy-five potential coaches, and I tried to get back to as many as I could. You've got to have your support staff quickly, and there are always good baseball men you know or have worked with before to choose from. Jackie Moore, for example, lived in Texas, and I knew he would make a great bench coach. He was the first guy I hired, and I filled the rest of the positions from there.

I had also promised George W. Bush when I interviewed with him that I would make it my business to meet the core group of players long before the season began. Because I lived in Palm Beach, Florida, all I had to do was drive an hour and a half to Coral Gables to meet Jose Canseco. He showed total respect for me immediately, even calling me Mr. Kennedy at first. We talked for four hours and only 10 percent of it was about baseball. In essence, we developed a great rapport, which we still have today. We quickly developed a relationship based on trust, and he always kept his word in all his dealings with me.

That's the way I went about meeting all the key players. Rafael Palmeiro knew me somewhat from winter ball, but we talked again anyway. I flew to Puerto Rico just to meet with Juan Gonzalez and Pudge Rodriguez privately in their homes. I was already confident that I wouldn't have any problems dealing with a group of stars, but I wanted to meet them all personally.

These are all things that have to be done as quickly as possible after being hired. You've also got to prepare for the general managers' meetings in November and then the main winter meetings in December, which last about five days. So you have to be familiar with any players who might be available and be prepared to give your input into projected trades, signings, or other player moves.

You're also meeting with your coaches to begin formulating spring-training plans. Perry Hill and Jackie Moore were extremely helpful to me at Texas. We also began going over the signs we were going to use and how we wanted our defense set up. Also, in January there was a minicamp for young prospects from within the system, and a few of the big-league guys, too.

Like so many other players and managers, I always loved spring training. It's more personalized than any other time of the year. The fans have a chance to meet the players, and the manager and coaches are working closely with everyone, often on a one-to-one basis. Players are divided into groups for workouts, with the manager often jumping between as many as four different fields to see all his players. The preseason games begin around March 5, and because there are so many players in camp, you sometimes have split-squad games and play two different games against two different teams. Each squad is required to have four or five players from the big-league roster on the field, maybe four regulars and the starting pitcher. After all, it is still a game for paying customers, and the fans won't be happy to see nine rookies or players they don't know on the field. They want some familiar faces.

Either way, you're on the field for a good part of the day, then have all kinds of meetings, both morning and night, full of evaluation, planning, and possible player moves. Once the preseason games begin you also have to begin evaluating the competition in your division and throughout the league. And, of course, the media are always there. But the core of the day is spent on baseball.

I always put my starting team together for the final ten days of spring training and let them play the rest of the way until the season starts. It gives them a chance to play alongside each other on a regular basis and get a feel for the rhythm of each other's game, and offers a preview of how I function as their manager. So by the time the season begins, the new manager has already been working nonstop for five months, and of course he doesn't stop there. Managing is a twelve-month job. If you survive the first year it all begins again, win or lose, as soon as the season ends. But that's by no means a bad thing. For a real baseball man, there's nothing better than being part of the game, year after year after year.

A Manager on Game Day

Most fans will see a game as a three-hour event. If they come to the ballpark early, they might catch batting practice and then hang around a few minutes after the game to watch the players leave the field. On TV, the game can be caught in spurts or in its entirety, depending how much a fan flips the channels or how often he leaves the room, gets a phone call, has a visitor, or other potential distractions. Game day for a manager lasts much longer.

What the average fan doesn't know, however, is that a manager's game day begins very early and ends very late . . . that is if he can sleep at all. Since the average fan has no idea what a manager does each day, I'd like to take you through a day leading up to a night game beginning at 7:05 P.M. It may not be exactly the same for every manager, but I'd venture to say it's pretty similar because baseball is baseball, and a conscientious manager can do it only one way.

Mornings are usually filled with media commitments. It may be an early TV or radio appearance, spending some time on a call-in show, or meeting with an individual reporter. If I have to speak with the general manager or other front-office personnel about team issues, I'll do it in the morning. After that, I get ready to leave for the ballpark. In Boston, I would usually go to Fenway with Tim Johnson, my bench coach. One of us would drive and we would arrive about 1:00 P.M. Then we might send out for a sandwich before getting down to business.

If it's a Friday with a new club coming to town for the weekend, we start by looking over the advance reports on that team from one or more of our scouts. I'll study the reports and make notes about anything that strikes me as important enough to speak to the team about. I also want to look at the upcoming pitching matchups. Suppose Kansas City was in and Kevin Appier was scheduled to pitch. I would begin gathering information for the lineup, check who hits Appier well and who doesn't, and also check which of my bench players have had the best success against him. To do this with any accuracy, I like to see at least 25 lifetime at bats before making a judgment on a hitter-pitcher matchup. Four or 8 at bats really mean nothing. I'll also look at the last several at bats to see if anything has changed or if any trends are developing.

I usually begin working on the starting lineup by 2:00 p.m. This is done quickly unless I'm waiting on an injury report to see if a specific player will be ready to go that night. Injured players get there early to receive treatment. That's scheduled by the trainer, and he'll let me know as soon as he can if he feels a questionable player will be ready. If it's a Friday with a new team in town, I might also have a quick meeting with the entire club. Occasionally, I might push the meeting back until 4:00, which is usually reserved for the media. If that becomes necessary, the media take the hit and the session is canceled, not always a popular choice.

Every day we then have what we call our "early work." If we're home, we'll come out on the field at about 2:00 p.m. and work for about an hour. These early sessions are for players who might need some extra hitting work, guys trying to break a slump, or a player who wants to work on something specific such as hitting the opposite way. Hitters always love to hit, and when we take normal batting practice, they don't get that many swings. So the early work gives them a chance to swing the bat a few more times. Early work can also include fielding. We might bring our double-play combo out to work on their timing, or if a new player has joined the team, we'll work on integrating him into the system. Then at about 3:00 p.m. we'll leave the field and give the visiting team equal time to do any early work of their own.

Sometimes this routine is altered by where you are playing. In Texas it's often very hot during the summer months, and the ballpark has hitting tunnels under the stadium so batters can get their work in and not be worn down by the heat. I never felt this was the best situation, since most hitters like to see live pitching out on the field. During this early work, I'm not always out on the field. Sometimes I'll come out if there is a player I want to watch or instruct, or if there is something specific I feel I should see. If I'm not there, the coaches handle it, and I might use the time to talk to certain players if they have any problems or issues they want to discuss.

By 4:00, everyone is in uniform. Only the starting pitcher doesn't have to be there early. He doesn't have to come in until two hours before game time, about 5:00 p.m. Of course, he can come in sooner if he needs extra time to go over the opposing hitters. Being there two hours ahead of time also gives the pitcher the chance to prepare, both mentally and physically, for the game. Also at about 4:00 P.M. the media people are brought into the clubhouse to talk with me. It's almost a mini–press conference every day. Players are sometimes involved if a media guy catches up with them. But I always wanted all the pregame media activities done by 4:40, when batting practice began. In Boston, I had a rule that all the players had to be out on the field by 4:20 to stretch with our trainer. The players had about twenty minutes to get loose before batting practice began at 4:40.

Players will hit in groups of four or five, with the bench players taking turns before the starters. On the road, you usually have only forty minutes, so you basically hit in three groups. At home, with more time, you can break them into four or even five. In the American League because of the designated hitter, the pitchers don't take batting practice. In the National, for obvious reasons, they do. Most of the coaches throw batting practice, with some, of course, being better at it than others. Tim Johnson was a former shortstop with a great arm who threw crisp, hard batting practice, the kind hitters like.

The starters prefer to hit off the best batting-practice pitcher because he'll throw closer to game speed than batting-practice speed. This was especially true of big hitters like Jose Canseco, Mo Vaughn, and Mike Greenwell. Most major-league hurlers throw between 85 and 95 miles per hour. A good batting-practice pitcher throws about 80, which Tim did. Some coaches can throw only 65 to 70, which sometimes can be too slow to be entirely useful. To compensate, we'll move those guys closer to the plate, putting a mat down in front of the mound. Some throw from as close as forty feet to make the pitches appear quicker and to save wear and tear on their arms. I had a strong arm as a catcher and always enjoyed taking my turn throwing as well.

I could usually go from the high 70s into the low 80s, and in the big leagues I liked to throw to the bench players, who were in the first group, because I didn't see them hit in games as much. Sometimes I'd prefer to stand behind the batting cage, watch the hitters, and talk with the hitting coach. Other times during BP I would go to the outfield and mingle with the players there, talking to them and watching them. Either way, it was always hands-on. As a manager I wanted to be on the field with them and watch all aspects of practice. Batting practice is also a good time to find any holes that a player might have in his swing. Bill Haselman, the backup catcher in Boston, was a low-ball hitter. When I threw up at his hands I could see he had more trouble. This kind of thing helped me when deciding on pitcher-hitter matchups during games. I could also spot the guys who stepped across their body and lunged at the ball, something we could then work to correct, and I learned which hitters were more patient, because they wouldn't swing at balls out of the strike zone even in BP. So you spot tendencies in batting practice and gather information that will help to make each player a better hitter.

With the extra guys, the ones who came off the bench and ordinarily didn't see much game action, I would often play situational-hitting games in BP. As a hitter got ready I might yell, "First and third, one out." Then I would mix the pitches up and tell him to try to get the run in. I felt this would help get these players ready for the same situations in games and give them a good positive routine, instead of just letting them swing for the fences on each pitch. Batting practice was also a time to practice bunting and hitting to both the left and the right side of the field, and also for players to try to get the ball in the air, practicing for the time a sacrifice fly was needed. And of course we always had runners on the bases to simulate the situations, even practicing squeeze plays for both the hitter and the runner on third. You definitely want your hitters to be able to execute in all these situations, and that makes batting practice a great training ground. It should be more than just a home run derby.

Batting practice lasts until about 5:40. Then the visiting team takes the field to hit until about 6:20. As soon as they're finished, we come back for infield practice, which lasts about ten to twelve minutes. We begin by having the main fungo hitter out near the mound hitting flies to the outfield. The left fielder makes two throws to second and two to home. The center fielder will throw two to third through a cutoff man, then two throws to home. The right fielder throws a couple to third and a couple to home. Then the outfielders all go to the deepest part of center field and work on catching both line drives and high fungos with a second fungo hitter, who stands down the right- or left-field line. The first fungo hitter now begins hitting grounders to the infielders. All the infielders will practice the throws they are likely to make during the game. We'll also practice double plays, bunts, and first-and-third double-steal defense. All has to be run very smoothly so that in just twelve minutes each player has the chance to practice what he will likely do once the game begins.

During infield practice I usually watch from the bench. I'm always looking for anything that doesn't look quite right, a player not moving the way he should, pushing the ball instead of cutting loose with his throws, not running as well as he normally does. That way I can see if anyone might be hiding a minor injury and should be checked out before game time. Once we're finished, about 6:30, the opposition comes out for infield and I stay, looking at all their players the same way I watch mine. This was another thing I learned in the minors. By watching the opposition you can see whether a player on their team has a strong arm, whether he has quick feet and how well he moves laterally, and what his release time is. It's also important to watch the opposition's catcher, to see his arm, his release, and his footwork. All these little things can dictate moves you'll make later in the game.

At 6:40, the grounds crew come out. They usually need about twenty-five minutes to get the field ready. At the same time, the starting pitcher goes to the bullpen and begins to work, stretching first, then taking his warmups. Most pitchers need about that same twenty-five minutes to get ready. At 7:05 P.M. the game begins. What I do in the dugout during the action will be discussed in the next segment. For the purposes of my entire day, the game usually ends sometime after 10:00 P.M.

Win or lose, I'll give the players ten or fifteen minutes in the clubhouse before allowing the media in. There is always a spread ready because some players haven't eaten since 2:00 P.M. I never like to eat immediately after the game, win or lose. I also rarely have team meetings after games unless there is something extremely important to discuss. I always feel it's best to pick your spots for after-game meetings. In my mind, it's better to collect your thoughts first, and have the meeting the next day. When the media arrive some of the guys come into my office while others mingle with the players. If the game ends at 10:30, the media ordinarily hang around until between 11:00 and 11:30. With all that going on, it's usually near midnight, or even a little beyond, before I'm dressed and ready to leave.

On occasion, the general manager might come down after a game to talk about possible player moves or trades, so there are times when you're at the stadium even longer. Rarely do you leave much before midnight, and I've always found that it takes a while to shut it all down after a game, making it tough to go right home and sleep. Usually I'll go out with one or two of the coaches, grab a bite to eat, maybe have a beer or two, and continue to talk baseball. While this routine enables me to relax, it's still a time completely devoted to baseball. There were many nights when I didn't get to sleep until 3:00 or 4:00 in the morning. Winning or losing doesn't make a difference. The only times I would try to get home quickly after a game were if we were playing the next afternoon. But that doesn't guarantee a good night's sleep, and in the morning I'd start the same routine all over again.

As a manager, I always prepared a few days ahead. I knew who was going to pitch and had my lineups set. If I wanted to rest one of my starters, I'd tell him after the game the night before. Players who know they won't start might want to prepare differently. As a player, if I knew I was getting a night or day off, I would take extra hitting and even take extra infield from different positions, just to get a better sense of the overall game. If I felt a guy needed a rest, I would tell him so he could practice and prepare in a different way if he chose as long as he understood he had to be ready to go into the game at any time, even if just to pinch-hit.

The manager is totally involved in every aspect of the game on an everyday basis. There is no time to relax, no time to look away from that field as long as there's a single player out there. The more you watch, the more you see, the more you know, the better prepared you'll be for any conceivable situation that might arise.

Managing in the American and National Leagues

I was always an aggressive, make-things-happen manager, never a guy who would sit back and wait for the three-run homer. A lot of that had to do with how I was brought up on the game. When you grow up watching how much havoc a Maury Wills can cause on the base paths, it makes an impression on you. Being a catcher only confirmed the idea that you can always make things happen on the bases by putting people in motion.

The managers you play for also influence you. Frank Robinson was one of my managers at Triple-A and he was an extremely aggressive guy. Ken Boyer, another great former player, also managed me at Triple-A. Kenny was a strong silent type of manager, but he always had an open-door policy for his players. Even if you were struggling, he would always wait until you came to him. His feeling was that if you came to him, you were ready to listen. If he had to come to you, you might just turn him off. Doc Edwards, another of my Triple-A managers, always talked about being a professional. That was his theme. Be a pro both on and off the field and always take pride in your profession.

I also respected the way Del Crandall managed. He reinforced my feelings about setting runners in motion. I was playing on a power-hitting team at Albuquerque in 1982. This was the Dodgers' Triple-A team, a step away from the majors, and that year the team had power guys like Mike Marshall, Greg Brock, and Candy Maldonado. Yet Del insisted on moving all his runners on certain counts. It didn't matter if the runners had speed or not, he moved them. I remember one game in which we were down one run in the bottom of the ninth. I led off with a base hit. Alex Taveras was up next, and the logical thing was a bunt to get the tying run into scoring position. But when I looked at the third-base coach I saw that Del had put the hit-and-run on. Sure enough, Alex slapped a base hit to right, and because I was running I made third easily. Ross Jones, who would make it to the majors for parts of three seasons, was up next. After he pulled the first pitch foul, Del called him back, then met him at the on-deck circle. He asked him to try to hit to the opposite field, to right. Jones did it, stroking a gapper to right center. Both Alex and I scored and we won the game.

Del's thinking was that had Alex bunted, it wasn't a sure bet I'd get to second. I didn't have good speed, so the bunt would have to be perfect. Even then, we might have only tied the game, then lost in extra innings. After considering all that, he decided we had a better chance with the hit-and-run in that situation. I was impressed by the way he had gone for it—an aggressive gambit—and it was something I never forgot. I also recall Maury Wills telling me that even if you're down three, four, or five runs in the first inning, don't stop managing and wait for the three-run homer. Do the little things to peck away and close the gap.

Whitey Herzog used to say that he always managed to win the game in nine innings. If you need to make a switch in the eighth inning, do it. Even take the cleanup hitter out if you have to and don't worry about his next at bat, because it might not come until the eleventh or twelfth inning, and the game might be over by then. He's absolutely right. One time with Albuquerque in 1991 while playing on the road at Las Vegas, I made a double switch in the ninth inning of a tie game, taking out my cleanup hitter, Eric Karros, bringing in John Wetteland to pitch and putting him in the fourth spot in the order. I needed John to pitch a couple of innings and didn't want to have to remove him for a pinch hitter. Because of the double switch, I brought Brian Traxler in to play first base for Karros and had him batting in the ninth spot.

When that spot came up in the tenth, however, Brian, who would have a brief stint with the Dodgers in 1990, got a hit to drive in the go-ahead run and Wetteland closed it out to win it. Karros was proud of never having missed an inning of any game in his professional career to that point, and asked why I had pulled him. I explained that my thinking was based on the big picture, and thus putting the team in the best position to win. It wasn't about anyone's stats. Then I explained the philosophy of the double switch and trying to win the game as quickly as possible. I told him that we might not have gotten to his next at bat. If I'd had to pinch-hit for Wetteland, then I'd have had no one to pitch the bottom of the tenth.

I incorporated all of these elements, learned from my former managers, and added my own intensity. I already had a great deal of experience when I finally got my big-league shot, having served a lot of games behind the bench, including eight years in the minors, then several more in winter ball, and a few in the Instructional League. So I knew that players will come to respect you if you're emphatic and strong as a manager, and give your team a game plan, direction, and leadership.

Because of my years in the Dodgers organization as a manager, I grew up managing more with a National League style. Yet I was familiar with both styles. In fact, even at Triple-A, if you play a National League team the pitcher has to hit, and if you're up against another AL team, then you use the DH. By managing both styles in the minors, I became familiar with double switches and handling a pitching staff.

When you manage National League style, you've got to be more careful in handling your pitching staff so that you have the right guy available for certain situations. If there was a designated hitter in the game I just described, it would have completely changed the scenario I related above. With a DH, Karros would have stayed in and I would have had the option to pinch-hit for the ninth hitter. But none of that would have affected Wetteland, who could have remained on the mound for as many innings as I needed him. Also, with the designated hitter you have more high-scoring games because there are theoretically no "outs" in the lineup. Stats show American League teams score a full run more than those in the National League. Managing in the AL, you have to be real careful not to blow out your pitching staff.

I remember one game in Texas where my starter, Kenny Rogers, gave up ten runs in the first two innings. Ironically, he was throwing well and we had already made several errors behind him. Kenny was pissed and wanted to come out, but I convinced him to stay in because I didn't want to use my long man that early. I let him go several innings more just to save my staff for the rest of the series. In the National, if you're down three or more runs by the fifth inning, in most cases you pinch-hit for the pitcher. But in the AL you don't have to worry about pinch-hitting, so you can let a starter who is getting rocked early go into the sixth or seventh inning if by that time he has settled down and is throwing well.

When I managed in the American League I missed the strategy of having the pitcher batting in the ninth spot. Sometimes I felt the games resembled slow-pitch softball. You win or lose games by 13–10 or 11–9 in these slugfests. When I talk about this I can't help but remember a game at Boston when I was managing the Rangers and Jose Canseco hit three homers as we won, 13–8. That's typical of the wide-open game with the designated hitter. Another characteristic in the American League is that it often seems as if the one and nine hitters are interchangeable. At Boston in 1995, for instance, I had the speedy Lee Tinsley leading off. Then I had power hitters right down to the eight spot. Batting ninth was Luis Alicea, my second baseman, who was also a switch-hitter. When he got on at the bottom of the lineup, I had speed on the bases and then the guys to move him along.

The Angels did the same thing in recent years. They had David Eckstein, a speed guy, leading off. The slowest guy, catcher Bengie Molina, didn't hit ninth, but rather eighth. Adam Kennedy, who had good bat control and some speed, batted in the ninth slot, but could also have led off. In 2004, Chone Figgins also filled that ninth-spot role for manager Mike Scioscia. So in the AL, teams like to have fast guys in both the nine and one spots, back to back, and that often sets the table for the middle of the order. In the National League, sometimes the two and eight hitters can be interchangeable—usually good bunters and guys who can hit-and-run—or the two and seven. Cesar Izturis of the Dodgers, for instance, has hit in both the two and eight spots. Years ago Butch Hobson was batting ninth for the Red Sox and hit 30 home runs. He kind of snuck up on everyone and had a perfect home run swing for Fenway. So you can't let up in the American League because every lineup is filled with so many offensive weapons.

A good manager has to think about his lineup and decide where certain players can be the most productive. When I joined the Red Sox before the 1995 season, John Valentin had been the sixth hitter. He had maybe 12 to 14 homers and drove in 60 runs the year before. I could see that John, who batted right-handed, was a good fastball hitter and had the perfect swing for Fenway. He could jack it over that wall, but he also had the ability to go the other way. I decided to hit him second, knowing he would see a lot of fastballs by hitting in front of Mo

Vaughn. Val was always a slow starter, and by May he was batting about .180. I remember Mo coming up and telling me that Val wanted to switch back to the sixth slot in the lineup. So I had a meeting with Val, Mo, and Tim Johnson, my bench coach.

"Skip, I've always hit in the sixth spot and been pretty productive," Val said. "Is there a way to get me back there? I'll drive in 60 for you in the sixth spot."

I just laughed. "While all that's true," I told him, "the two slot is perfect for you with this team. Stick with it and you'll bat .300, hit 25 homers, drive in 100 runs and make millions. Hitting in front of Mo you're going to see all fastballs."

So he stayed with it and ended up with 27 homers and 102 RBIs and was rewarded with a big $25 million multiyear deal after I left, but unfortunately he never had a year quite like that again.

In the National League, a manager might have to carry a couple more pinch hitters. There isn't a whole lot of pinch-hitting in the American. I don't think Cito Gaston pinch-hit at all the two years Toronto won the World Series. With Texas and Boston, I carried fourteen regulars and eleven pitchers. You would think that because you make fewer pinch-hitting moves, you'd need fewer pitchers, but you carry more pitchers because there are no easy outs in the opposing lineup. In the National League, you might want fifteen regulars and ten pitchers, which is ironic because you need more pitchers but carry fewer, since you need more players to pinch-hit.

In both leagues, I've always felt that the key to managing is handling a pitching staff. It's different if you're managing Sandy Koufax, Don Drysdale, Juan Marichal, and Bob Gibson. With guys like that you don't have to worry about having a setup man, a long man, or a closer. But today, guys rarely go nine innings. Even when I managed Roger Clemens at Boston, I had to watch the pitch count so I didn't burn him out. If you burn a staff out, all the hitting in the world won't help. I always felt I was lucky in that respect because, as a former catcher, I had a leg up when it came to working my pitchers.

Additionally, there are variables that a manager must consider. Clemens used to walk a few guys a game almost intentionally. Maybe there was a runner on second and a hitter coming up who'd had a lot of success against him. So he pitched him carefully. If the guy went deep into the count, fouled off a couple, he would then see ball four. Because Roger knew he could get the next guy, he basically gave him an unintentional intentional walk. Adding that kind of situation to the pitch count is a mistake. You have to ask yourself, Has it been a tough 115 pitches or a free-flowing 115 pitches? Maybe a pitcher has had a very rough second inning, throwing 32 pitches, and the effort has exhausted him. But you also have to ask yourself whether he has had five tough innings or one tough inning and four easy ones. So you always have to look at more than just the total number of pitches as your absolute. Though Clemens may have thrown 120 pitches by the seventh inning, he may still be fine, throwing 98 miles per hour with good mechanics.

I could always trust Roger to be honest, and I would start talking to him about the fifth or sixth inning. He might say, "Skip, I have a few bullets left, but keep an eye on me." That's the kind of communication you need with your pitchers and the kind I had with Roger. It's also good to have a balanced staff. If you have three young starters who normally won't make it through the lineup three times, it's almost necessary to have a horse or two who'll help save the bullpen.

Most American League teams carry five starters and six relievers. I always liked to have two lefties in the pen, one for the early and middle innings, and one to come in late. If I didn't have any southpaws or had just one, then I couldn't turn the lineup around the way I'd like. For example, if I bring a lefty in during the middle innings and the opposing manager starts using his right-handed pinch hitters, then late in the game he can't counter me. He has to leave his righties in to face my right-handed relievers. You get the idea.

Managing a Game

If I were hiring a manager, I'd want a guy who could handle the pitching staff and a guy who knew how to manufacture runs. I always felt I could create runs by putting men in motion. For that reason, I never worried about power hitters, though I certainly had them. It's better to know how to massage those starters, keep them confident and out on the mound; and because you play almost every day, you've got to be able to handle your bullpen as well. That's huge today. You have to look ahead to your upcoming games. There are times when you may have to sacrifice one game in order to win the next two. That's why I always had my teams concentrate on winning a series, not always individual games. In other words, while you obviously try to win every game, you can still win a series despite losing one game. You can't use all your pitchers every day. Even if you're in first place there are times when you have to make a pit stop. As I've said before, the baseball season is a marathon, not a sprint, and you don't see marathon runners going full speed all the time. You can't use your closer in five straight games, so you've got to be smart and pick your spots. Yet as a manager, you've got to try to find something positive in every situation. If your closer needs a rest, you may find out that one of your setup guys can handle that role in an emergency, and this can help you at the end of the season or in the playoffs, or in the event of an injury.

If you play .600 ball in baseball you'll most likely win your division. That's three wins out of five games, and that's why a manager should think in short spurts, not too far ahead. Take care of business and try to win each series. If you pick up just a couple of games a week you'll suddenly find you're just where you want to be. Each game has its own rhythm, its own flow, and its own set of problems for a manager to solve. Sure, once in a while there's a blowout. If you're up or down by ten runs in the sixth inning, then you pretty much play out the string either way, protecting your important players or pitchers, and already looking for tomorrow.

As a rule of thumb, I've always told my teams that the first three innings of a game are theirs; the middle three innings are ours, as I become more involved; and then the last three innings are mine. Those final nine outs are often the toughest ones to get. While you still take opportunities to make things happen, during the first three innings you generally watch the flow of the game. You observe everything as both teams go through their lineups. By the third you know how your starter is working that day, and if you have to try to manufacture a run or two. Then, as the pitch count mounts for the starter and the game goes into the seventh inning, you really have to take over. It's time to manage the bullpen while trying to get those last nine outs.

This is crunch time for a manager and why the bullpen has become more important to a team's success during the last fifteen years. Starters just aren't conditioned to go nine innings anymore. Look at both Boston and the Chicago Cubs in the 2003 playoffs. Both teams were just five outs away from going to the World Series. Pedro Martinez was left out there a couple of hitters too long. He said he was okay, but in reality he had lost it. In fact, the stats show that at this point in his career, the opposing team's batting average becomes dramatically higher after he exceeds the ninety-pitch mark. Grady Little felt that this was his horse, the guy to get him to the World Series, stats or no stats. And it backfired.

The same thing happened to Dusty Baker and the Cubs. They had a couple of bad breaks: the fan interfering with the foul ball to left that Moises Alou might have caught, then an error at short. But Dusty left Mark Prior in the game though he was pitching on short rest. Would they have won if he had brought his normal bullpen rotation in? We'll never know. However, that poses the sixty-four-thousand-dollar question. How do you manage those final nine outs? A manager has to figure the best way to do it. If he makes a decision that backfires, then the second-guessers come charging out of the woodwork.

It's the flow of the game that normally dictates your early strategy. When Tom Gordon was starting for me in Boston he always seemed to have trouble getting out of the first inning, but after that he often began putting up zeroes. Sometimes he'd come off in the first and we'd be down 3–0 or 4–0, which in the American League isn't a helluva lot. If I pulled Gordon early, then I would be using middle guys from the first or second inning on, and it might take five, six, or seven pitchers to finish the game. In a case like that, you sometimes have to be patient, let Gordon weather the first and hope he settles down. I always looked at myself as more of a late-hook guy, a manager who would stick with his starter longer than some others. My feeling was that we could always manufacture some runs and get back in the game.

There are also times when you simply don't have a bullpen and need 100 pitches from that starter no matter what. If the starter knows he has no help behind him, he'll tend to battle through to give you six or seven innings. When Larry Dierker was managing at Houston, he felt that his starters should learn how to get themselves out of early trouble and settle down. So he didn't have an early hook either. As a pitcher, Dierker had more than 100 complete games, and he would tell his starters not to look for bullpen help when they got in trouble early. By doing that he made them tougher, and they all learned how to get deeper into the game.

In 1995, Roger Clemens was coming back from an injury and working in a June game. That was a strike year, and when the players came back late in the spring, Roger threw too hard, too soon, and strained his shoulder. He was placed on the DL, and when he was activated in early June, he was still pitching like it was spring training. In one of his first starts he got battered for 10 runs. When I went out to the mound he told me he wanted to stay in because he needed the work. The game was already lost, and Roger said flat out that he didn't care about his earned run average. That's the kind of guy he is. I left him in to get the work and he ended up with a 10–5 record that year, pitching extremely well in the second half of the season as we won the division. Roger knew he had to get stronger to be in shape for the long haul, and I agreed. Those are the kinds of early-game decisions a manager often has to make.

I also had some of my own little quirks that I used every inning. When our defense started to take the field I'd always say, "Let's put a zero up there." And when they came in, I'd holler, "Come on, guys, we gotta go, gotta go, we gotta get more." The guys used to tease me about it and smile, but it was part of my intensity, not wanting the team to let up, even for an inning. Most of the time, I stood in the dugout looking for something that might help the team. In my mind, I was still a catcher and I was always trying to pick up signs, thinking pitch by pitch, looking for any kind of tendencies I could spot. I also watched the opposing dugout, watched the third-base coach, and kept looking to see if the defense moved. I just wanted to be ready to use anything that might give my team an advantage, even a slight one.

I would use motion at any point during the game when I thought

it could help us. I had seven different running signs and always studied each pitcher's moves to give my runners the advantage. I had a sign
with a left-handed pitcher on the mound that I called "first move" or
"first move on a lefty." That meant the runner should break as soon as
the pitcher moved his front foot. I felt I was pretty good at picking up
the pitcher's move and tendencies, and usually knew when he would
go home with the pitch. Otherwise, a lefty with a good move is often
difficult to run on. I told my players that I would let them know when
to run, and if they got picked off, I'd take the heat. I remember one
game in Boston when we had Mike Greenwell on first with two out in
the ninth, tie game. There was a left-handed reliever on the mound
facing switch-hitting Luis Alicea. With the count deep, I had picked
up the pitcher's tendencies and knew he was going home on the next
pitch, and that's when I put on first move for Greenwell, not normally
a base stealer, and it took them by surprise. The pitch was a ball and
Greenwell stole second easily. Now he was in scoring position. On the
next pitch, Alicea hit a line drive to left center for a single. Greenwell
came all the way around and we won the game.

I also had a "must-run" sign, which meant you go on the pitch,
good jump or not. In that instance, I felt the pitcher was going to
throw something my guy could handle. In reality, it was a run-and-hit
play. The batter didn't have to swing at the pitch if it was way out of
the strike zone, because I didn't want to take the bat out of his hands
by having him go after a bad pitch. If a runner misses the sign or de-
cides not to go, then it changes the count and the situation. That's why
there was a must-run sign. The runner had to go, no matter what.
There was also a "steal-on-your-own" sign, which gave the runner the
option. I might take the steal sign off if I thought the opposition was
going to pitch out, or even throw one up and away. So it was a constant
cat-and-mouse game from the very first inning, especially when I felt
I knew the signs.

In close games getting those last nine outs or that winning run
across the plate is often the toughest thing to do. And that's when a
manager's moves can most influence the outcome of the game. In
1993, my first year in Texas, I was grooming Darren Oliver to be an
occasional closer. He was a southpaw with a nasty, sharp curve and

could be especially tough on left-handed hitters. But when he had the good curve going, he could also get righties. In a game against the Yankees, who were being managed by Buck Showalter that year, I had a chance to make what many considered an unconventional move.

Kenny Rogers took us deep into the game and we had the lead going into the ninth. He got one out, then gave up a bloop single and a walk. Now it was decision time. Everyone thought I would go to Tom Henke, the outstanding closer we had obtained from Toronto. Buck had started a right-handed lineup that afternoon and had dangerous lefties on the bench, guys he was resting after a night game: Paul O'Neill, who was leading the league in hitting, Wade Boggs, and Don Mattingly. So I brought Oliver in to face the righties. I wanted to keep those .300-hitting lefties on the bench, and if I went to Henke, my usual closer and the obvious move, I knew Buck would have unloaded the bench on us. Darren could be wild sometimes but I still felt it was a better bet to have him face their right-handed hitters.

I just didn't want to see Paul O'Neill coming out of the dugout with a bat in his hands. It came down to whether I wanted to see Oliver face Mike Gallego or have Henke face O'Neill. The on-deck hitter was another righty, Jim Leyritz. So I brought in Oliver, and when he got Gallego to hit into a 6-4-3 double play, we won the game.

Other times, a combination of logic and experience will dictate an unconventional move. We were at Fenway in '95 hosting Toronto, and in the top of the ninth we had a two-run lead. The Blue Jays started to rally, and with two outs they had the tying runs on second and third with switch-hitter Otis Nixon up. I had a hard-throwing right-hander, Heathcliff Slocumb, on the mound and knew that Otis liked to hit the ball the opposite way. After he slapped a couple of fouls into the third-base dugout I was more convinced than ever that he wouldn't pull the ball. I called time and walked to the mound, but I wasn't there to change pitchers. I interchanged right fielder Darren Bragg with left fielder Troy O'Leary. My thinking was simple. If Nixon got a hit with two outs, the runners would be going on the swing—because there were two strikes—and would likely score. O'Leary had only an average arm and was a lefty thrower, so his ball would naturally tail away from the catcher to the first-base side of the plate. Bragg, on the other hand, had a powerful right-handed arm and often threw strikes. So I switched them. If a right-hander's throw tails, it will veer into the runner on the catcher's glove side, giving him a chance to make the tag.

Sure enough, on the next pitch Otis slapped a sharp single between third and short. Bragg charged quickly and fired a bullet to home plate. One run scored, but the third-base coach held the trailing runner at third. That made it a one-run game, and then our pitcher got the next guy to end it. You don't see that kind of move too often. It isn't one you make by design, but often by gut instinct and using what you have learned over the years. If a manager is willing to use his experience, prepare properly, and stay in tune during a game, he can exert some kind of influence almost every day. Obviously, the players are key, but they need direction. You can't have an orchestra without a conductor, even if it's full of superstars.

◆

CHAPTER FIVE

The Texas and Boston Years

People have told me that I managed during one of the toughest times in baseball, with the strike of 1994 coming in just my second year. But while you're living it you don't think about the politics and the ugliness. You simply do the best you can day in and day out.

My tenure as a big-league manager was a short one (admittedly shorter than I would have liked): two years in Texas and another two in Boston. Despite the premature endings, those four years were unforgettable in many ways, not the least of which was proving to myself that I was more than ready to direct a big-league team and knowing I had an impact on the outcome of many games as well as on the lives of some very successful players.

Bobby Valentine had been the Rangers manager for eight years, but when the team was struggling just to reach .500 midway through the 1992 season, he was let go and Toby Harrah, one of his coaches, finished as interim field boss. After the season, the team decided to bring in fresh blood. I was hired by then owner George W. Bush, about eighteen months before he resumed his political career. The problem I saw with the Rangers wasn't unusual. Despite having a core group of outstanding players, superstars and superstars in the making, they were not a balanced team. While I was inheriting players such as Jose Canseco, Juan Gonzalez, Dean Palmer, Rafael Palmeiro, Julio Franco, Pudge Rodriguez, Kevin Brown, and the great Nolan Ryan, I wasn't comfortable with the team's makeup. We could score a ton of runs, but I wanted more speed and defense. We also needed a deeper pitching staff. The year before, I had been the bench coach in Montreal under Felipe Alou, and that team had the elements I liked—speed, defense, balance, and a top closer.

The Rangers were weak up the middle, leaving unacceptable holes in the defense. The corners were solid with Palmer at third and Palmeiro at first, Gonzalez and Canseco were set in left and right, Pudge was a coming star at catcher, and Julio Franco was a fine DH. Up the middle and on the mound was where we needed help. So we tried to shape the team by adding these elements. Aside from pitching, up the middle are the positions you build your ball club around. We had already signed Tom Henke as a free agent from Toronto to be our closer, and later added a starter in Charlie Leibrandt. Then I gave David Hulse, who came up from the minors, a chance to play center. He was a slap hitter with speed who could also steal bases. Both Billy Ripken and Doug Strange were already in camp and they shared second, with Strange getting more playing time. Manny Lee, another free agent from Toronto, became our shortstop, though he was injured part of the year. Just these few moves made the club considerably stronger, and definitely more to my liking in terms of speed.

Nolan Ryan was in his final season, a great elder statesman who, at forty-six years of age, could still throw his heater but was breaking down a bit with a variety of leg problems and would spend some time on the DL. So we put Craig Lefferts in the rotation when Nolan was out, with Kevin Brown, Kenny Rogers, Charlie Leibrandt, and Roger Pavlik. Even with that group, there were still times when I had to improvise. Kevin and Kenny were solid, but the other guys weren't always reliable. In fact, I remember my old friend Robin Yount saying to me one day early in the season, "Kevin, of all the teams to manage for the first time, you got yourself a tough one."

I knew that, and when I brought the team together for the first time I told them, "It's going to take six weeks to get used to my motion style of offense. There will be times you will run yourself out of innings, but I'll take the blame for it. Believe me, in the long run it will pay off. By having our opponents constantly thinking about us taking the extra base, stealing, and executing hit-and-run plays, you guys are going to get more fastballs and the power hitters will all have better numbers. That's the kind of pressure a running game can create. By running and moving runners enough, the threat of it happening again is always there and you always get more of those nice fastballs to hit."

By telling them I would take the heat, it took the pressure off them if we struggled out of the gate. When we started the season at 6–1 it almost seemed too easy, and it was. Soon the team was struggling and I had to deal with a number of situations, one of which had the potential to derail my managerial career before it got out of the station.

Prior to 1993, Kenny Rogers had almost always worked out of the bullpen, mostly using his fastball. During one of our preseason promotional caravans, Rafael Palmeiro called me one day and said that Kenny would like a chance to start. Little did they know that assistant GM and scouting director Sandy Johnson had already recommended that to me a few weeks before. We knew Kenny had great stuff with a variety of pitches—a fastball in the nineties, a good curve, and an outstanding changeup. I thought about it, watched him pitch, and then talked with him before deciding to give him a shot. To spur him on a bit, I told the media that I thought he could win 15 games as a starter. He began the season as if he were going to prove me right by compiling a 3–1 record with an earned run average around 2.25. Then, suddenly, he imploded for four or five games, pitched poorly, and I could see his confidence eroding almost daily. The media began speculating that I would probably put Kenny back in the pen, and that he simply wasn't tough enough mentally to start. However, I'd seen this kind of slump during my time managing in the minors.

I told Kenny flat out that I felt he had the ability to start. "The media think I'm gonna take you out of the rotation," I told him. "At this point, it's up to you." Then Claude Osteen, my pitching coach, and I began telling him stories about other pitchers, guys who questioned their own ability and had to work through lapses in confidence. Claude mentioned John Denny, who pitched for several teams in the

1970s and 1980s and won 19 games for the Phillies in 1983, as one guy who had to battle, and told Kenny it was time to stop doubting himself. There are pitchers who have both fear of success and fear of failure. I had seen guys in the minors who were more comfortable with mediocrity. Sometimes a guy goes out there with the fear of success. He starts off hot and soon everyone expects him to win. But deep down inside, the player simply doesn't feel he's that good. He finds a way to bring himself back to mediocrity and then never becomes the player he is capable of being. But I thought Kenny was a winner and shouldn't allow himself to settle for less.

Others can't perform because they fear failure. Kenny was a free spirit in a lot of ways. Yet when I evaluated him and watched him, I saw a guy looking for an excuse to fail. I think most of us have had that mind-set at some time or another. So after telling him stories from our experience and trying to convince him that he had the ability, we left it up to him. We had the meeting on a Sunday afternoon after the game ended. I finished by saying, "Don't tell me anything now. Go home and sleep on it. Your next start is Wednesday. If you come in tomorrow and tell me you want the start, it's yours. You've got it. If not, I'll put you back in the pen. But I'm not gonna make the decision for you. You are."

The next day we brought him into the office, and without hesitation he said, "I want to start."

That was it. We kept him in and it was a turning point in his career. At the end of the season I had a chance to kid the writers. "You guys said he'd never win 15 games," I reminded them. "And you were right. He didn't win 15. He won 16!"

The next crisis involved Jose Canseco, a great player and a five-tool guy in his prime. I used to say that managing Jose was like managing Elvis Presley. He was like a rock star. Even when he came out on deck the girls would walk down the aisles to the railing to get a closer look at him.

That spring, Jose came to my office and told me that he used to pitch in high school and volunteered to be an extra pitcher for an inning or so if I never needed him in a blowout game where I didn't want to burn out anyone else on the staff. Other players had done it for an inning or so, including big stars like Ted Williams, Rocky Colavito, and Wade Boggs. He said it had always been a dream of his to throw an inning in the big leagues, something I understood completely, but my first reaction was, "If I put you out there and you get hurt, I'm done as a manager."

I understood how he felt because I had actually pitched twice in Triple-A. But the big-money guys are the ones you really try to protect, for a variety of reasons. Not wanting to just spring the idea on everyone cold turkey, I went to the GM, Tom Grieve, and to George Bush, making them aware that Jose had volunteered to pitch and really wanted a chance to throw an inning. Basically, I was given the green light to make the call. I told them I'd have pitching coach Claude Osteen work with him just to make sure his technique was sound and that he didn't hurt himself. That's what we did, and Jose listened to everything Claude told him. Then in May, we had an off day but had to play our Triple-A club at Oklahoma City, a kind of goodwill thing. It gave us a chance to look at the Triple-A players and to use some of our guys who were usually on the bench. The regulars got one at bat and then came out of the game.

That's when I gave Jose his first chance. We felt he was well prepared, and he came in, set them down one-two-three, had a strikeout, and was throwing at about 95 miles per hour. We all thought, Hey, he did it and he brought some real heat. He really looked comfortable out there. Then on the same road trip we began struggling a bit, suffering through some rough games. One day we were getting killed by the Red Sox at Fenway, a real blowout, and I had used up the pen the day before. Jose was DHing that game and I really needed a pitcher, the perfect spot to let him throw his inning. I told him to get ready to pitch the ninth. He went down to the bullpen and in a minute I could hear the ball hitting the catcher's mitt—hard. Pop! Pop! Pop! Pop! Because there were all kinds of fans down there watching, I think he was trying to show how hard he could bring it. I told Claude Osteen to call the bullpen to sit him down. He had thrown enough. Unfortunately, he never sat down.

Then we called him in to pitch the ninth and right away I noticed that he was having trouble. Instead of his 95-mile-per-hour fastball, he was throwing knuckleballs, almost lobbing them in. The Sox got a couple of hits and he was still not throwing a fastball. The next day he admitted he had felt some pain while throwing in the pen but hadn't said anything, and then he told us his arm was a little sore. The irony was that he continued to play for a couple more weeks, hit some homers, and seemed fine. Then in June we were in Seattle, and Jose made a throw from the outfield. As soon as he released the ball he clutched at his arm. That's when we finally had him checked, sending him to Los Angeles to be examined by renowned orthopedic surgeon Dr. Frank Jobe. I was in Tom Grieve's office when we got the news. Jose had a torn ligament in his elbow and would need Tommy John–type surgery. He was out for the year.

To call this a crisis for a first-year manager defines understatement. One of the team's best players was lost for the year with a severe elbow injury after I green-lighted him to pitch an inning. Sure, I needed an extra pitcher that day, but in truth I was simply allowing Jose to scratch an itch he had had for some time. The report from Dr. Jobe took some of the heat off. He explained that this was a progressive injury, a tear that was becoming greater over time and probably had begun the year before. Jose's full-fan performance in the bullpen might have enhanced it, and then the throw from the outfield finally blew out the elbow. When I heard that, the light went on. Dr. Jobe said a ligament problem affects everything the player does, including swinging the bat. The more I thought about it, the more I realized that Jose hadn't had quite his usual bat speed before the injury, and I also recalled him pushing the ball from the outfield on occasion, not throwing like I thought he should. He was always the kind of guy who played injured and didn't ask out unless he was hurting very badly.

To the credit of everyone in the organization, from George Bush to Tom Grieve, the finger was never pointed at me. But that didn't matter. I took full responsibility for putting Jose out there. Though I felt he was as prepared as any extra pitcher, progressive injury or not, I was still the one who had allowed him to pitch. Once a month the Rangers had a meeting of their minority stockholders, maybe seventy-five or eighty people. When I was asked to address the Canseco injury,

I never mentioned that I had gone to upper management with the possibility that Jose might pitch, and that they had cleared him to pitch. I simply said that, as the manager, I took full responsibility for what had happened and that the club would continue to do everything it could to win.

That meeting might have been the defining moment of my initial year as a big-league manager. By taking full responsibility, I earned more respect from the media, the players, and club officials, including George Bush.

Losing Jose was a blow to the team, but one we hoped we could overcome. While I don't want to minimize his loss, the team was headed for an even greater crisis, one I knew I had to cut off at the pass. If I didn't, we would continue to do something that I never could accept—lose.

By June 25, we were ten games under .500 and had just come off a disastrous 2–8 road trip. It was the last straw. Though we came home 2–8, I honestly felt with better situational hitting we could have been 8–2 during that stretch. That's how important it was. We had become the kind of team that simply depended on its natural talent. For example, we would have the bases loaded with none out, and the opposition would get out of the inning because our guys were trying to hit the ball a mile for a grand slam. I remember it happening in Baltimore early in the year. The sacks were full with Canseco, Gonzalez, and Palmer due up. Arthur Rhodes came in and struck all three of them out. Each one of them went down swinging for the fences, just like a lot of other guys on the team. They simply weren't playing situational baseball, forgetting things like how to hit with a runner on third, one out, infield playing back. You don't even need a base hit to drive in a run. A long fly or a well-placed ground ball will do the job. But the hitter has to find a way to get that run home. With good situational hitting you can manufacture runs and not have to rely on the three-run homer at the end.

We were simply not driving in runs from third with less than two outs, were striking out too much as a team, and were pulling the ball instead of using the entire field. I wasn't worried about the batting averages. Pure stats can be deceiving. What you have to do is break each game down and find the places where you know the game was lost. If a guy hits a three-run homer when you're already down 10–1, it doesn't mean much. I decided to challenge the team. On June 25, I called a voluntary workout on what would have been an off day and told them what they had to do, and said, flat out: "We'll find out right now who wants to win and who doesn't." The Basic Agreement said the players didn't have to show up on an off day, but in this case, everybody was there.

I didn't have to name specific guys. Julio Franco, for one, was a fine situational hitter because he naturally hit the ball the other way, a true professional. But when the big guys got into the home run mode they would pull the ball all the time. A player must recognize the situation and shorten his swing. He's got to know counts—which are the pitcher's counts and which are the hitter's counts. For example, if you're down on the count 0-2 you can't be looking for a fastball over the heart of the plate. You simply won't get it. If the count is 2-0 in your favor and you want to take a shot at getting that fastball, that's different. If a team is conceding the run from third, you've got to drive it in. Each player *must* know counts and situations, as well as who's on the mound, but most of all he's got to know himself and exactly what he's capable of doing.

For example, if your leadoff hitter doubles and the next three guys hit ground balls to the left side, then you're not thinking, not doing it right. Players have to be unselfish in certain situations, sometimes giving themselves up for the good of the team. Take a shot to right or try to hit the ball in the hole. All too often during the first months of the season our guys were hitting those three ground balls to third base with a runner on second. I remember another time when I asked Pudge to bunt against the Red Sox. He fouled the ball off with a half-hearted attempt. He looked as if he didn't want to bunt because he would have preferred to drive the run in. These were the types of things I addressed at that June 25 workout.

Practice that day was mainly for the hitters. Claude Osteen went to the mound and did the pitching, and I gave the hitters the situations. The catcher was instructed to call whatever he wanted, making it resemble a real game situation where everyone had to think. I made it a challenge, not a threat. The reality was that I couldn't bench a Juan Gonzalez, Dean Palmer, or Pudge Rodriguez. They had to play. But if they met the challenge of situational hitting they would not only make themselves better hitters, but enhance the team's chances to win. They didn't want a young manager calling them out on their days off, so they got the point quickly.

The point was that they *had* to do the right thing in these situations. Jose had been hurt on the previous road trip and everyone knew he was gone for the season. That made the session that day all the more important. I can say now that the entire team responded. No one becomes a great situational hitter overnight, but they made the transformation well enough as a team to make a difference. It was a turning point. We went from ten games under .500 to ten games over .500 over the remainder of the season. I always look back at that June 25 workout—or challenge as I prefer to call it—as the defining moment of the season.

The team played much better in the second half and finished at 86–76, in second place, but eight games behind the White Sox. We simply didn't have the talent the Sox did, especially in the pitching department, where they had four very solid starters. We also had some injuries at the end. Donald Harris had to come up and play center for us after David Hulse was hurt. Juan Gonzalez, our cleanup hitter, had a bad hamstring and was out almost the final three weeks. But Palmer, Palmeiro, and Franco had great second halves, and all in all, I was proud of the way the team played. I felt even better when George Bush came up to me at the end of the season and said, "It looks like we hired the right guy."

One of the other highlights from the 1993 season was a retirement party for Nolan Ryan on September 12. Nolan pitched that day and got lit up pretty good. It was tough yanking him, especially with many of his friends and former teammates in town for the party. But he had had a great run and could still bring high heat at age forty-six. It was his legs that slowly betrayed him. There was a postgame ceremony on the field and a party that night at Gilley's in Forth Worth, complete with some top country music people. Nolan wanted Sandy Koufax there, so I had Claude, a former teammate of Sandy's, call him initially, and when I spoke to Sandy he was only too happy to attend. Roger Clemens, a Texas guy, came in from Boston, so three great power pitchers from three different generations were together. I wound up managing two of them, and learned a ton of baseball from the third.

While there were plenty of highlights at the end of 1993, it didn't take long for them to be replaced by a series of *lowlights* to begin 1994. The agreement between the owners and the players' union was expiring and talk of a strike was in the air from day one. We came into spring training not knowing whether the season would be interrupted, or even completed. Spring training opened February 15, but without the usual buoyancy and good cheer. On the twenty-second I attended a banquet in Dallas, and on the dais that night I was sitting alongside George Bush, and during the festivities he leaned over to me and dropped a bombshell. "I just want you to know, Kevin," he whispered, "that I've decided to run for governor and I'm going to beat Ann Richards."

After I got over the surprise, I realized this was pure George Bush. Always positive. *And I'm going to beat Ann Richards.* There wasn't a doubt in his mind. I wished him good luck, but then added that I would miss him because he said he wouldn't be around the team much, and he was also the person who had hired me. He told me that Tom Schieffer would be running the team from upstairs and then suggested I relax. "Don't worry," he said. "All you have to do is win and you'll be fine."

The old bottom line again. Just win. But whenever there's a change at the top, everyone below should worry. I knew Tom Grieve was concerned as soon as he learned the news. I could see it on his face. He seemed to know that there would probably be a change in the general manager's office, sooner rather than later.

Of course, you can't go onto the field worrying about those things. I had other worries, not the least of which was that we had lost Rafael Palmeiro to free agency. Raffy was just coming into his own as a power hitter and he wanted to stay in Texas. But the word was out that someone had offered him a $40 million deal and it blew ownership away. They were also negotiating with Will Clark, and when Raffy's agents continued to play hardball, Tom signed Clark. Raffy ended up with Baltimore and put together some great seasons before returning to Texas years later. Though Clark was a fine ballplayer, Raffy was a quiet leader whom players respected and leaned on. In fact, he had leadership qualities no one knew, and it didn't hurt that he had just come off a 37-home-run season. Will was more vocal and tried to help direct the club. He wanted to win but did things in a different way, and it changed the dynamic of the clubhouse.

Once again I had to address the pitching. Nolan had retired, and Henke had hurt his back and wouldn't have a great year. Juan Gonzalez had bulked up quite a bit after having signed a huge deal, getting about $7 million per. He had blasted 46 homers the year before, but in '94 he didn't have the same touch or bat speed, and wound up with only 19 by August. Jose had promised to come back from his elbow surgery better than ever, which he did. He was in the midst of one of his best years when the strike hit, having already hit 31 homers, and he was well on pace for another 40-40 season.

The labor problems led to a negative aura around the entire club all spring. Kevin Brown was the team's union rep, and Juan was late to a lot of the meetings he called because he never wanted to strike, since he had all that money coming to him. The managers and coaches, of course, weren't involved, which put us in a tough spot. I was the go-between with the players and owners, carrying messages to each group. I remember the late Mark Belanger, the former great Orioles shortstop who was working for the union, telling me in the spring that there would most likely be a strike sometime in August.

As the season progressed and the impasse between players and owners continued, there was an increasing sense of bitterness in the clubhouse. The chemistry on the club, which wasn't the same with Raffy and Nolan gone, was further altered by the specter of the impending strike. Though we struggled most of the year at .500 or slightly below, we still managed to keep the lead in our division. It was the first year of the wild card, and while we had a losing record, I still wanted to finish in first place. That way, if a strike came but was then settled, we would be named division champs and could go right into the playoffs.

When the players went on strike after the games of August 11, I remember outfielder Chris James coming up to me and saying, "See you in about two weeks, Skip." I just shook my head. George Bush had told me earlier that week that if the players went ahead and struck on August 11, the season would definitely be canceled. He wanted me to be sure to tell that to the players, but they struck anyway and sure enough, the season was canceled. We finished at 52–62, one game ahead of Oakland. I remember the A's playing a late game on August 11 and we watched on TV, hoping they would lose so we'd maintain a one-game lead, just in case the season resumed for the playoffs.

I went from one of the most exciting years of my life, becoming a big-league manager in 1993, to one of the lowest points just a year later. After the season ended, the Rangers hired a new general manager, and true to baseball politics, he decided he wanted one of his guys to manage. Again, this is all part of the managing merry-go-round so many of us face, and how it all came about will be detailed in the next chapter. This wasn't the usual dismissal. As I'll explain later, it was almost a prearranged scenario. I was let go by the Rangers on Wednesday, and was announced the following Tuesday, at a media-filled press conference, as the next manager of the Boston Red Sox. Wow!

Boston

Did I grow as a manager during my two years in Texas? You bet I did. I grew fast, especially in 1993 after Canseco's injury, when I saw all over again that good or bad, the manager must accept responsibility for everything that happens with his team. When I got to Boston I was calmer. In Texas I'd often get angry when we lost. But I learned in making the transition from Texas to Boston that you have to pick your spots to get mad, reserving outbursts for those times when you want to make a point. I don't think I showed much emotion in the dugout at Boston. One reason was that the media coverage was so intense, and if an opponent hit a homer, the camera would always swing over to me.

The Red Sox were coming off three straight losing seasons, but I knew they had some ballplayers and certainly the potential to win.

Roger Clemens was a horse and on his way to becoming an all-time great. I knew Mo Vaughn would be a big player. One of the first things we did was pull off a trade for Canseco, so I was quickly reunited with one of my favorite players and a guy who might still be a force. Getting him at that time was nearly the equivalent of the Yankees getting A-Rod in 2004. Big, big news. John Valentin and Mike Greenwell were both productive hitters. Aaron Sele was a solid number two starter, though we didn't have a set three, four, or five—a potential problem. Then we signed Mike Mcfarlane to be our catcher. So there was a solid core and a lot of other players moving in and out. GM Dan Duquette was always into the waiver wire, picking up free agents. In my two years in Boston we had fifty-three and fifty-five players on and off the big-league roster—a roster that normally hovers around forty. The acquisitions weren't always successful, but sometimes we were able to make a pickup that counted.

There was one problem with this pretty little picture. When I first joined the team, the players were still on strike and things were very much in a mess. There was talk of starting the season with replacement players, which infuriated the union. On top of that, I wasn't allowed to hire my own coaches. I wanted Ron Perranoski as my pitching coach, but it was nixed. I had to fight to get a few of my own guys, like Tim Johnson and Dave Oliver. Frank White was a returning coach whom I kept, but because Mike Easler, who was hired during the winter as hitting coach, refused to work with replacement players and was subsequently fired by GM Duquette, I had to replace him. Jim Rice was one of the minor-league hitting instructors and a guy I always liked, so I hired him to take Easler's place.

But because the strike had not been settled in the off-season, no one knew exactly when, or even if, the season would begin. Talks had reached the impasse stage between the two sides, and the owners felt they had the legal right to implement their own set of rules. They did that during the off-season, making players free agents after four years instead of the six described in the collective-bargaining agreement. They shortened the free agency requirement as a concession because they wanted to do away with or change the arbitration procedure, which they felt was driving salaries upward. Arbitration was the vehicle that allowed even mediocre players to receive multimillion-dollar contracts.

With four-year free agency, certain players were suddenly on the market. The Red Sox signed both Sammy Sosa and Kevin Appier. That meant if the strike ended and the new rules stuck, we'd have both players in the fold. But the federal government stepped in and filed an unfair-labor-practice claim, returning the old rules, and both those players went back to their respective teams. This is the kind of uncertainty we all faced during the off-season.

Then there were the replacement players. Each team had to put a roster together, and since the managers and coaches are paid year-round, it was our responsibility to get a team ready—any team. I remember Sparky Anderson saying he wouldn't manage replacement players. Sparky could get away with it. But a guy like Mike Easler couldn't. And Easler lost his job because of the stance he took.

It was also tough for the replacements. Dan Duquette told the minor-league guys in our organization to play or be released. Minor leaguers were not part of the union, but those who played were looked upon as scabs. These guys were good players, but not necessarily huge prospects. Some were organizational players who had been there for years, like infielder Tony Rodriguez, who said if he didn't play he would be out of baseball. Tony and others like him were forced to cross the line. Nomar Garciaparra had signed and worked out with us, but wouldn't play in the replacement games because everyone knew he was a coming star. So he wasn't about to cross the picket line. Rick Reed, who wasn't in our organization but would later become a very good pitcher for a number of years, had to play to support his mother. Randy Brown, who was in the Sox minor-league system, had lost his father to a heart attack the year before while the two were sitting at dinner. Now Brown had to play to help support his mom. The team also signed some free agents who were not in baseball at the time, and we had to prepare these guys to play in the bigs.

Some became useful players. Randy Brown was a good defensive shortstop and fine Triple-A player. Ron Mahay was a minor leaguer who had talent, was a solid outfielder, and a very good Triple-A player. Most of these guys were either released or sent back down once the strike was settled, but the better ones were called up again during the season. I would say that just about every team had two or three of these replacement players on its roster at some point in the season, and all of them had a tough time. The bitterness was so deep that the regulars were not about to forgive the scabs. I would always tell regulars who asked that many of the replacements had to make a tough choice and should be judged accordingly.

Later, after the strike was settled, some guys on our team wouldn't take ground balls with Randy Brown, whom we kept up for workout purposes. John Valentin was one. He was a thinking player but felt very strongly about the union. Ron Mahay was brought up to fill in during the regular season when my center fielder, Lee Tinsley, pulled a hamstring. Ron was a good defensive player with some home run power who was later converted to a pitcher, something he had done in college. Mike Greenwell was the player rep on the team then, and I spoke with Mike, explaining that some of these guys were forced to cross the line and that he should try to talk the other guys into accepting Ron as a teammate. "Be fair," I told him. "Treat him as a human being. You don't have to have dinner with him, but remember, he was facing release if he didn't play."

Mahay played pretty well and Mike handled it extremely well. In a game in Anaheim Mahay hit a key homer, and Mike was the first guy out of the dugout to shake his hand. The Angels weren't too happy that a replacement player had gone yard against them, and the next time Mahay came up, someone on their team yelled for the pitcher to hit him. Sure enough, Ron was drilled, and the first guy out of the dugout was Greenwell. So things slowly returned to normal. But there were a few players who harbored resentment against the replacements for some time to come.

The strike was finally settled just before the season was due to begin using the replacements. So it was spring training all over again with the regulars, and eighteen games lost to the continuing strike were lopped off the schedule. Once the season began, we got off fast despite some problems. We had lost Roger Clemens to an arm problem in the spring. We had also made a trade for Mark Whiten, positioning him to bat behind Canseco, but he had problems hitting in

Boston and was soon being booed, a problem compounded in a game when a long fly popped out of his glove and into the stands for a homer. We had picked up Troy O'Leary on waivers from Milwaukee during spring training, and Troy began to do something every time he got into the lineup, including hitting a big three-run pinch homer in Detroit. Finally I decided Troy had to be in the lineup, and we optioned Whiten down to the minors. He had gotten off to a bad start, and if that happens in Boston, it becomes a very difficult place to play.

The team also needed a closer. We had the chance to pick up one of two veterans, Bob Montgomery from Kansas City or Rick Aguilera from Minnesota. Both were righties, but I wanted Aguilera, who could get lefties out with his great splitter. He joined us right after the All-Star break and saved something like 19 of 20 games the rest of the way. Aggie really made the team complete. We now had a balanced ballclub with great clubhouse chemistry. Mo Vaughn and John Valentin had great years. Canseco hit well. Tim Naehring was playing like a Gold Glover at third, and Greenwell could play the wall in left. I also had speed with Lee Tinsley in center and Luis Alicea at second, and we ran as a team, stealing nearly 100 bases. Even Mo Vaughn swiped 11, a perfect example of the old adage that you don't need speed to run.

We led the division from the beginning, getting off to a 13–5 start. Tim Wakefield, a knuckleballing castoff, became the ace of the staff soon after joining the team by winning 10 of his first 11 decisions. Clemens returned in June and we had a three-game lead over the Yankees at the All-Star break. With Aguilera coming on board as the closer and Roger beginning to pitch like himself in the second half, we really began to roll.

We had what seemed like a comfortable seven- or eight-game lead in the final weeks, and it began to look as if we'd win it. We were very consistent, not having lost more than four in a row all year. But I think we began pressing as we neared the finish line, and we found ourselves in the midst of a six-game losing streak. I could see the guys pressing. They couldn't relax. Then one night in Baltimore I had to use Dwayne Hosey in center because Lee Tinsley had strained a hamstring. Hosey was a little switch-hitter with great speed who also had some power. I led him off that night and on the first pitch he hit one out, just one swing of the bat that seemed to break the ice. We stopped the losing streak and went on from there.

We clinched it in Boston on September 20, against the Brewers. Someone coming to Fenway for the first time and not knowing what it was all about would have thought we had just won the World Series. The Boston police were out there on horses, and one by one all the stars got on and began riding around. Then a group of players grabbed me and pushed me onto one of the horses. It was a special moment and a special time. But as great as it was, it was just step one. The 1994 season was supposed to be the first with the wild-card teams in the playoffs, but the strike took care of that, so 1995 would be the first to have the extra series. There were two more series to win and I had to get the club refocused, and fast. Waiting for us was the team many considered the best in baseball that year, the Cleveland Indians.

The Indians had a phenomenal ball club, and they proceeded to sweep us. We wound up losing the first game in 13 innings when Albert Belle hit a homer off a hanging splitter from Rick Aguilera. Erik Hanson started for us the next night and they beat us 4–0, and then Tim Wakefield was roughed up in Game 3. It was over just like that.

The funny thing was that we had no fear of the Indians. We respected their talent but had played them just about even in the regular season, winning 6 of 13. Mo, for one, was pressing in the playoffs, 0-13 to be exact. He fell into a trap that isn't uncommon, the one that makes a guy think he has to do something special. When a player gets that mind-set he begins taking the game to the pitchers instead of letting the game and the pitchers come to him. It doesn't work. They beat us and I really thought they would go on to win the World Series, but the baseball can take funny bounces, and the Indians came up short against the Braves.

Despite losing in the playoffs, it was a special year for me. We led wire to wire and won the division over our longtime archrivals, the Yankees. I remember after we clinched on September 20, it took only about twenty minutes for me to get a congratulatory telegram from

Peter O'Malley. The next day I received a similar letter from George Bush, who was then governor of Texas. It was handwritten with the governor's seal on it. Tom Grieve also sent a telegram. Perhaps the most surprising one was the letter I received from Yankees owner George Steinbrenner, congratulating me and my entire staff. That was a class move by the Boss, a guy who wants to win as much as anyone.

Though I didn't know it at the time, my tenure in Boston would follow the same pattern as my time in Texas. A great, exciting, satisfying year followed by disappointment, disillusionment, and eventual dismissal. The change began in the off-season when I felt certain contractual obligations weren't being met. But my contract problems weren't the only signs that 1996 would not be a repeat of the previous season. Every manager knows that teams make personnel changes yearly. To that end, the manager should know best, and if he's got a good working relationship with his general manager and both trust their evaluators, they should be able to agree on what makes a good deal and which free agents should be pursued.

I could sense the difference, however, as soon as we started to think about '96. Instead of calling me for advice on personnel, Dan Duquette was operating on his own and any contact with me came via his assistant, Mike Port, whom I liked very much. Through this pipeline I heard they wanted to trade center fielder Lee Tinsley and pitcher Ken Ryan to Philadelphia for their closer, Heathcliff Slocumb. They wanted this deal because they didn't pick up the option on Rick Aguilera, who actually wanted to re-sign after doing such a great job for us the year before. Slocumb had saved 30-something games for a last-place team and had a good arm, but he was an outfielder converted to a pitcher. Tinsley led our club in stolen bases and was a switch-hitter and a good center fielder. Ryan had an iron arm and could throw 97 miles per hour but was having trouble with his mechanics. I still felt, however, that we could straighten him out. You also tend to get suspicious when you know there are two solid baseball men looking to deal in Philly, GM Lee Thomas and manager Jim Fregosi. Why would they want to trade their closer . . . unless?

I told Mike I did not want do the deal. Dan went ahead and did it anyway.

Duquette had also traded for Montreal's Wil Cordero during the off-season, and then halfway through spring training released Luis Alicea, who had been our leading hitter in the postseason and a good second baseman. He wanted Cordero to be our second baseman. Cordero was a shortstop turned outfielder, and now we were told to teach him how to play second. Just like that. Wil was a solid hitter, but he looked totally out of sync when trying to turn a double play. Mike Stanley, a fine clutch hitter, was our new catcher. Greenwell was back, so was Jose and Troy O'Leary. Then the club signed Kevin Mitchell, another veteran slugger, late in the spring. Starting to get the picture? By trading Tinsley and Alicea, we had lost our speed at the top of the lineup and our two table setters. While there was still a solid core returning in '96, the dynamics of the club changed. Suddenly I had five or six guys who could DH, with no choice but to put them out on the field. Even some of the veteran players, like Clemens and Vaughn, couldn't understand the moves that had been made.

Not surprisingly, it didn't take long for things to fall apart. The first week of the season we lost Tim Naehring and Kevin Mitchell, our third baseman and right fielder, to hamstring pulls. Then Slocumb, the closer I didn't want, blew a handful of saves, several of them games Clemens could have won. Slocumb could throw, but his control was erratic and the team didn't have the same confidence in him they'd had with Aguilera the year before. We started the season at 2–10, and right away Dan Duquette called me to his room when we were in Baltimore during a road trip. I figured he wanted to talk about the state of the team, maybe about some possible changes. I can still hear the words that greeted me at that meeting. It's as if they're recorded on a cassette embedded in my brain: "I'm not calling you up here to fire you!"

Not calling me up here to fire me! We're two weeks into the season with 150 games left. A year earlier with the same core we had won the division, and now, after 12 games, he's telling me that he wasn't going to fire me. It didn't take a genius to realize that if he had brought it up he must have considered it. Then he had a meeting with the coaches and got all over Tim Johnson and Frank White, basically threatening their jobs. *If Cordero doesn't turn double plays, I'll have to make changes.* Well, Cordero simply couldn't learn to turn the double play and wound up breaking an ankle in midseason on an aggressive slide by George Williams of the A's because he didn't know how to get out of the way. Poetic justice? Maybe. But that wasn't the worst of it. By threatening Tim and Frank, Duquette had alienated them. Now, half my coaching staff had lost their respect for the general manager, and that was detrimental to the team.

I kept my cool and simply told Dan not to panic. "We're 2–10 now, but we'll be fine," I said. "Let me handle the club. I know what I'm doing. We won last year, but if you keep panicking, you'll start to pull things apart here."

After the meeting I went to lunch with Tim and Frank. They were livid, feeling that Dan was questioning their integrity and ability to teach. Just two weeks into the season and I knew it wasn't going to be like last year, but I wasn't about to quit. From 2–10 we went to 6–19, not exactly the earmark of a defending champion and not much of an improvement. The players knew what was going on and the coaches had all stopped believing in Dan. We had been a very close-knit team the year before, but now we saw the actions that were being taken and heard the statements being made. To make matters worse, I realized that Dan was capable of firing his mother. I always felt his tough-guy approach was a huge mistake on his part. He was still a relatively new GM, hadn't been in this position before, and had never worn the uniform. For him to challenge the integrity of longtime professionals with a history of success, without first talking to them in detail about the situation, was a mistake.

Among other things, it was also suggested that we still had a hangover from the previous year and were simply going through the motions with the expectation that we would win the division again. My coaches and I had all been in the game for some thirty years and were used to competing on an everyday basis, so nothing could have been further from the truth. Only someone who hadn't been in uniform could make a statement like that, someone who obviously didn't know me as well as he thought, and didn't know the way I compete. All anyone wants in any position is mutual respect. Once you feel disrespected, it's hard to stay focused. In my case, it was a matter of my pride and passion, as well as my own integrity for the game. If nothing else, that would force me to continue to the best of my ability, game in and game out.

In the following months it didn't get much better. Two months into the season, our pitching coach, Al Nipper, was sent back to work in the minors and was replaced by Sammy Ellis. We'd had two pitching coaches the year before and got through it, but when you don't have continuity, it becomes difficult. I think Duquette's modus operandi was to keep everyone guessing and on their toes. But when you make countless changes just for the sake of making them, you're bound to upset the team. For instance, in those two years, we had 108 players and four pitching coaches on and off the roster. That's way too many.

By the All-Star break we were 36–49, already fifteen games or so out of first place, and appeared to be going nowhere. We still didn't have a second baseman and Jose had a herniated disc in his back that needed surgery, not to mention that the players felt the front office had quit on them. It wasn't a pretty picture. Yet I kept assuring the players we would get it together. Finally, we were able to make a couple of pickups that helped change the face of the team. We got outfielder Darren Bragg from Seattle for Jamie Moyer. Bragg played hard and became my leadoff hitter. Then my third-base coach, Dave Oliver, learned that Jeff Frye, a second baseman who had played for me in Texas, would become a free agent if he wasn't in the majors by June 1. We got him for next to nothing and he became our starting second baseman.

With Bragg leading off and Frye batting second I had my speed guys at the top of the lineup again, as well as a pair of good hitters who could do the little things to set the table for the big guys. Once they were in place we could make things happen—hit-and-run, steal a base, the same kinds of things we had done so successfully the year before. After the All-Star break I simply told the team to concentrate on winning each series we played. We didn't have to sweep every one, just take two of three or three of four, and we would get back in the race.

Bragg was doing the job at leadoff and Frye would hit .300 the rest of the way. Finally, I began feeling good again. When we swept Detroit four straight right after the break it gave everyone a big lift. Now we had something to build on, and by August we were red hot. We went over the .500 mark in a month that saw us go something like 22–7. It was a good feeling because in all my years of managing my teams have always gotten better as the season wore on.

We had a strong September following a great August and finished the season at 85–77. That made us 49–28 after the All-Star break, the best record in baseball for the second half of the season. We had a mathematical chance at the wild card until the last series of the season, but too many things had to break just right and we fell a couple of games short of the Orioles, in third place. Yet I was proud of the way everyone on the team had responded and felt once again that I had gotten the most out of the team. I'm not saying that if we'd had Bragg and Frye from the beginning that we would have won it. That's something we'll never know. But judging by the way the team played after those two guys were inserted in the lineup, I have a pretty good idea what would have happened had they been in there all the way. Having baseball's best mark in the second half of the season pretty much makes the point.

One of the highlights that year, and something I'll never forget, occurred with about two weeks left in the season. Clemens was on the mound and both Roger and I already felt that he wouldn't be back in '97. I also knew that he had some personal goals in sight. He had a chance to tie Cy Young's all-time Red Sox records of 38 shutouts and 192 wins. On this day he was pitching extremely well against the Tigers, carrying a shutout late into the game. As I sat on the bench I thought about a story Maury Wills once told me. Maury was at short for the Dodgers during a game in the 1960s with Sandy Koufax on the mound, and on that day Sandy had a rare laugher, leading 7 or 8–0 in the ninth inning. Because the Dodgers were such a weak-hitting team, Sandy often had to work hard to win games 2–1 or 3–1, or even 1–0.

In the ninth, there was a runner at third, less than two out, so the infield was playing back. You don't worry about the run in a game like that. The batter hit a grounder to short and Sandy looked to first. But Maury surprised everyone and fired home to nail the runner at the plate. Sandy then finished his shutout and after the game asked Maury why he'd thrown home instead of doing it by the book and going to first for the sure out. Maury looked him in the eye and said, "With all those times we didn't score for you we wanted to get you the shutout. You deserved it."

I told Roger the story in the dugout between innings, then added, "We all want you to tie Young's records, and if we have a chance to get the runner at home, we'll do the same thing."

Roger had a shutout going and about the seventh inning we realized he also had a shot to tie or break his own record of 20 strikeouts in a game. After seven, he had 17 strikeouts, and he got 2 more in the eighth, leaving him 2 short of a new mark. Needless to say, in the ninth we were all rooting for both the shutout and the strikeout mark. Alan Trammell opened the inning by popping to first. Then Ruben Sierra singled and went to second on a wild pitch. Tony Clark was next and flied out to left. Finally, Travis Fryman came to the plate. A base hit and the shutout would be gone; any kind of contact out and he wouldn't tie his strikeout record. But being the kind of competitor he is, Roger reached back and struck out Fryman swinging. To see him do that and tie the long-standing records of a baseball immortal was something to remember.

Despite a division title in '95 and another winning season in '96, things had fallen apart between Dan Duquette and myself, and as happens so often for so many different reasons, the Sox decided to let me out of my contract. So it was another two years and out. Disappointing? Of course it was. But winning the division in 1995 will always mean something; to ride that horse around Fenway that day, savoring the feeling of accomplishment, still means something, even though we didn't go all the way. Building relationships, seeing your former players make it to the majors, visiting different parts of the country, managing against rivals like the Yankees—nothing can replace those experiences.

There are so many special moments from those four years, too many to recount here. Watching Kenny Rogers overcome a crisis in confidence and then throw a perfect game about a week before the strike in '94 was incredible. Seeing the work ethic of Roger Clemens and the breakout year of John Valentin, watching Mo Vaughn surprisingly steal 11 bases and win the MVP, all of it will always have meaning to me. So there are no regrets. You just go on and keep looking forward to another opportunity in baseball. Like the game itself, you never know what might happen next.

CHAPTER SIX

◆

The Managing Merry-Go-Round

There is tremendous pressure on every single manager in the big leagues. Each year you can bank that five or six of them will be fired. It seems that as soon as the first one gets axed it opens the doors and more general managers decide they are going to move in another direction. There were even rumors of Joe Torre being fired early in 2003, and someone's job security is always fodder for the media. Yet despite all this I loved the job, cherished the job, and still miss an awful lot about it.

Unfortunately, managers aren't always hired and fired purely on merit and results—illogical perhaps, but something that I'm sure takes place in other fields. With baseball, as in those other fields, there are always unexpected twists and turns, personality conflicts, changes in management, egos, power struggles, and nepotism. A manager doing a good job can be fired just as easily as one doing a bad job. And in what may seem like the ultimate contradiction in terms, a manager can be fired for exactly the same reason he was hired several years earlier. While these factors certainly don't make managing one of the world's most secure jobs, there are always a slew of baseball men coveting one of just thirty positions available. The days of a Walter Alston getting twenty-three consecutive one-year contracts from the same team are over. In fact, they have been over for some time.

As a rule, there is a tendency for a general manager to hire someone he knows and with whom he feels comfortable. There is almost always a relation between the two based on previous experience. Either they were teammates at one time, or they worked together in another capacity with a different organization. Suddenly one becomes a GM, and he looks for that old friend to take over the field job. If there's an incumbent manager in place, he may very well lose his job for the simple reason that the new GM doesn't know him or doesn't feel comfortable working with him. In many cases, the new man doesn't even give the relationship a chance to develop, the assumption being that he will be more successful if a friend has the managerial post alongside him.

There are a few managers whose reputations are so strong that if they were fired tomorrow they could pretty much write their own ticket. These are guys like Joe Torre, Lou Piniella, Dusty Baker, Tony LaRussa, and Bobby Cox. All have track records of handling players— i.e., the stars—successfully and winning. But even these so-called supermanagers needed a break along the way or it might not have happened for them. Torre, for instance, already had something of a label on him after losing managerial tenures with the Braves and Mets. He may not have gotten another chance had Dal Maxvill not become the general manager of the Cardinals. Maxvill and Torre were old friends from their playing days, and the new GM, as is the practice, wanted a friend working the field.

"I was a baseball man and wanted to get back," Torre once confirmed to me. "If Dal hadn't hired me to manage the Cardinals I might never have wound up with the Yankees."

After being in the broadcast booth for six years, Joe then managed the Cards from 1990 to 1995, when he was fired. His record was just 351–354, but a year later he was wearing Yankee pinstripes. The rest of the story, as they say, is history. So there is always a connection. Before George Steinbrenner hired Joe there were also recommendations from people like then GM Bob Watson, who had known Torre from their Atlanta days. That always helps. Another example: Before Terry Francona was hired by the Phillies in 1997, the club received a call from none other than Michael Jordan, recommending him for the job. Terry had managed Jordan in the minors and in the Arizona Fall League when Jordan went on his hiatus from basketball. Getting an endorsement from an athlete of Jordan's stature is pretty powerful stuff.

Terry is one of a group of former skippers who are always testing the waters, looking for another job. Prior to 2004 he got that chance when the Red Sox hired him after firing Grady Little the year before. Terry and the Sox went on to win the World Series in 2004, so he is safe for now. There is also a small group of guys who always seem to be on call. For example, whenever a potentially winning team has a tough situation, Jim Fregosi's name seems to come up. Jim knows a lot of people in the game and has a ton of experience, and having him on the field gives people in front offices a certain comfort level. He is a very safe bet for certain situations, or to fill a gap in an emergency.

Let me give you a few other recent examples of the connection between GM and manager. The owner of the Pirates, Kevin McClatchy, hired Lloyd McClendon in 2001 because Lloyd was always one of his favorite players. Bruce Bochy in San Diego is a very close friend of GM Kevin Towers. They knew each other for years before Towers hired him to manage. When Chuck LaMar hired Larry Rothschild as the first manager of the Tampa Bay Devil Rays, he was hiring a longtime friend he knew from their days in Cincinnati together. And it didn't hurt me when I was interviewed in Texas that Sandy Johnson, who was part of the Texas front office, was the brother of my good friend Tim Johnson. So there is almost always a personal tie of some sort when a manager is hired.

By the same token, managers who are doing a pretty good job often get the short end of the stick when the friend who hired them departs and is replaced by someone who doesn't know them. It happened with me in Texas when the owner left and the general manager was replaced. After I left, Johnny Oates, Jerry Narron, and then Buck Showalter followed in quick succession. Just as the days of a single family owning a big-league team are now gone, in most cases keeping one manager for a long tenure is also a thing of the past.

A successful organization must have continuity, and following along that line, in order for a manager to be successful he must have loyalty. That's why choosing your own coaches is so important. You've got to have loyal coaches working with you to build a winning team, not guys with ulterior motives who may be looking for your job. There are even some owners and GMs who have had a mole in the clubhouse, usually a coach who isn't loyal to his manager and is carrying clubhouse tales—maybe even his own version of them—upstairs to the front office. There's no quicker way to undermine a manager. Once an organization or the people running it begin operating as if they're the CIA, things are going to fall apart.

Another phenomenon of the managing merry-go-round is a skipper being fired for the exact same reason he was hired. I know this sounds crazy. If they hire a guy for a specific reason—whether it's his personality or the way he builds a ball club, disciplines his players, or handles a pitching staff—why would they fire him for the same reason? Believe me, it happens.

Larry Dierker had been a very good pitcher for the Houston Astros back in the 1960s and 1970s. After he retired he became an Astros broadcaster, doing games for about seventeen years. During that time, the front office obviously listened to his broadcasts and knew he had a good baseball mind. Toward the end of his broadcasting tenure, the Astros manager was Terry Collins, a fiery, vocal type who was never afraid to voice his feelings. Terry is a good baseball man with a very strong personality. At that time, the Astros felt they needed this type of manager to get the team over the hump. Under Terry, the team had a couple of second-place finishes, but soon the execs began hearing complaints from a number of players who didn't like his style. That's when the front office decided that maybe they needed a manager with a milder temperament. Collins was out and Larry Dierker came down from the broadcast booth to take his first managerial job.

Larry was well respected, and his strong point was knowing how to handle pitchers. He wasn't the best game manager, but he was aware of that and hired Bill Virdon to be his bench coach, allowing him to learn on the job. Under Dierker, the Astros won four division titles in a row. Unfortunately, they never made it to the World Series. What did they have to do to get there? The same front office, general manager Gerry Hunsicker and owner Drayton McClane, decided they needed someone who ran a tighter ship, an opinionated leader who stuck to his convictions and hopefully would get them to that elusive next level. So Dierker was fired and Jimy Williams was hired.

Think about it. When the fiery Terry Collins was brought in, he replaced Art Howe, who was considered too laid-back and easygoing. Then Collins was fired because he was too abrasive for some players and the laid-back Larry Dierker was hired. After four division titles, Dierker was let go because someone felt he was *too* laid-back to get the team further into the playoffs, and Jimy Williams, whose style of managing fell somewhere in between Dierker's and Collins's, became the manager. Thus both Collins and Dierker were fired for the exact same reason they were hired. Strange, isn't it? Sure, the Astros didn't win in the playoffs, but was that Larry Dierker's fault? His team wound up playing the Braves almost every year. If Craig Biggio and Jeff Bagwell didn't hit in the playoffs, was that Dierker's fault? Jimy Williams came in and didn't win the division right away, so the team went out and signed Jeff Kent prior to 2003 and still came up short.

Prior to the 2004 season, the club signed top pitchers Andy Pettitte and Roger Clemens, hoping their postseason experience and strong arms would take the Astros to the next level. Even though Clemens was outstanding, the team was flat and underachieved. Just prior to the All-Star break Houston traded for a five-tool player, center fielder Carlos Beltran, and it still didn't make a difference. Then, right after the All-Star break, Jimy Williams was let go and whom did they bring in . . . the more fiery and aggressive Phil Garner. Soon after, the Astros got red hot, came on strong to win the wild card, beat the Braves in the division series, and took the Cardinals to seven full games before losing in the NLCS. Now Garner will be back in 2005, but if the team falters again . . . who knows? With all the changes over these many years, the Astros have become a perfect example of what I call the managing merry-go-round.

There's an additional irony to the story. After Terry Collins was fired by the Astros for being an overly aggressive manager, the Anaheim Angels organization began eying him. At the time the Angels, with all their ability, had a reputation for being a laid-back team. In 1995 they had a ten-game lead in the AL West late in the season, then played poorly as the Seattle Mariners overtook them. Marcel Lachemann was the manager at the time, another laid-back type who had previously been well respected as the team's pitching coach. Jim Leyland, the former Pirates manager who also won a World Series with

Florida and had a great reputation, made a call to the Angels front office and recommended Terry Collins, telling them he was also a kick-ass, no-nonsense guy who would shape the team up. Sure enough, he was hired.

After a while, Terry's style once again began to rub some of the players the wrong way. Word began leaking out that Terry had lost the team, and it wasn't long before he was fired, once again for basically the same reason he was hired. After that the front office changed, and that's when Mike Scioscia got the job. With everyone on the same wavelength, the team had the magic ingredients you need, loyalty and continuity, and the result was a World Series triumph in 2002.

My Story as a Managerial Microcosm

From previous chapters, you already have a good idea of the highs and lows I experienced during my tenures with both the Texas Rangers and Boston Red Sox, as well as the casts of characters involved. Now I'm going to detail how I got and then lost both jobs. This will serve as an example of the way baseball works and how there has always been a good-ol'-boys' network where everyone either looks to hire friends or finds someone who won't challenge his power base.

By the end of the 1991 season I had been a minor-league manager for eight years, all of them in the Dodgers organization. I knew in my heart I was ready for the big leagues. The problem was the one many aspiring managers face—getting my foot in the door. Though I would have preferred to remain with the Dodgers, I understood that there were no openings with the big club. Tommy Lasorda was a fixture as manager and very loyal to his coaches, *his guys.* Those two words would come to mean a lot more than I thought they ever could when it came to the way baseball is run.

Knowing there was no chance with the Dodgers, I sent out eight résumés, to Boston, Houston, San Diego, and Toronto, among others, just looking for a big-league job. At that point, coaching would have been fine. I already had an offer on the table from Dan Duquette of the Montreal Expos that I had pretty much ignored, at first. As it turned out, it would signal the beginning of a chain of events that would stretch out over the next five years. Dan had known Ray Poitevint, the scout who had signed me out of San Diego State years earlier. Ray followed Harry Dalton from Baltimore to the Angels, then to the Milwaukee Brewers, where he met Dan, who was just an intern at the time. From what I understand, Ray took Dan under his wing and later became a strong reference for me. Eventually Dan moved on to become the general manager of the Expos when Dave Dombrowski left to join the Florida Marlins. My friend Tim Johnson was already working in Montreal and put a good word in for me, as did Del Crandall, who had managed me at Albuquerque. So the recommendations were piling up (without them, your chances are nil).

What Dan offered me was the farm director's job, not exactly what I had in mind, but he made it a point to tell me that Whitey Herzog had been a farm director for a while, and that eventually led to a very successful managing career. I guess he was trying to convince me that it would be a good stepping-stone, and when he offered me a two-year guaranteed contract I simply couldn't turn it down. I signed in November and began the 1992 season as the farm director of the Montreal Expos. I also felt good because I knew that Dan was aware of my ultimate goal, returning to the field as the manager of a big-league team.

Then some eight months later, on May 22, a day I'll always remember because it was the same day that Johnny Carson was scheduled to do his final show, Dan called me at my home in West Palm Beach and told me he had fired the team's manager, Tom Runnells. Hearing that, the excitement began building immediately. Maybe I was about to get my chance. But Dan squelched that quickly. He told me that he had already decided to make Felipe Alou the team's interim manager, indicating that he wanted to name me, but was reluctant to have two young first-year managers hired back to back. In addition, Felipe was already very popular in Montreal. Then Dan asked me to become the team's bench coach while he observed how the team responded under Felipe as manager. Again I accepted. In all fairness, Felipe had been in the organization for a long time and deserved his chance.

At least I was in the big leagues, back on the field, with a strong feeling that my time was coming. Once Felipe took over, however, the team perked up and began playing very well. The Expos had a solid club that year, and under Felipe's direction the team began putting it all together, sprinting from last to second and nearly overtaking the Pirates for the top spot. After the season, Dan told me there was no way he could make another change considering how Felipe had helped turn the team around. Though I wasn't managing, Dan had kept his word by getting me on a major-league field, so I trusted him. I considered Dan Duquette a good friend, someone who had my best interests at heart.

Now I had to make a decision. With Felipe now entrenched as a manager, I decided to try again. A little over a year earlier, I had sent a résumé to the Texas Rangers. Sandy Johnson was the assistant general manager and scouting director there and, as I said, the older brother of Tim Johnson, one of my best friends. Sandy had called me in the winter of 1991, even before I took the Montreal job, and said he had given my résumé to Rangers owner George W. Bush, with the recommendation that I be hired as the team's manager. But it had never gone any further than that. In fact, at the time I wasn't even aware it had happened. Then, in the middle of the 1992 season, Bobby Valentine was fired and Toby Harrah was named to manage on an interim basis. Toward the end of the year I got a call from the club informing me that they were planning to interview me for the manager's job. The encouraging part was that they had told me there would be just three other candidates—Harrah, Jerry Royster, and Rene Lachemann. In truth, I would have been just as happy if there had been twenty candidates. That's how badly I wanted a chance to manage in the bigs.

Sure enough, after the season ended, the Rangers called Duquette and received permission to speak with me. Then the process began. In October, Sandy Johnson and Rangers general manager Tom Grieve flew in to Florida to speak with me as a kind of preliminary interview. I met them at the Fort Lauderdale airport, where we went into a private conference room. They asked me the usual questions, about my philosophy of handling a pitching staff, running the game from the dugout, how I would handle spring training, and the kinds of team rules I would institute. They also asked if I believed that the manager should be allowed to hire the coaching staff or whether it should be done by committee. I said: "If you're going to trust a manager to run your ball club, then you've got to trust him to get the coaches he wants."

Grieve apparently loved that, adding only that he had promised the current coaches that the new manager would talk with them first, and eventually I did, hiring two of them. I made it clear at the time that I wanted the best people. It wasn't as if I was going out to hire six friends. But I'm getting ahead of myself. Another important question they asked was how I would handle the players, especially the stars. They knew I had a long background working with Latin players from my winter ball days, and at that time there were many Latin Americans on the Rangers, the guys I've already spoken about—Gonzalez, Rodriguez, Franco, Canseco, Palmeiro. I answered the way I felt, only I didn't know at the time that I would soon be asked the same question in a much more important meeting by a much more important man.

All in all, I felt good about the interview, especially since I knew I could return to Montreal as bench coach if I didn't get the job. But I had spoken from the heart, something I've always done. It worked for me because it only took a few days to get a callback. This time they wanted to meet me again in Fort Worth, at the office of Tom Schieffer, one of the team's partners.

The Rangers organization had many investors, about eighty minority owners, but three men essentially ran the team. Tom Schieffer, the brother of longtime CBS newsman Bob Schieffer, was an attorney and dealt with the club's overall operations; Rusty Rose handled the finances; and George W. Bush, the managing general partner, always did the main hiring of the baseball people. We met at eight in the morning. The three managing partners were there, along with Tom and Sandy Johnson, but it was apparent from the first minute that George Bush was the centerpiece. He was the one who kept asking the questions.

One of the first questions George Bush asked me was if I thought the team had too many Latin players to win a championship. I knew where he was coming from immediately. It wasn't that he had anything against Latin players, but there were rumors that the team hadn't played up to its potential because of too many cliques and entourages. I responded as quickly as he asked the question.

"No," I said. "There aren't too many Latin players. When we won championships in the Dominican and Puerto Rico I had about twenty-five Latin players and six Americans."

He gave me that little smirk of his, and I think he not only liked the answer, but was impressed with the way I had responded so quickly, making it apparent that I wasn't searching for a politically correct answer. There were, however, two other questions that stood out, and I remember them quite clearly, even today.

"You weren't a star player in the big leagues," he said, as if I had to be reminded of that, "but we have a bunch of stars and are a very high-profile club. If I give you this job, just how are you going to handle these guys?"

Again, I didn't hesitate. I told him I would want to see each player immediately, going directly to their homes and meeting them there on a one-to-one basis. It was important, I told him, for the core players to know me and vice versa before spring training began. I think he liked that as well. Then one other question struck me. It came near the end of the interview. George Bush looked me in the eye and said, "Well, I'm not saying you have the job yet, but if I give you this job would you take a one-year deal?"

Again, I didn't hesitate. "No," I said.

"Why not?" he asked. "You had one-year deals all those years you were in the minor leagues."

I was surprised he knew that, and I realized immediately that he had done his homework. That impressed me. But again, I answered quickly. "That's the point. I've always had one-year deals," I said. And he got that little grin of his once more. "It has to be more than one year. When you get to the big leagues as a manager you need more than just one year to do the job right." My feeling was that to have time to implement your program you need a minimum of three years, with the optimum being five. A manager has to have time and security. As I've said before, it's too easy to fire a manager who has one year, or one year with an option. I explained my feelings to Bush and told him how it takes time to shape the type of club you want, implement your system, and get the entire organization on the same page, the way the Dodgers had done it. If you don't have security, as well as the backing of the GM and owner, the players begin to think you might be gone in six months and you can lose the team.

I left feeling pretty good and it took only a few days for the phone to ring with a decidedly Texas twang, as I always like to tell people. It came as a surprise because I didn't think they would make a decision so quickly. Tom Grieve was on the other end, telling me what I had wanted to hear for so long a time: "We'd like to offer you the managing job with the Texas Rangers with a two-year contract."

I had waited for so long to hear those words, yet despite all my previous advice about a manager jumping at that first big-league job, I didn't accept immediately. From the first day I signed with the Orioles years earlier I had learned that baseball was a business. I wanted my lawyer to talk with the Rangers first, and Sandy Johnson told me later that I made everyone a little nervous with that move. But a few days later I flew in to Texas to be announced and have my picture taken with Tom Schieffer, Tom Grieve, and the man who would later become president of the United States, George W. Bush.

My first year managing the Rangers was one of the best of my life. The team had a winning record and a great group of core players, so there was no reason to suspect that things wouldn't continue to go smoothly. At that point, I was hoping not only to lead the Rangers to a championship, but to have a long run at the helm as well. Then during the off-season, George Bush dropped the bombshell about running for governor and predicted he would beat the incumbent, Ann Richards. When I replied by saying I'd be sorry to see him leave the ball club, adding that I felt he had always been in my corner, he kind of teased me by saying, "Don't worry, all you have to do is win." I felt that way too, and actually went on a radio show prior to the 1994 season and said flat out that there were no excuses for us not winning in the upcoming year. In hindsight, maybe that was a mistake.

What I didn't know when that ill-fated 1994 season began was that I was about to experience the managing merry-go-round first-hand, and also learn that backroom baseball maneuvering is certainly not always what it seems to be. Though I didn't know it at the time, it began before spring training even started. My old friend Dan Duquette called me at home in Texas to tell me he was leaving Montreal to become the general manager of the Boston Red Sox.

I remember that May, after we swept the Red Sox in a series at Fenway, Dan took me to a friend's restaurant in Boston. His buddy came over and sat down with us. After we talked for a few minutes the friend looked at me and said, "How big would it be to have a Kennedy managing in Boston?" Dan answered without taking a breath, "Well, yeah, that very well could happen someday," and agreed it would sound good. Of course, all I was thinking about then was how to get the Rangers to win more games. I didn't know at the time that the exchange between Dan and his friend was anything more than playful talk. You'd have to be living on another planet, however, not to make the association between the Kennedys and Boston. But Kevin Kennedy? That just wasn't part of my thinking then.

Then soon after the strike hit, I got a surprise call from Dan Duquette on my cell phone, asking how things were going in Texas. That immediately struck me as odd. I had already talked with Tom Schieffer, who had said my job was safe, that everyone thought I was running the club well. In fact, at the end of 1993 they had put another year on the contract so that I would begin the next year with two years still on the deal. Sandy Johnson told me the Rangers always did it that way. With the contract extended, I fully expected to return to the team in 1995.

When Bud Selig officially canceled the season in September, I got a call from Tom Schieffer, who was setting up a meeting with Tom Grieve, Sandy Johnson, and me. This time, George Bush wouldn't be there. We went in one at a time to meet with Schieffer. Tom Grieve was first, and as soon as he came out a half hour later I could see the look on his face. He turned to us and said, "They let me go." Just like that. Sandy and I must have looked as if we had lost our best friend, because Tom quickly added that we shouldn't worry, that both of us would definitely be fine.

Yet it didn't sit well with me. I was already thinking that the guy who was most influential in getting me hired, next to George Bush, had just been dumped. Now Tom was gone and the reality of the game was starting to knock on my door. Sandy went in next and when he came out he told me he was now the interim GM, but that Schieffer was going to go through an interview process to find a permanent replacement for Grieve.

When I finally entered Schieffer's office the first words I heard were that while Sandy would be an interim GM, I was going to remain the manager . . . no matter what. *No matter what!* No hidden meaning there. To me, those words constituted a total endorsement as much as anything could. Case closed. Schieffer then elaborated by telling me again that I had done a great job, so when I left his office I called my coaches and told them they, too, would all be safe. It was a difficult time for them as well. Coaches sometimes worry even more than the manager, often with good reason. When some owners and GMs need a scapegoat but still don't want to replace the manager, they ax a coach.

We all waited while Schieffer went through the interview process for a new general manager. At first there were rumors that Walt Jocketty, now the GM of the Cardinals, was a leading candidate. Jackie Moore, one of my coaches, knew Walt well and said if he got the job we'd all be fine. Again, a matter of someone knowing someone. But soon after, there was another name thrown in the mix. Doug Melvin. From what we heard later, Doug had come in armed with stats and numbers, and proceeded to tell Tom Schieffer what was wrong with the organization and what had to be done. He must have made an impressive presentation, because he was subsequently hired. I already knew that Doug was close to Johnny Oates, and that Johnny had just been fired as manager of the Orioles. Now I was about to learn another lesson. It's the old proverb that says it isn't what you know, but who you know.

Maybe I'm oversimplifying things a bit, because it's also a matter of finding a comfort zone, and guys can sometimes achieve that only by working with someone they know, or someone they can intimidate and dominate. Doug Melvin had been in the Orioles front office and a few years earlier had hired Johnny Oates to be their Triple-A manager. When Doug got a higher position with the Orioles, Oates had followed him and become the team's manager. Knowing this, the wheels began turning in my head. I didn't have to wait long before the spokes began to break.

First, Butch Hobson was fired in Boston. Dan Duquette had never really wanted him there in the first place. Oates, of course, was already out in Baltimore, and suddenly I began getting calls from Duquette, one or two a week, asking me about my situation in Texas. I kept telling him I had been assured my job was safe. He simply said, "If anything changes, let me know." Technically, he hadn't offered me a job and thus didn't break the rules of tampering, but he came close, obviously inquiring about more than my health and happiness. Looking back, I'm pretty sure he knew more than I did at the time.

My next wakeup call came at the press conference to introduce Doug Melvin. After introducing himself and speaking briefly about the team, Doug began fielding questions. It didn't take long for one of the reporters to ask, "What about Kevin Kennedy?"

Doug waffled for a second, then said, "We'll see. I have to talk with him."

Whoa. This certainly wasn't the ringing endorsement I thought I had received from Tom Schieffer just a short time earlier. In fact, it wasn't close to any kind of endorsement at all, and that's when I really began to feel the heat. What happened to *no matter what?* I wondered. I wasn't exactly burying my head in the sand and waiting. After all those years in the minors, then finally getting the Texas job, I made no secret of wanting to stay. I liked the team, liked the Metroplex—the Dallas–Fort Worth area—and simply didn't want to go anywhere else. Finally, Melvin set up a meeting with me—the moment of truth, as it turned out.

He began by asking me about the clubhouse, telling me he had heard there were problems. It wasn't a very happy clubhouse, according to his sources. Hey, it was the strike year. It was an ugly atmosphere. There were some guys who wanted to strike and some who didn't, and that certainly doesn't make for harmony. I'd venture to say there probably weren't any happy clubhouses in 1994. At any rate, I told Doug that what you hear and what is actually happening aren't always one and the same. I also reminded him that while it was an ugly season in a lot of ways, we were in first place when the season was canceled. But as we continued to talk, the line of questioning he was pursuing began to strike me as that of a guy looking for an excuse, digging for something he could use to justify getting rid of me. When the meeting ended, he said he would call me the next day.

I didn't get the call until a couple of days later, and he asked me to meet him at his office at 9:00 in the morning. I knew right then I was done. Talk about a kiss-of-death phone call. Not let's have lunch or go somewhere to relax and chat about the team. It was simply, "Meet me at my office at nine." I'll say this much: Doug was very gracious about it. He said, basically, "Kevin, I just don't know you. I want to bring my own guy in." Bingo! There it was. I just nodded and told him I had suspected that all along. Then I began talking to him about the team and the players, especially how to deal with the stars. Later, I was told that he was impressed by the fact that after he had fired me I still spent time talking to him about the club. All that was well and good, but it was the last thing he said before I left that morning that struck me as strange.

"Besides," he said. "I think you're going to be fine with Duquette."

Now the merry-go-round was starting to turn. I was still wondering what he meant when I called Dan. As soon as I got him on the phone I laid it right on the line, telling him I had been fired and then in the next breath saying I wanted to work for him. No sense pussyfooting around. I needed a job. Dan and I had always been straight with one another, and as I said, there was a large element of trust between us. He asked me when I could fly to Boston and I said the next day.

I was let go on a Wednesday and landed in Boston on Thursday. I met with their former GM Lou Gorman, who was still in the front office; Mike Port, the assistant GM; and Duquette. Team owner John Harrington came in and said hello but stayed only ten minutes. A far cry from team owner Bush, who had personally conducted an interview lasting several hours. After Harrington left, I went to lunch with the other three. Then I spent part of the afternoon talking with Dan almost informally. It wasn't really an interview. After that, I flew right back to Texas, with Dan telling me he'd keep me informed without really tipping his hand. I learned later that he had called Sandy Johnson to do another reference check on me, asking what had really happened in Texas. I assume he wanted someone to confirm the kind of job I had done there.

Early the following Monday Dan called me again and immediately offered me the job of managing the Boston Red Sox. I accepted as quickly as he had offered it, a one-year deal with a convoluted option, a strange contract that was structured differently from other contracts I'd previously had. If I was fired after 1995, I was guaranteed only half of the money I'd earn in 1996. That part was a bit disappointing, but because it was Dan, I agreed. Yet there was some additional language in the contract that was odd. It gave Dan the option of removing or reassigning me after just a couple of months. In other words, if he fired me two months into the 1995 season he could reassign me to Triple-A and I'd have to go. In fact, he could send me all the way down to Single-A. There was also a confidentiality clause, stating that if I was fired I couldn't talk about it while my contract was still in effect. Before I signed, my lawyer got the reassigning clause out, but it certainly wasn't the greatest of deals.

On the upside, I did receive a raise and would still be managing in the big leagues. Dan asked me when I could fly in because he wanted to announce me quickly, then have us go immediately to the Instructional League and start working. I said how about tomorrow. It was almost an unheard-of situation. I was let go by Doug Melvin in Texas on a Wednesday, hired by Dan Duquette in Boston the following Monday, then announced as the new manager of the Boston Red Sox on Tuesday. Talk about a whirlwind courtship!

But the more I thought about the whole scenario, the more I began to see things clearly, and the more I began realizing that there was more to this game of revolving managers than just wins and losses. Here's my understanding of how things happened, and why, for the first time, I began to question my own trust in Dan Duquette just as I was about to go to work for him.

Before Dan knew I was going to be fired, he apparently talked to Doug Melvin about Johnny Oates. He would tell me later that Melvin advised him not to hire Oates because he (Oates) wouldn't be able to handle the tough Boston media. Of course, Melvin had his own agenda for Oates, so he wasn't about to encourage someone else to hire him. I also found it odd that when I was announced as manager of the Red Sox the headline of a Boston paper read, DUQUETTE GETS HIS PAL, NOT HIS MAN. To me, that was a read-between-the-lines piece of journalism. I had known that Dan was looking into the possibility of hiring Tony LaRussa before Tony re-signed with Oakland, a turn of events I found kind of interesting . . . and more than a little bit disturbing.

Dan told me they were looking at LaRussa "because we have to sell tickets." In other words, he would have preferred a high-profile manager; but I knew the line about selling tickets was pure bull. The Red Sox were always at 93 percent capacity in Fenway no matter who was managing. That was the first line of nonsense I ever got from Dan, and I said so. When I called him out, he just smirked. The same day I was announced, LaRussa signed a three-year extension with Oakland for about $1.75 million per year, and I remember Dan saying the GM who signed him for that amount should be fired. That also struck me as odd. I told him I felt LaRussa deserved that much, then pointed out how much some NBA and NFL coaches were getting. A good manager is worth that, I said. But the exchange also made me wonder what he really thought about managers and their ultimate value.

The way the whole thing had come down so quickly still stuck in my craw. It didn't seem right, and it certainly wasn't a coincidence. Here's how I think it happened. I'm pretty sure that when the two general managers talked, they both agreed to what almost amounted to a swap. Melvin wanted Oates and Duquette wanted me. So Duquette might have said, *Look, both guys are going to be managing in the big leagues. You let Kevin go and I'll hire him, and then you're free to bring Johnny Oates to Texas.* For those reasons, I never considered that I was out-and-out fired in Texas. It was more of a political thing, the politics of the front office, and it goes on all around the league.

Here's a more recent example of what I mean. Oakland A's GM Billy Beane didn't rehire Art Howe before the 2003 season because he wanted bench coach Ken Macha to stay with the team. With Howe gone, he got Macha to stay the only way he could, by naming him

manager. The A's wouldn't give Macha permission to interview in
Boston. The funny part is that Macha, Howe, and Lou Piniella have
the same agent, Alan Nero. It was almost as if Nero orchestrated all
the moves. The Mets made no secret of the fact that they wanted
Piniella, but Lou wanted to go home to Tampa. Nero got that done
first, then probably told the Mets, *Piniella's gone, but Art Howe is available and he's coming off two straight divisional titles. Why don't you hire
him?* That done, the door was open for Macha to take over in Oakland. The circle had closed, and therein lies the politics of the real
world.

I always knew in my heart that my firing and hiring, all in the
blink of an eye, was an orchestrated tradeoff among the two general
managers, and now I see it with other GMs and their managerial
choices as well. It's a system that's firmly entrenched in today's game
and I don't know if it will ever change. Does that also mean it's the best
way to run a ball club? Not necessarily. Otherwise, there wouldn't be
so many changes every year.

Now It's Boston

My demise in Boston was an example of something else, something
that can not only hinder a manager's ability to operate to the best of his
ability, but also keep the franchise as a whole from succeeding. It has
to do with loyalty and continuity. If you don't have that, things will fall
apart. And if a GM is driven by ego or power, and doesn't want to
defer to or work with the manager, the team will also eventually be
sabotaged.

As I described earlier, the Red Sox went wire to wire in 1995 and
won the division before we were eliminated by the Indians in the first
round of the playoffs. So there was no reason for me not to feel good
about my job. Yet when I brought up the matter of a contract extension with Dan, he began to do the shuffle. I already knew that Mike
Hargrove had gotten three more years in Cleveland, and Dan himself
had a five-year deal. But all he would say at first was, "Well, we're set
for next year. Then we can talk about '97 and '98."

During the winter he continued to be slow to negotiate, seeming to go out of his way to avoid the issue. A month after the season ended I still didn't have a deal in place. Other managers were getting extensions, and we had just won the toughest division in baseball. I felt it was finally my time as a manager, and it would feel even better if I had the security that went with the success on the field. After all the years in the minors and in winter ball, the struggle to get there, then finally winning, well, opportunities don't come along that often. I had a businessman friend from Dallas helping handle my contract negotiations. Back then you could have a businessman or lawyer, but not a baseball agent. My friend flew from Dallas to Fort Myers, Florida, to meet with Dan, and when he returned he was puzzled.

"I don't know what this guy said," he told me, referring to Duquette. "He didn't go anywhere, just kept saying don't worry, we'll get it ironed out, but I think he's trying to play hardball and I'm starting to sense an edge about this."

By November, when I was out at the Arizona Fall League, I still didn't have a deal. Finally, Dan told my friend he would make an offer, the first and final one, and we would have seventy-two hours to decide. It called for just a one-year extension with a very small increase in salary. In a way, he was challenging me through my friend-agent.

I couldn't believe what was happening. After having the time of my life the past season I thought, Why do I have to go through this? Thanks to me, Dan had given my bench coach, Tim Johnson, a two-year deal at just over $100,000 per. He knew Tim was managerial timber, so he already had someone who knew the team if I left. That gave him an ace in the hole. See how the game is played? Under these circumstances, I decided I simply wasn't going to accept the one-year extension as it had been put on the table. I also spoke to a friend from the *Boston Globe,* who wrote an article that insinuated there was a problem developing between Dan and me. That same day the club announced it was raising ticket prices, so they took a double hit with the fans, who were solidly in my corner.

The next day I got a phone call from Dan, who was on his way to Arizona. He left a message on my voice mail, saying, "I think we can come to an agreement that will satisfy you and the ball club. We'll talk when I get there." It was very businesslike, nothing like our relationship had been before. When we picked Dan up at the airport there was an obvious uneasiness. My trust in him had been shattered. I had always considered him a good friend, but now I was thinking, I've worked for this guy twice and suddenly he's treating me like any other Joe. By this time I felt as if I had been disrespected, and it was bothering me.

I remember taking out the letter he had written me a few months after we had been eliminated from the playoffs. I read it again and couldn't believe this was the same guy I was dealing with now. The letter, dated October 18, and with a copy sent to team owner John Harrington, said:

> *Congratulations on winning the American League Eastern Division and for your contribution to a great 1995 season. Your leadership and stability on the field, and in the clubhouse, played a key role in the success of our team. Our record of 86–58 ranks 2nd in the American League, and 3rd in all of major league baseball. We are particularly pleased with our 35 game improvement between the 1994 and 1995 seasons. These are significant accomplishments considering the new coaching staff and a franchise record 53 players on our club this season. We have laid the foundation for us to continue toward our goal of a world championship in 1996.*
>
> *I am pleased to enclose your bonus check and to commend you on a job well done. Best wishes to you and your family this winter.*

While the letter obviously put some pressure on us to win again, it could also be interpreted as the proverbial ringing endorsement. Then again, I'd thought I had the same kind of ringing endorsement from Tom Schieffer in Texas. Remember *no matter what?* At my next meeting with Dan he stuck to his guns for '96, but he added '97 at a fair salary and guaranteed me half of 1998. Because of everything that had happened, I'd be a liar if I didn't admit that my goal was to make it more difficult for him to let me go. So I agreed to the deal, which meant I would be getting money through 1998, no matter what might unfold.

Looking back now, it was ironic. Strange as it may sound, I finally had something closer to the deal I wanted, and it wound up getting me fired. Things began going downhill from that point, even though we turned it around in the second half of the 1996 season, just missing the wild card by a couple of games while compiling the best record in baseball during those final months. Yet my problems with Dan hadn't stopped. The option date for the Red Sox to pick up my contract was September 20. We were still in the race when I had a meeting with Dan, who said he knew the date was coming, but wanted to wait until after the season. By this time I knew I had to take a stand, so I told him I couldn't wait until after the season; the contract said the option had to be acted upon by September 20. I told them either you pick it up or you don't. He repeated that he wanted to wait, yet I couldn't understand why, not after the great second half we were putting together, not to mention that we still had a chance for the wild card. At that point, I couldn't conceive that the guy would let me go. Maybe he would decide not to pick up the option, but at least I would manage the team again in 1997 as a lame duck.

What he did was put the onus on John Harrington, the owner, telling me that it was Harrington who didn't like the date, that they didn't normally talk about extensions until October. I reminded him that it was the team lawyers who had drawn up the contract and had put the September 20 option date in there, not me. Then I suggested they read the contract before they made a decision. But the situation wasn't getting any better and they never acted on the option.

The day after the season ended—after we had finished so strong—Dan called me up to his office. The conversation must have lasted all of two minutes.

"Kevin, it isn't all about winning," he said, then added quickly, "We're going to let you out of your contract, and by the way, Mr. Harrington is on board and knows what we're doing."

Just like that. Boom! From my trusted old friend. All the while I'm thinking, Not about winning. In Boston, of all places! Of course it's about winning in Boston. Is he kidding me or what? If it wasn't about winning, why did he panic and begin threatening everybody's jobs when we were 2–10 at the beginning of the season? So don't tell me it's not about winning. I knew right away that this guy had made up his mind in April. But when he said it, all I could do was look at him and say, "Dan, until you learn to communicate you're going to miss out on people and have problems. Good-bye."

The man basically fired me without giving me a reason, just that it wasn't all about winning. Sure, he was looking for an excuse, but he never gave me a real, logical reason. I was told by someone shortly afterward that he did indeed want to fire me in April, but held off because we had won the division in '95, and he probably would have heard all kinds of flak for making such a quick and impulsive move. Obviously, it's always about winning. To me, that was always the ultimate bottom line. There are certainly other factors involved, and there have certainly been other cases where winning managers have been canned, but the oldest axiom in the managerial book is that you have to win, sooner or later . . . usually sooner.

In Boston I thought I was working with a trusted friend, but instead I found myself entangled with a guy who had to control everything and didn't want anyone around him to taste the power. He always had me dangling on the end of a bad contractual situation and then all but took away my ability to put together the kind of roster I wanted, and needed. It was almost as if he thought any manager could win with him pushing the buttons upstairs. The fact that he ran so many Red Sox stars out of town, including Roger Clemens and Mo Vaughn, speaks volumes. Not surprisingly, Dan himself was fired just a couple of years later. In fact, with the Red Sox, it seems as if they're always starting over, never quite finding a way to stop the merry-go-round of changing managers.

Managing and security have never gone together. I'm not about to go back and make a list. But look at the history. Casey Stengel was fired more than once. Leo Durocher was fired more than once. Both are Hall of Fame managers. And Billy Martin, always a winner, was fired more times than I can count. Need I go on? Maybe one way to avoid some of the problems would be to have the manager and general manager be one and the same. It has been done in the past and it's done in other sports, most notably the NFL. I think Whitey Herzog was the last to do it in the big leagues when he took over the Cardinals in 1980.

August Busch hired Whitey and gave him all the power to put together a winning team, which he did. Once he made all the moves he felt necessary, he relinquished the GM job because he really didn't want both.

In today's game, it's important to have a front-office guy who knows contracts, but that doesn't necessarily have to be the GM, yet most owners want their general managers to handle negotiations. It certainly wouldn't be difficult to have a contracts man working with the GM. It might not be a bad idea to just let a good baseball man run the whole show, except for contracts. A manager with a particular vision should have input and a strong voice in all personnel moves. After all, he's the one running the team on the field. There are financial restrictions, of course, but that doesn't mean every winning team has to be the Yankees, with a $200 million payroll. You can win with a few stars and the perfect role players to complement them. The Angels proved it in 2002 and the Marlins even more so the next year.

The most successful organizations are those with the manager and general manager on the same page, working together for a common goal. Bobby Cox and GM John Schuerholz in Atlanta are like brothers. Walt Jocketty and Tony LaRussa in St. Louis are the same. Kevin Towers and Bruce Bochy in San Diego are a tandem, great friends. Lasorda and Campanis did it with the Dodgers for years. GM Brian Sabean and manager Felipe Alou in San Francisco both had their contracts extended to 2005. In New York, George Steinbrenner is the ultimate boss, but he wants to win so badly that he knows he needs people like Brian Cashman and Joe Torre around him. That's the way it works best, and that is definitely the best situation for a manager. Of course, it always helps when the organization is winning.

Today, more of the general managers are nonbaseball people, guys who haven't played the game. Ten or fifteen years ago maybe 90 percent of the GMs had played at some level. But since the strike of 1994 it seems that a lot of the GMs who were baseball men have lost their jobs. If a GM hasn't played, then he needs good evaluators around him, as well as a manager he trusts and whose advice he will take seriously. Many of the GMs today are smart young guys who mirror the world as it is today—fast news, the Internet, computerized analysis. They use all this to come up with their own formulas for success, and the managers of the future may find more of these computerized breakdowns as part of the interview process.

But in reality, you can't reinvent the wheel. Al Campanis had the same kind of statistical analysis they have today, just in a different form. He also had people skills, evaluation skills, and teaching skills . . . and he led an extremely successful organization for many years. In addition, the older owners were more hands-on, no one more so than Walter O'Malley when he ran the Dodgers, or Charles O. Finley when he owned the A's, and of course there is George Steinbrenner today. Done correctly, this can only serve to promote that all-important continuity right down the line and can only help the manager.

My experiences are a perfect example. In Texas, George Bush was hands-on, conducting nearly the entire interview before hiring me and keeping track of the team's pulse until he decided to enter politics. On the other side of the coin, John Harrington in Boston only dropped in to say hello when I was interviewed and basically allowed his general manager, Dan Duquette, to run the team—and he almost ran it into the ground before he was finally let go. In any case, the manager knows he's on a merry-go-round going in, and unless he winds up in one of that handful of successful organizations with loyalty and continuity, he will stay on the merry-go-round until it inevitably spins him off.

◆

CHAPTER SEVEN

The Most Important Positions
on the Field . . . and Why

Despite all the emphasis today on the home run and the sluggers who hit them, good baseball people know that it's pitching and defense that win championships. These two ingredients have traditionally been the hallmark of most great teams. Look what happened in the 2004 World Series. The Cardinals' pitching didn't hold up while the Red Sox' did. The result, a four-game sweep for Boston.

Over the last decade baseball has entered yet another home run era. With the record-breaking exploits of Mark McGwire, Sammy Sosa, and Barry Bonds, followed by the speculation about how the possible use of performance-enhancing drugs, especially anabolic steroids, might taint these new marks, the home run has been baseball's biggest story for more than ten years. There is constant debate about how the new ballparks with shorter outfield dimensions, livelier balls, diluted pitching, and performance-enhancing substances have all helped bigger, stronger hitters dominate the game. Unfortunately, all this long-ball hoopla has relegated one of the most important elements of the game to the back burner. During much of this period you simply haven't heard much about defensive ball clubs and how playing superior defense can affect the outcome of a game. Yet almost any coach or manager—in any sport for that matter—will tell you that defense wins championships, and in baseball the combination of pitching and defense has traditionally been the hallmark of most great teams.

Look at the Yankees ball clubs that won four championships beginning in the late 1990s. The team's strength was always pitching and defense, with timely hitting a final touch. A deep rotation, a quality bullpen, and strong defense up the middle are always winning ingredients. The successful Dodgers teams in the early 1960s did it the same way, with Koufax and Drysdale leading a stingy pitching staff and players like Maury Wills, Wes Parker, John Roseboro, and Willie Davis giving them a fast, sure-handed defense. Same with the Cardinals teams of the early 1980s—pitching, defense, and speed. They were especially strong up the middle with Ozzie Smith at short, Tommy Herr at second, and Willie McGee in center field. All three clubs were built basically the same way, though the Yankees had more hitting and the Cards more speed because they played on turf.

The Boston Red Sox finally reached the pinnacle in 2004, winning the World Series with a stirring comeback from a 3–0 deficit against the Yankees in the ALCS and then sweeping the St. Louis Cardinals in the World Series. The difference in this Red Sox team from those of the past was the addition of Curt Schilling, who won 21 games and became the team's ace, and defensive players such as first baseman Doug Mientkiewicz and second sacker Pokey Reese, who often came in during the latter part of the games, especially when the Bosox had the lead.

The best way to emphasize the importance of pitching and defense is to look at something called "lineup turnover." Lineup turnover can give players on the offensive team an extra at bat, but can also be avoided by a combination of solid pitching and tight defense. Look at it this way: There are twenty-seven outs in a game. If you allow a team four walks and commit two errors, that's six opportunities for outs that you just gave up. Now the team receiving those gifts theoretically has thirty-three outs, a bonus of two innings. Lineup turnover. Say a team makes an error in the second inning, but gets out of it without giving up a run. Okay, no damage done, you say. Think again. That extra out has just turned the lineup by one player. It could come back and haunt your club later in the game. Here's another example. Two National League teams are playing and with two outs and none on in the middle of the game, the number-eight hitter draws a walk. Now the pitcher has to come up to make the final out. So instead of the pitcher leading off the next inning, you've got the top of the order, a decidedly more dangerous situation. What might seem like a harmless walk has turned the lineup and could ultimately affect the end result of the game.

That's the importance of lineup turnover. How many times have you seen the three, four, and five hitters come up in the ninth inning of a close game? It's one thing if they come up because of base hits earlier, but if the culprit was a couple of careless walks or an error, then unnecessary lineup turnover has given them a fifth at bat. Balls that get past a mediocre infielder also lead to turnover, whereas the grounders Derek Jeter backhands in the hole at short to take away hits with his spectacular jump throws eliminate turnover. And, of course, a pitcher who can keep walks to a minimum also helps himself and his team.

Another potential game saver is the double play, often called a pitcher's best friend. If you don't have an infield that can turn the double play consistently, you'll wind up facing additional hitters throughout the game. Remember, one extra hitter can change the outcome with a single swing. That's part of the reason it's so important for a team to be strong defensively up the middle. However, the team that's solid defensively all around, with no weak links, has a big advantage each time it takes the field. Some positions may be more important than others, but the need to make a good defensive play at a key part of the game can happen anywhere. It may not be possible to have Gold Glovers at all nine positions in the field, but the importance of defense should never be diminished.

Ranking the Positions

Good teams are almost always solid up the middle—catcher, shortstop and second base, and center field. That allows them to control a great deal of the game by keeping base runners close, avoiding stolen bases, turning double plays, shortening the outfield gaps, and smoothly completing relay plays from the outfield. All this helps keep lineup turnover to a minimum.

While every position on the field is important, it should be apparent that some, by their very nature, can affect the outcome of the game more often than others. By ranking them in order of importance, I'm not denigrating certain positions while singing the praises of others. Rather, I'm discussing each position in relation to the responsibilities that go with it. Obviously, players at certain positions are going to be handling the ball more than others, and that in itself makes their defensive abilities extremely important. Here, then, is how I see the nine positions on a baseball field in the order of their relative importance.

Pitcher

Baseball is the only major sport where the team on offense doesn't control the ball. The pitcher puts the ball in play and knows where it's going, not the hitter. Ted Williams, among others, has said that hitting a baseball is the most difficult skill to master in all of sports, so it's little wonder why pitching is the most important element in the game.

Another baseball axiom says that good pitching always stops good hitting. When great pitchers have it all working, teams just don't hit them. Bob Gibson in 1968, Ron Guidry in 1978, Dwight Gooden in 1985, Roger Clemens in 1986, Sandy Koufax in any of his peak years—all were nearly unhittable. Josh Beckett in the 2003 World Series was a young pitcher who dominated the postseason and won the biggest game of his life, the clinching sixth game of the Series, with a command performance on three days' rest. So while this is really a chapter about defense and playing the different positions on the field, it still all begins with the pitcher.

Sandy Koufax used to say that he always looked at a pitcher's stat that showed how many total runs he had given up versus earned runs. If the numbers were almost equal, then he felt he was looking at a pitcher who bore down most of the time. He also said that the great competitor isn't the guy who keeps his team in the game, but loses 4–3. Rather, it's the pitcher who wins that same game, 3–2. The great competitor makes it his business *not* to let a run score when the team at bat has runners on first and third with less than two outs.

In a game against the Pirates in the 1960s the first two hitters that Sandy faced, Bob Bailey and Donn Clendenon, started the game by hitting home runs.

"I thought I had good stuff in the bullpen that day," Sandy told me, "and I threw good fastballs to both Bailey and Clendenon, but I'm suddenly down 2–0 before there was a single out. So I walked to the back of the mound to regroup, and decided I had to really bear down the rest of the game. I couldn't let them score again."

All Sandy did was retire the next twenty-seven Pirates in order, and the Dodgers won the game, 3–2. Very few pitchers, of course, have Sandy's talent. But as great as he was, he made himself even greater by his ability to bear down, pitch hard, and keep both himself and his team in the game.

Pitchers can also help themselves by developing a good pickoff move and by being able to field their position. If the starter has a terrible move and a speed guy representing the tying run gets on to lead off one of the last three innings, a manager might have to yank his pitcher for the simple reason that he can't hold runners close. If a pitcher can't hold runners, a burner can steal him blind. In that case, the opposing manager doesn't even have to waste an out with a sacrifice. Just let the man steal. So the importance of the pitcher goes beyond his ability to throw the ball toward home plate.

Andy Pettitte, who went from the Yankees to the Astros in 2004, has one of the best pickoff moves in the game. It's deceptive and effective, making it extremely difficult for a runner to get a good jump on him. He may stop the running game better than any pitcher in baseball. The trick is to keep a runner's feet from moving when leading off first. Rickey Henderson, the all-time base stealer, was famous for keeping his feet moving all the time. If the pitcher didn't keep him honest, didn't keep his feet from moving, then he could almost waltz into second base—as close to automatic as you can get.

Greg Maddux is the perfect example of an outstanding pitcher who helps himself even more with his great fielding ability. In fact, Maddux won thirteen straight Gold Gloves, more than three times as many as his four Cy Young Awards. Maddux is quick off the mound to field bunts and has good, soft hands to snatch those hot comebackers. As a manager, you tend to worry less in bunt situations when you have a good fielding pitcher out there.

The pitcher also needs the ability to make the short, quick throw to first or third on bunts, and be adept at starting the 1-6-3 double play and, occasionally, the 1-2-3 double play. The more things a pitcher can do well in the field, the better the chance for him and his team to win.

Catcher

The catcher is the quarterback on defense. To begin with, the catcher sees the game developing better than anyone on the field, and that's why a manager has to give him the autonomy to call most of the pitches. That doesn't mean a manager shouldn't take control in certain situations, but today more managers, or pitching coaches, are beginning to call the entire game, and I think that takes away from the catcher's ability to exercise the control he should have.

A pitcher needs to have total trust in his catcher's decisions, and once he does he can relax and just throw. The catcher has to know not only the strengths and weaknesses of each hitter, but those of his own pitcher as well. If the pitcher doesn't have good stuff on a given day, the catcher has to be able to nurse him through. He also has to be honest with his manager, letting him know as soon as he spots something that isn't right with the pitcher. In addition, he also has the responsibility of making sure that his defensive teammates aren't out of position. If the catcher plans to work a particular batter with off-speed stuff, but the defense is playing opposite field, he's got to move them because the odds are the batter will pull the ball.

Catchers and pitchers will sometimes disagree on which pitch to throw. You've all seen a pitcher shake off a sign at times. This can present a problem with certain battery mates because the ultimate decision is the pitcher's. However, if the catcher is convinced that his choice is the right one he should go to the mound and try to explain why he wants that particular pitch. When Mike Scioscia was the Dodgers' catcher he did that quite often and was very good at it. Once pitcher and catcher know each other well and have confidence and communication, there usually isn't a problem.

There are times, however, when a pitcher should take a stand. In 1993, my first year with Texas, Pudge Rodriguez was a twenty-one-year-old catcher trying to handle a veteran pitching staff. In one game, I brought in my closer, Tom Henke, to get a three-out save. Instead, he got beat on a fastball. When I asked him why he didn't throw his out pitch, the splitter, he said he went with the pitch Pudge called. This was an obvious case when the pitcher should have taken control. I reminded Henke that he had more than 280 big-league saves and that Pudge was just twenty-one years old and still learning. A veteran catcher should definitely take charge of a young pitcher, but a veteran pitcher must exercise more authority when working with an inexperienced catcher.

Needless to say, a good throwing catcher is one of the best assets a defensive team can have. To be a great thrower, a catcher needs more than just a strong and accurate arm; he also needs great hands and quick feet. You can teach other techniques, such as calling the game and blocking the plate, but if a catcher doesn't have a strong, quick, accurate arm, he's never going to be a great thrower, and smart managers will take advantage of that. Most of the time runners will steal off the pitcher, but this becomes infinitely easier if the catcher has a mediocre arm. At Texas and Boston I always had signs for the pitcher to go to the slide step or quick move to the plate to keep fast runners from getting a great jump.

When a pitcher is working out of the stretch position, the average time it takes for the ball to reach the catcher's glove from the time the pitcher makes his first move is 1.3 seconds. If it takes 1.4, 1.5, or 1.6 seconds, a fast runner can steal off him easily. That's how fine a line you're walking and why great throwers like Johnny Bench and Pudge Rodriguez can serve as equalizers. Pudge, for example, can throw to second in 1.8 seconds. That's from the time the ball touches his glove to the time it touches the glove of whoever is making the tag. It's also the reason why the catcher needs quick feet and must be able to square up and get into throwing position quickly. He also needs quick hands to transfer the ball from the glove to the throwing hand, as well as a very smooth and quick throwing motion. When you consider that Rickey Henderson could steal second in 3.1 seconds, you can do the math. If the pitcher is slower than 1.3 seconds to the catcher, even a great thrower like Pudge isn't going to nail a Rickey Henderson.

Most catchers will do some things better than others. Few are perfect. No one, for instance, was better at catching pop-ups than Gary Carter. Mike Scioscia blocked the plate better than anyone I've seen and called a great game, but he wasn't the best thrower. Carlos Hernandez, who isn't as well known as some of the others, could block balls in the dirt extremely well. Bill Haselman is an example of a backup catcher whom pitchers loved throwing to because he set up well and gave them a great target. Thurman Munson didn't have a cannon for an arm, but had a release like a middle infielder turning a double play.

There's no doubt that Pudge Rodriguez is the best I've ever worked with, and the best of his generation. Not only has he learned how to expertly handle a pitching staff and call a game (just check out the job he did helping the Marlins to win the 2003 World Series), but he also has the best arm of any catcher I've ever seen.

The importance of a good catcher simply cannot be overstated. The more things he can do well, the better chance you'll have to win because of the many ways he can influence the outcome of the game.

Shortstop

The shortstop is traditionally one of the best athletes on the team. That's because a shortstop has to track ground balls to all sides, and must be able to charge in quickly for slow rollers, go back for pop-ups over his shoulder, turn the double play, serve as the cutoff man on many different types of relays from the outfield, and make a variety of strong and accurate throws.

Not surprisingly, the shortstop has to take charge of the entire infield. He's the guy who will watch his catcher's signs with men on base and let the second baseman know which one will be covering on a play there. If you see a shortstop with his glove in front of his mouth he's signaling the second baseman. He doesn't talk, he just opens or closes his mouth. An open mouth means "you," that he wants the second baseman to cover the bag, that he'll hold his position on the field. If there is a fastball pitcher and a right-handed hitter who goes the other way, he'll clench his lips together saying "me," and he will cover while the second baseman holds. The shortstop also has to watch every pitch. Even without a runner on, if he sees the catcher calling a changeup, he might slide a couple of steps to his right with a right-handed hitter up, and to his left with a southpaw swinger. But he can't move too soon or he'll telegraph the pitch to the hitter. So timing is essential.

In addition, the shortstop also helps the third baseman with the signs, letting him know what pitch is coming. If he sees that a changeup is coming, he'll let the third baseman know that there's a good chance the ball will be pulled his way. And sometimes he'll even relay signs to the outfielders by signaling behind his back. There are always all kinds of things going on at the position, giving the shortstop a large number of responsibilities.

When I was managing the Red Sox in Game 1 of the 1995 playoffs against Cleveland, we were leading, 2–0, behind Roger Clemens in the seventh inning. Then Omar Vizquel walked and Carlos Baerga came up, batting left-handed. My shortstop, John Valentin, was the man covering on a steal. However, he should have known that Baerga hit to the opposite field quite often when batting lefty. On a Clemens fastball, he shouldn't have been the one covering. But as soon as Vizquel took off, John began moving toward second using a crossover step. Sure enough, Baerga got jammed and hit a slow trickler toward shortstop, where Valentin had just been. Because he left too soon and used the crossover step, he couldn't recover and the ball ended up dying in the outfield about thirty feet from shortstop.

Instead of our getting the third out on what could have been a routine grounder, the Indians now had runners on first and third. Then Albert Belle slammed a two-run double and Eddie Murray singled him home and we were down, 3–2. By leaving just a shade too early and using a crossover step, Valentin had created the difference between winning and losing. Maury Wills used to come in two steps and then cross over; that way, he'd give himself a chance in case the ball was hit to him. But if a shortstop uses the crossover step immediately, he can't recover. Maury would simply cut the angle down by moving in two steps. At any rate, it might seem like a little thing, but it was a big thing as far as the outcome of the game was concerned. We ended up losing in extra innings.

Remember the heads-up play Jeter made in the 2001 playoffs against Oakland? He saw immediately that the throw from right was going to sail over the cutoff man, so he ran straight to the spot where the ball would be, grabbed it in full stride, and flipped it backhanded to catcher Jorge Posada, who made the tag on Jeremy Giambi. Derek had the athleticism and instinct to make a totally unconventional and unexpected play that saved the game.

Obviously, the shortstop also needs a strong arm, more so than the second baseman, and has to make a variety of throws, often using different arm angles. Quick feet and a quick release on his throws are also a plus. Shortstops have to make different plays, from choppers to slow rollers to line drives that short-hop right in from of them. They have to throw off balance and quickly, or make a strong throw from deep in the third-base hole. Jeter has the jump throw from that position down to a science. Nomar Garciaparra does it differently, throwing the ball sidearm. Both can make it work. Omar Vizquel bare-hands choppers better than anyone, throwing in almost a single motion. Ozzie Smith had tremendous hands and phenomenal range. Phil Rizzuto, from an earlier time, didn't have a real strong arm, but he developed a lightning-quick release to compensate. He always had enough on the ball to nip any runner by a step or two.

One trend we're seeing today is more power-hitting shortstops. In the old days, only Ernie Banks had that distinction. Cal Ripken was the first of the modern-day shortstops to hit with power. Robin Yount developed power as his career progressed. He always had a great work ethic and told me years ago that he began using Nautilus machines because he said he was tired of hitting fly balls that died on the warning track. Today, guys like A-Rod, Nomar, and Miguel Tejada are true home run hitters. A-Rod, of course, began playing third base for the Yankees in 2004, and whether he'll ever return to short is now a matter of conjecture. But before he made the switch he was already being called the best-hitting shortstop of all time.

The shortstop has a huge defensive responsibility at a very active and difficult position. He's got to hold the entire infield together, give direction to the players on each side of him, and be prepared to make a variety of plays from the routine to the spectacular.

Center Field

Center field is the other position where a top athlete always plays. You can rattle off the names of the great center fielders right down through the game's history—Tris Speaker, Joe DiMaggio, Willie Mays, Ken Griffey Jr., and now Carlos Beltran. There are many others, of course, but those are five who do it all—hit, run, catch, throw—and do each exceptionally well.

The center fielder has to have great first-step quickness. He also needs speed and the ability to go back and come in on the ball. If you think about all these diverse elements you'll have a good idea just how valuable a center fielder can be. If a center fielder plays too deep, he's going to lose a lot of those shallow catches, so it's better to play in and have the ability to go back. Paul Blair, who played for the Baltimore Orioles in the 1960s and 1970s, was one of the best ever at going back on the ball, an ability that allowed him to play extremely shallow.

As a rule of thumb, the center fielder takes every ball he can reach. He has priority on both shallow pops and balls hit in the gaps. That means he has the authority to call off the shortstop and second baseman on pops, as well as both the right and left fielders on balls hit between them. Not surprisingly, the center fielder also needs a strong and accurate arm. Strong but erratic won't cut it. You want a guy out there who can hit the cutoff man or throw through him when necessary. Before being slowed by injuries, Griffey had the speed and ability to take doubles away by not only cutting the ball off in the gaps, but doing a full 360 and throwing the runner out at second. The ability to make plays in both left and right center field is called shortening the gaps, another important asset for the guy in the middle of the outfield.

The center fielder must also take charge and move his fellow out-fielders around, positioning them as different hitters come up or game situations change. As is the case with the shortstop, the center fielder must be aware of the situation and the count, as well as the score of the game. He may get a sign from the shortstop, or may notice something himself, such as where the catcher is setting up—in or out—on a particular hitter. As soon as he feels one of his fellow outfielders is out of position he's got to call it to his attention. In addition, there are a number of other intangibles of which he must be aware.

For instance, the center fielder has to be familiar with each stadium—the walls, the turf, the way the ball bounces and caroms. He must know just what to do as soon as a ball is hit toward a particular spot. When Fred Lynn was in center at Fenway Park and Jim Rice was in left, the two used to know just how the ball would carom from different spots on the Green Monster wall in left. As a result they would sometimes crisscross as they went for the ball, knowing how it would come off that wall. By doing that, they would sometimes decoy the runner and keep him from taking an extra base. Only time and experience can fully teach even a great outfielder how to play all the elements at ballparks around the league.

During my time I've seen a variety of center fielders, very good players who have compensated for one weakness or another and have worked hard to take on the responsibilities of a demanding position. Mays, of course, was the best. Griffey, before he was injured, wasn't very far behind. Fred Lynn was also outstanding. Speed and quickness are more of a priority than a cannon for an arm. Don't get me wrong, the rifle arm is a great asset, but if a center fielder can chase down balls in the gaps and can hit the cutoff man quickly, he'll be able to do the job.

Jim Edmonds isn't a real speed guy either, and doesn't steal a lot of bases, but he gets a very good read on the ball as it comes off the bat and thus gets great jumps. He also has no fear of putting his body on the line to make the circus catch, and he's made plenty in his career. Perhaps Steve Finley, the veteran center fielder who was with the Arizona Diamondbacks at the outset of the 2004 season before being traded to the Dodgers, is a perfect example of a guy who doesn't have all the physical gifts, but is smart and knows the responsibilities of the position very well. Finley, who joined the Angels prior to the 2005 season, has been solid out there his entire career. He plays the angles of the different ballparks well, is a fundamentally sound outfielder, and has a good arm. While he may not have the physical gifts of a Mays or Griffey, he has always played well and is a leader, and his teammates know he is going to do the right thing. He is constantly communicating with his corner outfielders, positioning them, and almost acting like a coach on the field. Bottom line, he is a winner and inspires confidence out there. That's as important for a center fielder as anything else.

Second Base

Having a good second baseman is essential to building a solid defensive foundation up the middle. The biggest priority for a second baseman is turning the double play. Not only does a second baseman need very quick feet, but he has to know the four or five ways to turn a DP, and know them well. This can be a difficult skill to master, partly because the second sacker often puts himself in a dangerous position when he's turning two. On the 6-4-3 or 5-4-3 he's looking to receive the ball from the shortstop or third baseman and can't watch the runner coming at him. Because his vision is partially blocked by the oncoming runner he's got to be quick, often needing to make an acrobatic move to get out of the way while still making a strong, accurate throw to first.

Robbie Alomar in his prime was the best I've seen at turning the double play. When Robbie and Omar Vizquel played together at Cleveland, they were an incredibly slick combo. You couldn't get the ball through those two, and any grounder hit with a man on first was a sure double play. Shortstop Cesar Izturis and second baseman Alex Cora of the Dodgers was the game's best combo before Cora was let go after 2004. They played as well as any shortstop–second base duo since Vizquel and Alomar. With guys like that patrolling the middle of the infield there are fewer seeing-eyed hits and more double plays to bail the team out of innings. The pitcher has more confidence because he knows the guys behind him are going to gobble up everything. There's no way to overemphasize the importance of having infielders like that.

Not only does a good second baseman have to turn two, he's also got to make the routine plays consistently, as well as the difficult ones in the hole between first and second and those deep behind the bag. Though most of the throws are shorter on the right side of the infield, the second sacker has to have a quick release, as well as the ability to occasionally cut one loose on the double play or after a stop behind the bag. Experience will teach the second sacker about the runners in the league. He's got to know which guys come in the hardest, which ones will try to take him out with a rolling block, which runners can be overly aggressive.

In fact, turning the 4-6-3 double play is actually tougher than the 6-4-3 because the second baseman has to turn his body to make the throw after he fields the ball. The shortstop is almost always squared up toward second.

A shrewd second baseman can also spot signs, just as the shortstop does, and make the same kinds of position shifts. He can also tip the first baseman, for example, if he knows an off-speed pitch is coming. He'll know when to shorten up and where to play the various hitters.

This *is* an extremely important position that people tend to take for granted. But watch a good second baseman turning two. Look at the way he has to concentrate on taking the throw, avoid being steam-rolled by the runner, and still make a strong and accurate throw to first. It's a real art to do that well, and it makes the second sacker an important and integral part of a winning infield.

First Base

Ideally, a first baseman should be a left-handed thrower for the same reason you have right-handed throwers on the other side of the diamond. A southpaw can make the 3-6-3 double play much easier and he can go to second or third faster on a bunt play. This isn't, however, an absolute. There have been some great right-handed first basemen down through the years. Steve Garvey is a perfect example. He was moved from third to first because he had an erratic throwing arm. But he was quick with great hands, and could both pick balls out of the dirt and leap for high throws.

A good first baseman can save a ton of errors by scooping throws out of the dirt and catching them on a variety of bounces. Good hands are essential because there are sometimes going to be fourteen or fifteen ground ball outs—especially with a sinkerball pitcher—during a game, and not every throw is going to be perfect. The same holds true with pickoff plays at first. Not only does the first baseman have to communicate with his pitcher but he's got to give a good target, and have the ability to make a quick tag. At the same time, he has to be ready to snag an errant throw to keep the runner from advancing to second.

There's a kind of myth that says playing first is easy, and a good place to stick aging veterans who maybe can't go in the outfield anymore because they've lost speed, or catchers who are taking too much of a beating behind the plate. Some can make the transition because they are great athletes, but others struggle with it. The Mets, for example, were trying to make Mike Piazza a part-time first baseman in 2004, but he didn't have the natural instincts and footwork to handle the position.

There have been many outstanding first sackers in the last few decades. Wes Parker, who played for the Dodgers in the 1960s and early 1970s, was a fantastic defensive player. When the Mets had Keith Hernandez and the Yankees had Don Mattingly, there was always an argument in New York as to who was the better first baseman. Today, both J. T. Snow and Derrek Lee are outstanding around the bag. Lee is a right-handed thrower, yet still makes all the plays. Both are great at picking balls out of the dirt.

As with all the other infield positions, the first sacker has a ton of defensive responsibilities, and the more he can do with the glove and the smarter he is, the more games he will help win. Remember, sometimes that key scoop of an errant throw for the third out with two men on will be even more important than if he hit a three-run homer.

Third Base

The hot corner! What a perfect name for the position. A good third baseman doesn't have to be fast, like a shortstop, but he needs first-step quickness. Add to that a pair of great hands and a cannon for an arm, and you've got the prototypical third sacker. Third is a reactive position, with the ball coming so quickly that it's often a hit-or-miss proposition. This lends itself to some spectacular, highlight-reel plays. Look what Brooks Robinson did in the 1970 World Series, and Graig Nettles in the 1978 Series. Both put on clinics, showing the world how a great third sacker can pick it. It seemed as if anytime you turned around, they were robbing another player of a hit. Just ask Johnny Bench about Brooks in that '70 Series. He still shakes his head in awe.

Besides having to make diving plays to both the left and right, the third baseman also must be willing to put his body on the line, often blocking hard shots with his chest, then picking the ball up for a quick throw to first. Backhand plays behind the bag require the proverbial gun of a throwing arm, and third sackers have to be able to charge the bunt or slow roller, barehand it, and throw in a quick, usually sidearm motion. Adrian Beltre of the Dodgers makes that play as well as anyone today. Tim Naehring, who played for me in Boston, had great hands and also did it well, as did veteran Robin Ventura.

The third sacker has the same wide variety of responsibilities as the other infielders. He must be able to make a crisp throw to second to start the 5-4-3 double play. Likewise, he has to learn the hitters and position himself accordingly. He also must serve as the cutoff man on balls to left and center, depending upon where the runners are located.

Quick hands, quick feet, lightning reactions, and a cannon for an arm. These are the ingredients that have always been the hallmarks of a great third baseman, and it continues that way today.

Right Field and Left Field

Of the two corner outfielders, the stronger arm should be in right because of the longer throws, especially to third base. There are a ton of right fielders known for their throwing arms. Roberto Clemente might have been the best of them. Dave Parker, who followed Roberto in right for the Pirates, made two incredible throws before a national

TV audience in the 1979 All-Star Game and ranks up there as one of the best. Reggie Smith had a fine arm, as did Jesse Barfield when he played for Toronto. Paul O'Neill could also throw well and played a solid right field for the Yankees. Today, Gary Sheffield is perfect for right field in Yankee Stadium. He can get to the ball and can throw. And Vladimir Guerrero of the Angels may be the best of today's bunch. His MVP season in 2004 was a tribute to his play in right field as well as his timely hitting.

The left fielder, as a rule, doesn't have to have the arm strength of a right fielder. Barry Bonds, for example, is an outstanding left fielder and in his younger days a guy who could get everything. But Barry simply does not throw as well as the right fielders I mentioned. There's an old expression that says, he has a left-field arm. That doesn't mean a left fielder doesn't have to do all of the same things the right fielder must do. He does. Only the throws, as a rule, aren't as long and the big arm will serve a team better if it's positioned in right.

Both left and right fielders must learn the caroms in the corners of all the different parks. Because it's more difficult reading the angles off the bat on balls hit to left and right, the quicker the corner outfielders are in getting to the right spot, the less chance of the batter taking the extra base. Just look how well Carl Yastrzemski played the Green Monster in Fenway. He knew every inch of that wall and could tell how any type of hit would bounce, the angle at which it would come off the wall, and where he would have to be to grab it quickly. Later, Jim Rice learned pretty much the same thing, and so did Mike Greenwell. But Yaz was the real master.

How much speed do you need in left and right? Speed never hurts, of course, but you can cheat a bit at those corner spots, play a bit closer to the lines, especially if you have a burner in center.

These rankings of defensive importance are based on the general structure of a team. For example, you can't get away from needing defensive strength up the middle. Have a weak link there and, sooner or later, the team will suffer for it. But you still can't take a player solely because of his defensive ability. If I had a chance to get a Roberto

Clemente or a J. T. Snow, I'd go with Clemente every time, despite the fact that first base is theoretically more important defensively than right field. Suppose you have a player like an Albert Belle, who just wasn't a good fielder. He was still going to hit 50 homers for you, so you find a place for him to play. Hide him in left field. But, of course, you can't have nine Albert Belles on the field because then you'll need all of them to hit 50 homers just so the team can reach the .500 mark.

There's no getting away from the fact that defense and pitching win championships. They minimize outs, minimize lineup turnover, and often deny the offensive team that dangerous fifth at bat. Good defense allows starting pitchers to go deeper into the game and saves the bullpen. Three errors, for example, can add another 25 pitches to the pitch count and may even affect the starter in his next outing. Another thing to remember is that speed and defensive ability never go into a slump. There's no reason for a player in the field not to be consistent. A ground ball is a ground ball. A 6-4-3 double play is a 6-4-3 double play. A solid, consistent defensive team makes the plays, over and over again.

As a manager, there's no better feeling than to have a defensive player you trust completely. I had that in Boston with Tim Naehring at third. I always knew he would make the play. He had great range and great hands, and because of that he didn't have to play as close to the line as some third sackers. Same with Billy Ripken playing second at Texas in 1993. He kept us in many games with his glove. Needless to say, it was also that way when Pudge was behind the plate. Even though he was very young when I managed him, I knew if anyone could throw a guy out, it was him.

Who were the absolute best in my time? That's never an easy question, but if I have to name names, I'm willing. As a manager, I would absolutely love to have any of these guys on my team and would feel very comfortable and confident watching them run out onto the field.

Pitcher. You can't ignore Greg Maddux since he won thirteen Gold Gloves in a row. Greg is always in good fielding position as soon as he delivers the pitch. He's got great hands on quick comebackers and knows how to turn the 1-6-3 or 1-4-3 double play. His fielding ability has often helped minimize big innings, which helps him as a pitcher as well as the rest of his team.

Catcher. As much as I obviously love Pudge Rodriguez, I can't turn my back on Johnny Bench. Both were the greatest catchers of their respective generations and very close in defensive skills. Bench, of course, revolutionized one-handed catching with the single-break glove, which is closer to a first baseman's mitt than the traditional catcher's glove. He also threw lasers to second. Pudge has incredible quickness and gets so much leverage from his legs that it creates arm speed. He loves throwing behind runners and picking them off. Because of his throwing ability, guys cannot get big leads or what we call secondary leads, and often can't score on hits that would normally drive them home, or go from first to third on a single. And in his day, Bench did much of the same. Both are masters at the position.

First Base. The best I've seen defensively was Wes Parker, even though I was just a kid when he was playing. Wes was so smooth and had incredible hands and was great starting 3-6-3 double plays. He also made quick, strong throws to third or home depending on the situation and had great range on ground balls or line drives. Nor did he hesitate to dive when the situation called for it.

Second Base. Robbie Alomar, in his prime, was tops in my book. He had exceptional range going both ways and the arm to make all the throws. His arm strength allowed him to play deeper than others, on the fringe of the outfield grass, and this also served to increase his range. Not surprisingly, he was also great at turning two, both starting the twin killing or being the man in the middle.

Shortstop. The Wizard of Oz. That's all anyone has to say. In fact, Ozzie Smith may have been the best ever defensively. He had great range, quick feet, and a strong arm, and could make acrobatic plays better than anyone. I've also always felt that Omar Vizquel has been unheralded. If I had to choose one guy I'd want to field a ground ball in a crucial situation, I certainly wouldn't feel too badly if he was out there. Vizquel can also come in, barehand a slow roller, and throw in one motion as well as anyone I've ever seen.

Third Base. This is a tough one. But if I had to pick one it would be Brooks Robinson. He exemplified that quick first step that every third baseman needs. Brooks had tremendous hands and an accurate arm but more than that, had the uncanny ability to make phenomenal, spectacular, game-saving acrobatic plays. Many feel he's the best of all time defensively, and I'm not about to argue with that.

Center Field. For me, the ultimate center fielder has always been Willie Mays, and it remains that way. A healthy Ken Griffey Jr. is close, but the Say Hey Kid is still number one. Willie was everything a center fielder should be. He had tremendous instincts, quickness, and aware- ness. He was never out of position, always got an incredible jump on the ball, and ran everything down. Who'll ever forget the catch he made off a Vic Wertz moon shot in the 1954 World Series, when he caught the ball with his back to home plate while running full speed some 450 feet away at the old Polo Grounds? Then he whirled and made an incredible throw back to the infield. Mays, obviously, had a great arm and always knew just where to throw. Flamboyant and al- ways exuding enthusiasm for the game, Willie would make that non- chalant, famous basket catch that no one can teach. He always put on a show, but to him it was just the joy of playing baseball.

Right Field. Once again I've got to go back to an earlier time. That's be- cause Roberto Clemente played from the mid-1950s to the early 1970s and remains the best I've seen out in right. He had the strongest arm in baseball during his playing days, and the accuracy to keep anyone from running on him. Just the threat of that powerful arm was enough to stop runners from taking the extra base. He also ran ex- tremely well and would chase anything down, not worrying about in- jury from outfield walls or from diving for a ball. There have been many great right fielders in the game since the 1960s, but Clemente still stands above them all.

Left Field. In a way, left field is the weakest defensive position. There have been a ton of power hitters who play left, but many of them were not great fielders. My choice for the top left fielder is Barry Bonds, an eight-time Gold Glover. Barry doesn't have a right-field arm, but he has speed and instincts, and no fear when he goes after a ball. His hitting exploits of the past few years have overshadowed everything else, but he's a great all-around player who, in his prime, played left field as well as anyone.

CHAPTER EIGHT

◆

The Importance of the Running Game

There are statisticians who say they can prove the stolen base is overrated. But a good running game isn't about stealing bases. It's about putting people in motion, shortening the defense, distracting the pitcher, the catcher, the second baseman, and shortstop. In other words, the running game can put pressure on the defense, and ultimately give your hitters an advantage. And if all that isn't enough, speed and motion make it helluva lot easier to create or manufacture a run in a close game.

I know I've touched on the importance of the running game in some of the preceding chapters, but I feel so strongly about this sometimes neglected part of the game that I want to devote more space to it. The running game has been in my baseball blood from the time I first saw Maury Wills stealing base after base for the 1962 Dodgers. As a player, I learned even more about the potential of a good running game when I was with Albuquerque in 1982. Del Crandall was the manager and was always putting people in motion, allowing me to see just how effective that could be.

Being a catcher during my playing days taught me how motion can change the complexity of a game. When we were playing a team where anyone in the lineup might run, on almost any count, I felt tremendous pressure. As a catcher, I knew if the opposing manager was aggressive and might start the runner at any time, the last thing I wanted was a curveball in the dirt. This same mind-set affects the pitcher. If he knows the runner might go at any time and I call for a curve, he begins to think about the pitch. He says to himself, If the runner goes and I bounce my curve, my catcher probably won't throw him out. So now he's worried about not bouncing the curve and being extra careful, so he just might hang one. See what I mean: motion changes the mind-set of everyone.

Time for a little history. Running and motion played a huge role in the early days of the game, especially in the first two decades of the twentieth century. Managers used the stolen base, the hit-and-run, the sacrifice, and the squeeze play on a regular basis, day in and day out. Everybody hustled because each and every run was important and home runs were few and far between. The stats will bear this out. In 1911, with just sixteen teams, big-league runners swiped 3,403 bases, an average of just over 212 steals per team. Ty Cobb led the majors that year with 83 steals, and just four years later set a new record of 96, a mark that would endure for forty-seven years. That same year, 1911, only 515 home runs were hit, an average of just over 32 per team. No way any team could stand around waiting for a game-winning walk-off homer back then.

This brand of baseball began dying in the 1920s, when Babe Ruth started showing everyone the special kind of magic in the home run, and the dead-ball era soon became a distant memory. Shortly after that, the running game almost became a distant memory as well. All through the 1930s and 1940s the stolen base numbers decreased as more hitters tried to hit the ball a country mile. Baseball became a station-to-station game with most teams trying to drive home runs with the big hit or homer, rather than trying to manufacture runs with the running game and "small ball."

By 1950, stolen base totals hit an all-time low. The sixteen big-league teams combined for just 650 steals, an average of just over 40 per team. The American League leader that year was Dom DiMaggio, a center fielder who could run, but he had just 15 steals as the entire league totaled an anemic 278. The National had a few more steals with 372, led by the Braves' Sam Jethroe with 35. But by then, it seemed as if the game had slowed to a walk, not the kind of game I would have liked to have played.

The revival of the running game started with the White Sox' Luis Aparicio in the late 1950s. Aparicio swiped 56 bags in 1959, and a year later Maury Wills of the Dodgers stole 50. Two years later Wills broke Cobb's long-standing record when he swiped 104, and not only was the excitement of the stolen base back, but the Dodgers as a team began showing what speed, pitching, and defense could do to help a ball club. That's when the game began to change once more.

Soon more great base stealers came along. Lou Brock followed Wills and upped the record to 118 for a single season in 1974. Rickey Henderson was next and in 1982 brought the standard to 130 steals. The Cards' Vince Coleman accomplished something no other player had done before when he swiped more than 100 bases for three straight seasons between 1985 and 1987. Teams that played on turf, such as the Cardinals and Kansas City Royals in the 1980s, built their ball clubs around speed and motion. Then in the 1990s the game began changing once again. Not only were the turf-covered stadiums beginning to disappear, but the home run reemerged with a bang, especially toward the end of the decade and into the twenty-first century.

Today there are smaller parks, perhaps a more tightly wound baseball, and more players who swing for the seats and can hit it out. Some teams today simply don't want to take the chance of running themselves out of an inning when one of their guys can hit a three-run shot. The prevailing attitude in many cases is why bother to run? It isn't necessary. In addition, the rewards for power far outweigh the rewards for running, both in the media and at the bank. There are still a good number of stolen bases today. In 2003, for example, there were 1,279 thefts in the American and another 1,294 in the National for a total of 2,573. However, that's the lowest total in the majors since 1975, not counting the strike years of 1981 and 1994. In 2004, the total was 2,589, nearly the same. While the speed burners will always steal, I think the lower total of stolen bases indicates a decline in the motion game in general, as emphasis continues to be placed on home runs.

There are some managers and organizations that will use the running game, and some who will oppose it. The Oakland A's simply don't believe in it at all. They use on-base percentage as their benchmark. They want the first guy on and are not concerned about whether he can steal or not. Felipe Alou in San Francisco has always believed in motion, and Joe Torre was always moving guys with that great Yankees team of 1998, which had ten players in double figures in steals. He didn't run as much in 2004, because the makeup of the team was different. Mike Scioscia of the Angels is another manager who fully understands the benefits of the running game.

I read an interesting statistic early in the 2004 season. The L.A. Dodgers at that time were hitting .272 as a team, third in the National League, but were thirteenth in runs scored. That told me two things. They weren't getting enough clutch hits, but they also weren't manufacturing enough runs. Don't get me wrong. By utilizing a running game you aren't taking the bat out of a power hitter's hands. You don't have a David Ortiz bunt with the game on the line. But if you utilize speed and motion maybe the game won't be on the line when Ortiz comes up in the ninth. There's an old baseball maxim that still applies today: Speed never goes into a slump.

Let's Talk Motion

A running or motion offense is not just about stealing bases. It's more about putting pressure on the defense, creating distractions, and making your opponent worry about what you *might* do. Two runners caught stealing early can give you an advantage late. Because the opposing manager knows you're willing to run, he might pitch out twice in the seventh inning, creating a hitter's count and giving you the advantage, an advantage created by the threat of motion rather than the motion itself. When I took over at Texas in 1993 and installed a motion game, I told my players not to worry about getting thrown out the first month of the season. I just wanted to establish the running game and the threat of it. You can always pull back once you've established the threat, because that threat won't go away . . . unless you stop entirely, of course. That threat to put players in motion makes it more difficult for the opposition to prepare for you and gives them more to think about when they try to defend you at any point in the game.

Motion doesn't always show up in the stats. You might see that a guy got a base hit through a hole in the left side of the infield, but that fact won't tell you that the shortstop left early because he had to cover second base. Motion is about shortening the defense and getting the catcher to call for more fastballs. That's why I have always said that you don't always need speed to run. What dictates motion is the pitcher, the score, the count, the inning, and the hitter. All of these things will tell you when you can and should run.

You've got to remember that for every run you put up there, your opponent has to score two to beat you. Manufacture a run early and they need two. Manufacture two and they need three. With a good pitching staff that may be all you need. I've always believed that, especially when I had a top-flight pitcher like Roger Clemens or Kevin Brown on the mound. I always wanted to get runs early because there was a good chance my pitcher would hold the lead. Conversely, if you think your pitcher is going to give up runs you may not want to try manufacturing runs or give up too many outs early. Then you're taking a chance on running yourself out of a potentially big inning.

But once you instill that mind-set and earn a reputation for running often and under a variety of circumstances, then you have a weapon that never goes away. When I was managing that first year at Texas I once had my guys run on fourteen straight 2-2 counts until someone had the guts to pitch out on me. Doing that created a lot of holes, as well as opportunities for run-and-hit plays. Sometimes I gave the hitter the option to swing. If he put the ball in play someone had to cover the bag because the runner was moving, and that opened holes in the infield for the batter. If the pitcher threw something off-speed, a breaking ball or curve, then it was a good pitch to run on and there was a good chance the runner would steal the base. So until someone realized what I was doing and began pitching out, I was giving my team a big advantage and a great way to manufacture a run. That's the kind of cat-and-mouse game you can play out there.

Speed at the top of the lineup changes many things. My Texas club in 1993 is a perfect example. I made David Hulse my center fielder and leadoff hitter because of his speed. I would often hit-and-run with him in the first inning. With the threat of David running, my two hitter would see more fastballs. That's why I liked a two hitter who could drive the ball. Doug Strange filled the bill in Texas that year, and John Valentin did it for me when I managed in Boston.

Using the combination of Hulse and Strange in Texas worked very well. There were a number of games when Hulse got on first to start the game, and either stole second or was going on the hit-and-run when Strange doubled. Two hitters and we're up, 1–0. That's a great way to start a game. In that situation, Strange had the best year of his career, winding up with 29 doubles and 60 RBIs. He never approached those numbers again, but with Hulse running or threatening to run, Strange saw more fastballs and profited from it.

Managing aggressively is one thing, but knowing when to run is another. A control pitcher is much easier to hit-and-run against because you know the pitch is going to be around the plate. If you're facing a guy who's wild and who may walk six or seven hitters, then you don't run as much because you may just run yourself out of the game, since there's less guarantee the batter will make contact on the hit-and-run. Using motion—hit-and-run, run-and-hit—makes your players shorten their swing and results in more contact. Running is also a great way to break a team's hitting slump or even an individual's slump.

Speed also creates different kinds of pressure on the defense. Fielders know which guys hustle every time and which ones don't. The guy who doesn't hustle out a routine ground ball gives the infielder all day to set and throw. The player who runs his heart out will make that same infielder get rid of the ball quickly, and the chance of an error increases. If there are fast, hustling men on the bases, guys who will go in hard at second, the defense has to think more and must execute faster. And that's when they might make mistakes.

Let's Talk Counts

There are hitter's counts, pitcher's counts, and running counts. Nothing, of course, is absolute, because you don't want to get into patterns, but the odds of using motion effectively are better on some counts than on others. To begin with, as soon as a pitcher falls behind in the count, whether it be 1-0 or 2-1, the offensive team has the advantage. Both of those are great hit-and-run counts because the pitcher doesn't want to fall further behind. In addition, a pitcher will rarely pitch out on a 2-1 count because he doesn't want it going to 3-1, so that makes it an even greater hit-and-run count. If the hitter fouls the ball off at 2-1, bringing the count even at 2-2, that's still not so bad because as you'll see, 2-2 is a great running count.

If the leadoff man gets to first and the count goes to 2-0 on the number two hitter, then you have a hitter's count, so you'll use motion less frequently, especially if the two hitter has power. If I put the hit-and-run on and the batter is forced to swing at ball three, I'm doing the pitcher a favor. It's also not a great steal count. The pitcher is already in the hole, and if the runner is caught stealing, it screws you out of a possible big inning, and gets the pitcher off the hook. If the count goes to 3-1, then you once again have a good running count, especially if you have a good contact guy up. In most cases, it becomes a run-and-hit play. If the pitch is out of the zone, ball four, you don't want the batter swinging. But on most 3-1 counts, the pitcher will try to throw a strike. If one of my power hitters is up, I want him swinging the bat, not thinking he has to put the ball on the ground just because I'm putting the runner in motion.

Remember, you can't get into patterns. If you hit-and-run consistently on a 1-0 count, the opposing manager will pitch out. That will only make it 2-0 and he'll still have a couple of pitches to work with. As effective as motion can be, it still has to be somewhat unpredictable. With a running ball club, the threat is always there, but it's still best to pick your spots.

When the pitcher gets ahead in the count it's a different story. Both 0-2 and 1-2 are pitchout counts, and many managers will even pitch out on both 0-1 and 1-1. Any time the pitcher gets ahead in the count he has a tremendous advantage. Maury Wills told me more than once that the greatest defense against a base runner like him was for the pitcher to throw *strike one* and *strike two*. I've seen managers pitch out on 0-1 and the runner doesn't go. They then pitch out again at 1-1 and he's going. I've done that many times. The worst scenario for the pitchout is the 2-1 count, but I did that as well because I wanted to create the mind-set that I wasn't afraid to do it. While 0-2 is a great pitchout count, if a team pitches out twice and the runner doesn't go, then the count goes to 2-2, and the advantage goes back to the offense because that's a great running count.

Why is 2-2 such a great running count? For openers, pitchers do not want to go 3-2 because they then *have* to throw something in the strike zone to avoid walking the batter. For that reason, you'll rarely see someone pitch out on 2-2. That in itself makes it a great running count. I'd often give the hitter the option. With the runner moving, there are going to be holes in the infield. If the pitcher is a guy who wants to put the hitter away with a ball down and away, or a splitter in the dirt, then again it's a great pitch to run on. If there's a sinkerball pitcher who throws strikes out there, then my guy is going to put the ball on the ground, again making 2-2 a great running count. The easiest pitch for the catcher to throw on is the fastball. And a fastball in the zone also gives the hitter a chance to drive it. So the pitcher also wants to make it happen on 2-2, and that's why I've always felt that count gave me the advantage when I had someone on base.

The count is always important. You've got to be acutely aware of the count as well as all the other elements, and always be ready to use motion to your advantage.

More on Motion

The threat of motion at any time also creates more power for your team. I've seen it all my baseball life, as both a catcher and a manager. Teams that have a lot of power still do better when they move runners. I proved it in both Texas and Boston. My big hitters always got more fastballs because opposing managers and catchers knew I could and would run at almost any time. When players like Mo Vaughn, Mike Greenwell, Rafael Palmeiro, and Jose Canseco take off and are successful, teams can't help but take note. Even if you had a bull elephant standing on first, they would have to think about him running because of what you've done with every player in the lineup.

While this is surely a home run era, most teams would be wise to consider using a running game as well. There was a statistic I read toward the middle of the 2004 season that said the Yankees, who had the best record in baseball at the time, were scoring about 45 percent of their runs on home runs. Knowing Joe Torre, I'm sure that stat bothered him a bit. Even though he had a lineup full of home run hitters, if the team suddenly went into a power drought and manufacturing runs became a necessity, would these guys be able to do it? Joe would almost have to start from scratch to reestablish a motion game, and in the middle of the season that isn't always easy. Like I said, speed and motion never go into a slump.

I remember young Chone Figgins worrying about making the Angels in 2004. I knew immediately that Mike Scioscia would keep him because he loves speed. Sure enough, Figgins was a great utility player early in the season before taking over at third for the injured Troy Glaus, and he led the team in steals. Having both Figgins and David Eckstein at the top of the lineup or batting one and nine, and both hitting over .300, was the perfect setup for power hitters like Garret Anderson, Vladimir Guerrero, and Jose Guillen who followed.

It's also a plus when you have one real speed guy on the bench. If you get your leadoff hitter on base in the last inning of a one-run or tie game, you can immediately send that speed guy in to pinch-run. That's just what happened in the ALCS between the Yankees and Red Sox in 2004. The Yanks were three outs from sweeping the series and up by one run when Mariano Rivera walked Kevin Millar to start the ninth. Manager Terry Francona sent Dave Roberts in to pinch-run, and everyone knew exactly what his job was—to steal second. That's just what happened, and when the next hitter singled, the game was tied. The Sox finally won the game and went on to take four straight. Without Roberts's steal in the ninth, the Yanks might well have wrapped it up in four.

The use of Dave Roberts in that situation is a perfect example of speed making a huge difference. These were two teams who generally lived by their home run hitters. But in midseason the Sox made a couple of deals to add speed and defense to their team. Roberts was the speed, and while he was relegated to pinch-running, he suddenly became one of the most valuable players on the ball club. You could see immediately in that ALCS game that Mariano Rivera was worried about him. He threw over to first several times because he knew that Roberts was going to run. If that guy on first makes the pitcher rush his delivery just this much, he can alter his effectiveness, and ultimately affect the outcome of the game. There's no greater proof than Game 4 of the 2004 ALCS.

◆

CHAPTER NINE

The Greatest Hitters I Have Seen

Early in his career, Mickey Mantle used to get a lot of drag bunt base hits batting left-handed. It's not like that with sluggers anymore. I remember Mo Vaughn kidding me in Boston, saying, "Why do I have to practice bunting? You're never gonna ask me to bunt in a game."

There's no doubt hitting strategies have changed over the years. In fact, if you analyze the facts using pure logic, you would think that today's hitters should be a lot better than those of yesteryear, but the stats certainly don't bear that out. More and more hitters are swinging from the heels today because they know that hitting home runs turns the baseball into a golden egg and will lead to the big bucks. We're in a home run era, and that's one way in which the philosophy of hitting has changed the game over the last thirty years. We no longer play classic baseball by the so-called book. Managers won't bunt a runner over to second with a power guy on deck because the opposition will just give the power guy an intentional walk.

Players today have one big advantage over players of yesteryear. When I played, a coach might tell you what you were doing wrong, might even demonstrate it, but you still had to visualize it because there were no tapes available. The coach served as an extra set of eyes, and you basically had to feel your way through when trying to correct a problem with your technique. Now there are all kinds of videos available from a number of different camera angles. A hitter can break down every at bat, using stop action and slo-mo, and isolate every phase of his swing. I remember the Dodgers having the facilities for a player to watch his at bats between innings and make adjustments during a game. Imagine Babe Ruth doing that. The Babe would probably rather eat a hot dog than watch a video.

Are today's players better hitters because of this? Not as a group certainly. The swing-for-the-fences mentality often leads to too many strikeouts. Likewise, many of today's players don't utilize the theories of situational hitting, nor do some know how to use the entire field. In effect, these guys become one-dimensional hitters or, in some cases, are asked to be one-dimensional. As Casey Stengel said a long time ago, home run hitters drive Cadillacs. Now it may be BMWs, Mercedes, or Hummers, but it's still the home run hitter who makes the big bucks and attracts the most attention. So many of today's hitters are just doing what is asked and expected of them.

Look at a player like Joe DiMaggio—a great hitter from the late 1930s to the early 1950s. Joe D. had a lifetime .325 average and blasted 361 career homers. He also compiled an amazing 56-game hitting streak, one of baseball's greatest records, and there's no way he could have done that swinging from his heels on every pitch. Even more amazing, perhaps, is the fact that he struck out only 369 times in his career. That's only eight more strikeouts than home runs. When you see a stat like that you know a guy is a complete hitter.

There has been a wide variety of power hitters over the past two decades. Guys like Gorman Thomas and Dave Kingman hit a lot of home runs, but their batting averages were often in the low .200s, and they struck out much too often. They were typical of the one-dimensional hitters I mentioned earlier. Mark McGwire hit 49 home runs as a rookie, so his power was never in doubt. He wound up with 583 dingers, including an amazing 70 homers in 1998. Though he never hit for a very high average, just the sight of Big Mac coming to the plate with a bat in his hands inspired fear in the opposition. I once saw him take a Zane Smith sinker in Fenway that was no more than two inches off the ground and hit it so far that I thought it might land on the Massachusetts Turnpike.

Juan Gonzalez is another guy with tremendous power, but he has proved he can also hit over .300. Same with Frank Thomas, who had some great all-around hitting seasons with the White Sox and is still a lifetime .300 hitter. I remember hearing Thomas say during the 2003 season that he knew his job for the rest of his career was to hit home runs. Sure enough, his batting average went down. The guys that can hit the 45 to 50 homers and still maintain a .300 average are always special. Mays, Mantle, Aaron, and Frank Robinson all did it back in the fifties and sixties, and Junior Griffey has done it when he is healthy. Likewise, Sammy Sosa batted over .300 in two of the three seasons he hit more than 60 homers.

Obviously the quintessential all-around power hitter of the modern era is Barry Bonds. Not only have his power numbers risen in the latter stages of his career, but his batting average has gone up as well. The year he hit his incredible 73 home runs, Barry also batted .328. The following year, 2002, he slammed 46 homers and led the league with a .370 average. In 2003 he whacked 45 more while batting .341, and then in 2004, at the age of forty, he led the National League with a .362 average, hitting 45 more homers and bringing his career total to 703. With a lifetime batting average of .300, it's very apparent that Bonds has become a better hitter with age, an old-fashioned all-around hitter who can lead the league in slugging percentage and hitting at the same time.

Unfortunately all the great numbers that Barry has put up since 2001 have now come under increasing scrutiny because of baseball's steroid scandal. While no one can dispute his fine batting technique and the outstanding all-around player he was in the early part of his career, Bonds's tremendous batting surge over the past four years will undoubtedly be viewed with suspicion by many people who wonder if he had the help of performance-enhancing substances.

Gary Sheffield is another who can slug and hit for average as well. I managed against Gary in the minors when he was just seventeen years old and even then he had great bat speed. He said he developed his trademark waggle because when he switched from aluminum to wood bats, they actually felt light to him and he didn't want to get out in front too soon. The waggle helps him stay back. Gary also walks more than he strikes out, another testament to his ability as a hitter and his keen eye at the plate. Young Albert Pujols of the Cardinals shows all the earmarks of being the majors' next great hitter. He has hit over .300 in each of his first four full seasons in the majors. In 2003 he finished with a .359 batting average, 43 home runs, and 124 RBIs and followed that in 2004 with a .331 average, 46 homers, and 123 runs batted in. Pujols, who now has a .333 lifetime average, has great mechanics, and if he continues to work hard there's no telling what he can do.

George Brett is an example of a modern player who wasn't a real slugger and always hit for average, but although he wasn't a genuine slugger he could also hit the long ball when necessary. Brett kept his weight on his back leg but was always in perfect balance when he hit and could go to all fields. A classic .300 hitter, Brett not only won batting titles in three different decades, but flirted with .400 in 1980, winding up leading the league with a .390 average. Yet when he had to turn on the ball, he could, hitting 317 home runs with a high of 30 in 1985, the same year he batted .335. Although Brett lost many games to injury during his career, he was undoubtedly one of the best of his generation.

Finally there are the pure hitters, guys who don't worry about home runs, but just want to get the bat on the ball and hit it where it can't be caught. There are three players who have done this exceedingly well—Rod Carew, Wade Boggs, and Tony Gwynn. All wound up with more than 3,000 hits and the trio won nineteen batting titles between them.

Gwynn had that pure line-drive swing and always used to say, "I try to hit it in the 5½ hole," which is between short and third. So you had a lefty swinger often going to the opposite field. Tony studied every at bat nightly on video and said that when he hit he would focus first on the logo on the pitcher's hat, then look for the release point of the ball. Boggs could also go the opposite way, learning to pepper the Green Monster at Fenway and hit the 5½ hole as well. I remember Jim Rice telling me that Wade could hit the ball as far as anyone in batting practice, but he wasn't about hitting 30 home runs. He worked on the art of pure hitting. They said the same thing about Carew, that he could have been a 25-home-run guy if he had wanted, but he wasn't about that either. Sometimes I think he got more of a kick from a perfectly placed bunt that he could beat out for a hit than from putting one in the stands.

Like all great hitters, these three players had a work ethic, great hitting mechanics, and excellent vision. Every single at bat was important to them. They conceded nothing, not even to the greatest of pitchers. I know that Tony Gwynn, for example, could locate the spin on the ball quicker than anyone else. He had outstanding focus. Reggie Smith used to call this ability "eye switch." That's when your eyes switch from one point to the next to pick up the ball.

People always ask if there will never be another .400 hitter. Most of the .400 seasons came in the early days of the game. The all-time record is .438, compiled by a player named Hugh Duffy way back in 1894. Guys like Ty Cobb and Rogers Hornsby did it three times, George Sisler twice. Hornsby may have achieved the greatest sustained batting feat in baseball history when he averaged .400 over a five-year span between 1921 and 1925. His averages for those five years were .397, .401, .384, .424, and .403. That, I can assure you, we'll never see again. No one, of course, has reached the coveted .400 mark since Ted Williams batted .406 in 1941. Gwynn gave it the best run when he hit .394 in 1994, the strike year. Had the season been completed, Tony told me he felt he would have hit .400 because he was totally locked in and getting stronger. Just three more hits and he would have been at .401.

Yes, I think someone can hit .400 again, but it will take the right set of circumstances and, of course, the right hitter. He's got to have a great eye and has to be totally locked in for six months. A left-handed hitter will have a better chance because he's already two steps closer to first. Gwynn, Boggs, Carew, and Brett, the guys who have come the closest, were all left-handed swingers. So were Cobb, Sisler, and Williams. Hornsby was the only right-handed hitter in that group. A southpaw also has more of a hole between first and second when the first sacker is holding a runner. In addition, the quality of the pitching is diluted today with thirty teams in the big leagues. I think Barry Bonds has the tools to hit .400, but he simply won't get the opportunity because of the way they pitch him.

A much more difficult record to break is Joe DiMaggio's consecutive-game hitting streak of fifty-six games. Remember, if you're trying to hit .400 and go 0-4 one night, then get four hits the next, you'll be right back on track. With a hitting streak it's different. You need that one hit every game, no matter what. It's possible to hit the ball right on the nose four or five times and not get a hit or find yourself victimized by a great fielding play. Remember, when DiMaggio's streak was finally stopped it took two great plays by Indians third baseman Ken Keltner to do it. After that game, Joe D. hit in another 16 straight, so if Keltner hadn't fielded one of those balls the Yankee Clipper might well have had a streak of 73 straight games.

And as for the home run record, Barry Bonds is well within reach of Hank Aaron's mark of 755 home runs. For a while it also looked as if Ken Griffey Jr. would have a shot, but injuries have robbed him of a good deal of playing time since coming to Cincinnati in 2001. A-Rod, with his 350 home runs by the age of twenty-eight, may also wind up in the top ranks of home run hitters. But as far as the single-season record, I don't think anyone will top Bonds's 73 homers, at least not for a very long time. If someone begins approaching the record and is as dangerous a hitter as Bonds, I think the pitchers and managers will take the bat out of his hands by walking and pitching around him before he can get close.

The Rankings

Picking the ten best hitters I've ever seen obviously isn't an easy task. First of all, it's very subjective. As with any kind of rankings, there is always immediate fodder for debate. No two people share the exact vision when it comes to greatness. Some may favor the slugger over the singles hitter, the guy who hits for average over the guy who drives in 130 runs.

The players I'm choosing are those I've seen play. Some are from an earlier time, but at least I got to watch them as a young fan. Obviously I can't put guys like Cobb, Hornsby, and the Babe into my rankings. Though there's no denying their greatness, there is no way I can evaluate their hitting skills from watching a few grainy old films from their playing days. By the same token, I'm also not in a position to judge the three greatest hitters from the late 1930s through the 1950s—Stan Musial, Ted Williams, and Joe DiMaggio. While there's little doubt that they could easily be very high in the rankings, I didn't see them play.

Here then is how I see the best hitters of my generation. The top ten are in the order in which I feel they should be ranked.

1. Roberto Clemente. I'm sure my pick for the top spot will surprise a lot of people. Roberto played in an era of great pitching, from 1955 to 1972, and could hit the best of them by using the whole field and taking what the pitcher gave him. He had something of an unorthodox style with a short stroke. Even though he opened up before swinging he kept his hands back and his hips in, and his front shoulder squarely aligned with the pitcher. Then if he was fooled, he could still get an opposite-field hit.

Roberto was great at hitting the down and away pitches—he could even hit them when they were just inches off the ground. He had no holes in his swing and, in fact, got even better with age, as his batting averages in the latter stages of his career attest. His lifetime mark was .317, but he had seasons of .357, .352, .351, .345, and .341. Though he drove in many runs with extra-base hits, he also had the power to go yard, hitting 240 homers, something that is often overlooked because of the many great sluggers who were playing at the time. Roberto was just an incredible all-around hitter who, in some ways, has never fully been given his due, both at the plate and in the field. Anyone who remembers his performance in the 1971 World Series (.414 average and two homers), when he was thirty-seven years old, simply cannot dispute his greatness.

2. Tony Gwynn. A pure hitter. If you want to teach a kid how to hit a line drive for a base hit, just show him films of Tony Gwynn. I actually faced Tony once when I was playing in Triple-A and threw an inning as an emergency pitcher. Guess what? He lined a base hit up the middle. Nothing changed much after that, except that he just kept hitting and getting better. Injuries were always a bugaboo to him, but he was a hitter without a weakness, a guy who studied his at bats diligently. Tony never jumped at the ball, and his great bat control allowed him to match up with anyone. He hit Greg Maddux exceptionally well, and not too many batters can make that claim. Later in his career Ted Williams got his ear and told him that he had the ability to turn on the fastball and hit more home runs. Ironically, 43 of his 135 career homers came in his last three full seasons. He had seasons in which he hit .351, .370, .358, .394, .368, .353, and .372. There is simply no way Tony Gwynn cannot be near the top of the list, not with seven batting titles, a .338 lifetime average, and a season in which he came within three hits of a .400 average.

3. Rod Carew. Another pure hitter who couldn't be fooled. Rod was totally relaxed at home plate, his bat laid back, his loose and relaxed hands enabling him to just flick his wrists and pop the ball to left for yet another hit. He was a guy who preferred flirting with .400, placing bunts for base hits, going to the opposite field, and occasionally pulling the ball down the line for a double to trying to hit home runs. Rod had one habit, however, that wouldn't be recommended today. He always kept a wad of tobacco in his right cheek when he batted. Not surprisingly, however, he did it for a reason. He said by holding the tobacco there it kept his right eye open more and helped him to see the ball better. Rod had batting averages of .366, .350, .364, .359, and .358 on his way to a lifetime .328 mark.

4. Wade Boggs. Like Gwynn and Carew, Wade had tremendous bat control. Watching him, you sometimes had the feeling he could put the ball wherever he wanted. Later, he learned to line the ball off the Green Monster at Fenway and one year even showed his power by hitting 24 home runs. He never did that again only because he preferred the hit-'em-where-they-ain't school of batting and hit over .360 four times in his career. There was simply no one way of pitching him that would guarantee you an out. Wade wasn't a speed merchant, so he didn't leg out a lot of hits, but since he had more than 3,000 of them, he certainly knew how to place the ball. Like Gywnn and Carew, he could hit .300—and challenge .400—in his sleep.

5. Barry Bonds. Barry is the only hitter in the game today who can change the way you manage from the first inning on. He inspires true fear when opponents see him coming to the plate, so much so that he's been given intentional walks in the first inning and with the bases loaded. Better to walk in a run than give Barry the chance to drive in four. He's the only modern-day power hitter who chokes up on the bat, but he feels this longtime habit gives him better control. Add to this almost perfect mechanics and quick hands, and you have the most feared hitter in baseball, one who can go the other way in addition to hitting moon shots into McCovey Cove. Barry passed his godfather, Willie Mays, early in the 2004 season to take over third place on the all-time home run list and finished the year with 703. Now Babe Ruth is directly within his sights and all-time leader Henry Aaron is not that far away.

Bonds may also be the greatest player ever between the ages of thirty-five and forty and, as of 2004, was showing no signs whatsoever of slowing down. He has a tremendous walk-to-strikeout ratio, attesting to his great discipline at the plate, and he is always willing to take the walk instead of chasing bad pitches. Not surprisingly, he also holds the record for intentional walks in a season, and in July 2004 he broke Rickey Henderson's record for the most walks in a career.

6. Willie Mays. Willie Mays may be known more today as Barry Bonds's godfather, but back in the day he was recognized as one of the greatest all-around players ever to grace the diamond. Willie debuted in 1951, the era of the eight-team leagues and four-man pitching rotations, a time in which only the best survived in the majors. He also had to hit in two very difficult parks, the old Polo Grounds in New York and Candlestick in San Francisco. The center-field clubhouse, in play at the Polo Grounds, was nearly 500 feet away, and the winds at Candlestick made it difficult to hit the ball out in left. Willie, of course, learned to hit them over the right-field fence, but had he played in smaller home parks he might have hit 800 home runs. As it was, he hit 660.

Willie was both a presence and a threat at home plate. If a pitcher knocked him down—which happened often—he didn't charge the mound or make threatening gestures. He simply got back up, dusted himself off, and got a hit, and he wound up with 3,283 of them. He had a power-packed body and the speed to leg out infield hits. As a hitter, he made great use of both his hands and his legs, and always brought that great energy and enthusiasm to the plate with him.

7. Henry Aaron. Even when he was on deck, Henry Aaron was always studying the pitcher intently. He had an effortless swing and great, quick wrists that made the ball just leap off the bat. Aaron also benefited from playing in two hitter-friendly ballparks, County Stadium in Milwaukee and Turner Field in Atlanta. But he was still a great hitter, and a hugely consistent one, hitting more than 40 home runs eight times, and topping .300 on fourteen occasions in a twenty-three-year career. Claude Osteen, for one, told me that Hammerin' Hank was very tough to pitch to because he had no holes. Those quick wrists could correct any mistake in an instant.

8. Mickey Mantle. A switch hitter with tremendous power from both sides of the plate, the Mick was the guy who invented the tape-measure home run. Early in his career, before the injuries piled up and dulled his skills, he was the whole package. The fastest runner in the league then, he often dragged bunts for base hits from the left side of the plate. In 1956 he won the Triple Crown, hitting .353 with 52 home runs and 130 RBIs. A year later he batted .365, and in 1961 was part of the M&M Boys' race for 60 homers. Roger Maris hit 61 and Mickey wound up with 54. Numerous leg injuries and a self-inflicted destructive lifestyle ultimately shortened his career and held his numbers down. With Mays and Aaron, he formed a big three in the 1950s and 1960s, and his switch-hitting ability made him even more dangerous.

9. Mike Piazza. Without a doubt, Mike Piazza is the best-hitting catcher of all time, but even without that distinction he's one of the greatest hitters I've seen. Mike finished the 2004 season with a .315 lifetime batting average and during the season passed Carlton Fisk as the most prolific home run–hitting catcher ever, with 352 dingers. Mike is very relaxed and quiet at the plate, then explodes from the hips with his hands following. He can generate great power and hits to all fields. The rigors of catching for many years have doubtless been a factor in his offensive numbers declining in recent years, but he remains a threat every time he comes to the plate. Mike has had seasons of .346, .336, and .362, so he's been a lot more than just another power hitter.

10. Pete Rose. Despite all his off-field problems, you can't ignore what Pete Rose did on a baseball diamond. He was a self-made hitter who taught himself to switch-hit, and was a tough, tough out. Batting out of a classic crouch, he would watch the ball right into the catcher's glove when he took a pitch. He became a good clutch hitter because he would always put the ball in play and simply never gave an at bat away. Some guys will get two hits early in the game and they're satisfied. Pete never was. He battled right until the last out, and it's no accident that he's baseball's all-time hit leader (4,256) with a trio of batting titles thrown in. In addition to all the singles and doubles, he could also go deep, slamming 160 homers during his long career. A vicious competitor, he compiled a dramatic 44-game hitting streak in 1978, tying Wee Willie Keeler for the National League record and the second longest ever behind DiMaggio's.

Who Comes Next

This next group consists of more outstanding hitters, some whose careers are over and who I feel are just a shade behind those in the top ten, as well as players still active today who have a chance to move up if they finish their playing days with a flourish. Once again the list is subjective. You may not agree with some of them, but here are more of my candid observations based on my own knowledge of the game as well as some personal experiences. These players are not ranked in order.

Frank Robinson. A former Triple Crown winner with 586 lifetime home runs (fifth on the all-time list), as well as the winner of a Most Valuable Player award in both the National and American Leagues, Frank Robinson was truly a great hitter and outstanding all-around player. Though he batted as high as .342 one year and slammed 49 homers in his Triple Crown season of 1966 with Baltimore, I feel he was just a cut below the likes of Mays, Mantle, and Aaron with the bat. And maybe that's why he doesn't get enough credit, having played in an era full of great hitters and sluggers.

George Brett. Using a balanced stance with his weight on the back leg, George Brett could hit for both power and average. George could hit to all fields and had a classic swing that generated more power than people thought. He was a determined hitter who once flirted with .400 and won batting titles in three separate decades.

Kirby Puckett and Don Mattingly. I put these guys together not only because they had similar numbers, but because both lost potentially productive years to injuries. If Puckett had not developed glaucoma and Mattingly's back had held up, both might have had a legitimate shot at the top ten. They were that good. Both were batting champs, could hit for power and drive in runs, and were multiple Gold Glove winners on the other side of the ball. Kirby Puckett had a quick bat and could use the entire field. He was a star for a decade and helped the Twins to a pair of World Series titles, compiling seasons of .356 and .339, and leaving the game with a .318 lifetime mark. Once he was diagnosed with glaucoma, he had to retire immediately, but he excelled long enough to make the Hall of Fame.

Mattingly was so good for a five-year period that he was universally acclaimed as the best player in baseball during the mid-1980s. He had a compact stance with his hands held low and could really uncoil. His quick bat enabled him to wait and use the entire field, and he worked hard, learning to be a power hitter, something he wasn't expected to be when he came up. He was an MVP, won the batting title at .343, and hit a career-best .352. Unfortunately, his career was compromised by a bad back, which took away the tremendous torque he generated when he hit. Because of the back, he was relegated to being no more than an average hitter the final half of his career.

Edgar Martinez. Edgar Martinez was without a doubt the greatest designated hitter in baseball history, and despite his time in the field being curtailed by repeated leg injuries, he will get votes for the Hall of Fame when he becomes eligible. He was a hitter with no holes in his swing, a guy with enough pop to hit 309 homers. His .312 lifetime average bespeaks his consistency, and he had as many as 37 homers and 145 RBIs in a single season, as well as batting averages of .356 and .343. Edgar also had the ability to go to right field, and not only was he a perennial Yankee killer, but he hit the Yanks' great closer Mariano Rivera as well as anyone in baseball.

Now some of the best hitters still active today.

Derek Jeter. A great clutch hitter, Jeter now has more base hits than anyone in postseason history, one of the bonuses of playing for the New York Yankees. But he always does it against good pitching, has natural power to right field, and can surprise with the home run. Derek also has those little intangibles and qualities of leadership that make him a winner. He's a .315 lifetime hitter with highs of .349 and .339, but he's got to keep that batting average well over .300 if he expects to make it into the top ten someday.

Alex Rodriguez. There is little doubt anymore about A-Rod's phenomenal ability. He has power to all fields and had whacked more than 350 homers by the age of twenty-eight. With his smooth swing and his desire to excel, he may not only crack the top ten before he retires, but have a chance to go well past 700 home runs. As of 2004, all eyes were on Barry Bonds to see if he can catch Henry Aaron. By 2014, the eyes may be on A-Rod to see if he can catch Bonds or Aaron, or both. Much more than a one-dimensional hitter, A-Rod has hit as high as .358, has slammed as many as 57 home runs, and has power to all fields. He only has to cut down on his strikeouts to be a complete hitter.

Manny Ramirez. Manny Ramirez was born to hit. He's simply a pure, raw natural hitter who makes it look easy. Manny keeps his hands back and doesn't move them until he's ready to swing. Yet he can also go the other way, hit to right, and is a big threat even when he isn't swinging the bat well. He's a guy who doesn't allow anything to bother him. In effect, he's a guy who just hits, and is always happy as long as he's getting his swings four or five times a game. With 390 lifetime homers through 2004 and a .316 lifetime batting average, Manny is surely one of the best hitters of his generation.

Ichiro Suzuki. Ichiro was a seven-time batting champion in Japan who wanted to play alongside the greatest players in the world. All he did after coming to Seattle in 2001 was lead the league in hitting with a .350 average, then win both the Rookie of the Year and Most Valuable Player awards. He's a left-handed hitter in the Rod Carew–Wade Boggs–Tony Gwynn mold, a guy who can place the ball just where he wants it and won't hesitate to lay down a bunt for a base hit. Though he keeps his hands back extremely well, he's so fast that he seems to be running out of the box as he hits, which gives him that extra step toward first. In 2004, Ichiro not only won a second batting title with a .372 average, but set a new major-league record with 262 hits, breaking the record of 257 held by Hall of Famer George Sisler and set way back in 1920. With his fine technique and speed, Ichiro may make a serious run at a .400 season in the next few years.

Ken Griffey Jr. By the 2000 season Junior seemed on his way to breaking the all-time home run record and establishing himself as one of the game's great hitters. Then fate took a turn and he lost a major part of the next four seasons to injury, derailing what had been a brilliant career. He had a smooth, fluid swing, had been a .300 hitter, and was the player of the decade in the 1990s until Barry Bonds began to take off. Still, Junior has hit as many as 56 homers in two different seasons and was a better all-around player than his slugging counterparts of the 1990s, Mark McGwire and Sammy Sosa. He finally hit his 500th career home run in 2004, but just when he seemed in the midst of a fine comeback year he tore his hamstring and was lost for the season once again.

Nomar Garciaparra. A first ball, fastball hitter, Nomar has been criticized for not being more patient at the plate, but it's hard to argue with success. He's a two-time batting champion—with averages of .357 and .372—who hits with power, runs well, and knows how to use the entire field. Nomar has made himself stronger over the years and should continue as one of the game's top hitters. Traded to the Chicago Cubs from the Red Sox midway through the 2004 season, Nomar should prosper in the friendly confines of Wrigley Field in 2005 and maybe beyond.

Albert Pujols. The Cardinals' first baseman is simply putting up numbers you can't ignore and doing it with tremendous technique. Not only does he have great balance, but he has great discipline and uses the field extremely well. He also has the ability to use his legs to generate great bat speed and can drive the ball out of the park to all fields. Pujols is a guy who jumped basically from A-ball to the Cardinals and was an impressive hitter from day one. In four full seasons he has a .333 average, 160 homers, and 504 RBIs. He is also the only player in big-league history to hit over .300 with 30 or more home runs and more than 100 RBIs and runs scored in each of his first four seasons. Albert is definitely a hitter who may make it into the top ten before he's through.

Gary Sheffield. When you think of Gary Sheffield you think about bat speed. He may have the quickest bat in baseball, and the result has been more than 400 home runs. Many of his home runs are laser beams, and he hits the ball with backspin as well as anyone I've ever seen. Like other great hitters, he has gotten better with age, moving his lifetime average up to .298 as of the end of 2004. He also has a great eye and walks more than he strikes out.

Vladimir Guerrero. In his first year in the American League in 2004 Vladimir Guerrero won the MVP prize by hitting .337 with 39 home runs and 126 RBIs for the Angels. This guy is a notorious instinct hitter who sees it and hits it. He can smoke the low ball as well as anyone, and with his long limbs can get the outside pitch as well. Vlad has hit .300 or better every year he's been in the majors, has a .325 lifetime average, and is yet another prime candidate to move into the top ten before his career ends.

CHAPTER TEN

◆

The Greatest Pitchers I Have Seen

I grew up watching Sandy Koufax and he became my favorite player long before I met him. He was always special. He had that one-of-a-kind charisma and there was always an aura about him. He was like a rock star. If Koufax was pitching either at home or on the road—sellout! Everyone wanted to see him, and he rarely disappointed. The guy had it all and that's why he's, by far, the best pitcher I've ever seen.

A great pitcher doesn't always have the strongest arm. Greatness can range from Sandy Koufax, who had a huge arm, to Greg Maddux, a pitcher without a blazing fastball but one with outstanding movement and command. What all the great pitchers have is a fearlessness and a competitive nature that drives them to be the best. These special pitchers want the ball. They want to be that Game 7 pitcher. There's no fear of success, no fear of failure. They all have a just-give-me-the-ball-and-let-me-pitch attitude.

Koufax always said that the real competitor is not the guy who pitches well enough to lose a low-scoring, close game. Rather, he's the guy who finds a way to win that game. When one of his teammates made an error behind him Sandy always reached back for that little extra because he didn't want that runner to score. That's when he would intentionally go for the strikeout. Pedro Martinez is a modern pitcher who can take it to the next level to keep his team in the game. In a 2004 interleague game against the Giants, Pedro didn't have his best stuff, but whenever Barry Bonds came up that night his fastball registered 2 to 3 miles per hour more on the JUGS gun. The special guys go beyond the capabilities of the average pitcher, way beyond.

The great pitchers have the ability to stop momentum from swinging to the other team. The night Koufax pitched his perfect game in 1965 he said he didn't have his best stuff warming up in the bullpen. As usual that season, the Dodgers weren't doing anything offensively, so Sandy had to bear down from the beginning. With a 1–0 lead he used his fastball—his best pitch that day—almost exclusively in the last three innings, refusing to let the momentum change, and he wound up perfect, and with a 1–0 victory.

Bob Gibson was one of the most fearless pitchers I've ever seen. He would always battle right down to the final out, putting on that game face early in the morning and keeping it on until the game was over. I was catching Gibson at a Hall of Fame Fantasy Camp about 1989 or 1990 when he was throwing for the retired pros against the fantasy campers. Gibby was about fifty-four years old then and some of the campers began getting on him, yelling that he couldn't pitch anymore, that he was too old. From behind the plate I could see his face change right before my eyes. Suddenly the fire returned, and the old Gibson, the guy who hated *all* hitters, was back on the hill. He cranked it up and blew them all away, striking them out one by one. Those campers weren't about to go home and brag to their friends about hitting Bob Gibson, not if he had anything to say about it.

It's still important for an organization to develop its best pitchers as starters in the minors. Even in the age of specialization, an organization shouldn't take a kid with great stuff, or three great pitches, and make him a closer. Work him in as a starter first. Then you can begin evaluating his mental makeup, whether his stuff remains good through six or seven innings, how quickly his arm bounces back, and whether he's able to keep his pitch count down. A pitcher can be converted to a closer at any time. Look at Dennis Eckersley and John Smoltz. Eckersley was a solid starter with a 20-win season under his belt before becoming a totally dominant closer for the A's. Smoltz was even better, a former Cy Young winner as a starter and a guy who won 12 games in the postseason, who changed roles because of repeated arm problems. But he had the tools and temperament, and also became dominant as a closer before switching back to the Braves' starting rotation in 2005.

Pitchers from the 1920s right into the early 1970s were conditioned to pitch on three days' rest, then jump right into four-man rotations when they reached the majors. The old-timers built arm strength and endurance by throwing more often than today's pitchers. On their scheduled day to throw between starts, some pitchers wouldn't just throw on the side, but would opt to throw batting practice to their hitters in order to stay sharp. You don't see that today. With good mechanics, starting pitchers prior to the advent of the five-man rotation could throw 150 to 170 pitches a game and then do it again four days later.

I remember reading about a game in 1965 when the great Warren Spahn was finishing his career with the expansion Mets. Spahn was forty-four years old then and one night hooked up against the Giants and their young ace, Juan Marichal. The game was scoreless after nine innings and the two kept pitching. At one point, Giants manager Herman Franks asked Marichal if he wanted out. Juan answered quickly: "If that old man can keep going out there, so can I."

The Giants won the game, 1–0, in 16 innings on a Willie Mays home run as both pitchers went the entire distance. Spahn had done that his entire career, but you will never see this today. Young guys being developed in the minors simply aren't being conditioned to pitch complete games. One of the reasons is that more organizations are putting credence in pitch counts and the stat of "batting average against." If the batting average against a particular pitcher rises dramatically after, say, 85 pitches, then the pitcher is pulled from the game. All organizations are paying attention to these kinds of modern-day statistics, so if the computer finds that in the long haul it doesn't benefit a team to let a guy go deep into the pitch count, they won't do it.

Some teams are now limiting starters in the minors to 100 pitches a game. It's an organizational rule from top to bottom. Thus, young pitchers are conditioned to throw only 100 pitches per start when they reach the majors. I know that I never believed in these kinds of limits as absolutes. If a guy is breezing in the eighth inning and has thrown 99 pitches, are you going to yank him? Do that, and you can disrupt the entire flow of the game. Nevertheless, some managers will do this, and the opposition will look out there and say thank you, because the starter was just blowing them away. Now, if the reliever is off his game, they still have a chance to win.

Good mechanics remain the key to long-term success for any pitcher. That begins by making good use of the lower half of his body. Roger Clemens, Nolan Ryan, Bob Gibson, and Tom Seaver are all examples of pitchers who used their legs correctly. Seaver had great mechanics from day one. I've seen pictures of Warren Spahn and I could tell immediately how he made good use of his hips and legs to create arm speed, and he proved it by pitching well into his forties. Greg Maddux, who doesn't have the big fastball, is nevertheless very sound mechanically, with great use of the lower half of his body, which creates perfect alignment of his feet and a consistent arm angle on all of his pitches.

One example of a talented pitcher who was having problems with mechanics was Mike Hampton, who joined the Braves in 2003. Though he has had success in the past, Hampton has a tendency to step across his body and land on his heel. That's why he's had problems for a number of years after putting together a great season with Houston in 1999. A pitcher simply can't have command if he doesn't have good mechanics. It's like driving a car that is out of alignment. You're always fighting your own body, and that's a battle a pitcher can't win. Working with Braves pitching coach Leo Mazzone, Hampton has improved his mechanics, and his confidence is coming back.

There have been some young pitchers who can't understand why the legs are so important. Their rationale is that you don't use your legs to pitch; you use your arm. These guys have to be taught quickly that leg drive is paramount to success. The first thing an athlete loses is usually his legs. Good pitchers know this, and that's why running is so important to them. If a pitcher's legs get tired late in the game he's going to lose that extra drive and then lose the edge with his stuff and

his command. I remember when I was drafted into the Orioles organization in the late seventies. One of the first things I noticed in spring
training was how Jim Palmer was always running, running, and running. He was a veteran then, with a long and lean build, but he would
run more than most of the young guys.

Not all great pitchers need a 98-mile-per-hour fastball, but they
do need sharp stuff, command, and ball movement, as well as the ability to get the big out in crucial situations. Greatness comes in all kinds
of packages, from six-foot ten-inch Randy Johnson to a six-foot, 175-
pound Greg Maddux. More often than not, it's really what's inside that
counts.

The Rankings

The following are my choices for the ten greatest pitchers I have seen,
followed by a secondary list of pitchers who are a cut below, though
outstanding in their own right. As with the previous list, this is a subjective list consisting of pitchers I have seen in my baseball lifetime and
who have impressed me for the reasons that will be given.

1. Sandy Koufax. Perfect mechanics, a great arm, a winning attitude,
and unbelievable stuff. I'd have to say that during his six peak seasons,
from 1961 through 1966, Sandy Koufax was as dominant as any
pitcher in history. Sandy used a high leg kick, led with his hips, and
generated great explosiveness from the lower half of his body. These
full-body mechanics produced great arm speed, and I'm sure he threw
pitches at 100 miles per hour or slightly more in the days before the
JUGS gun. He had not only the fastball, but an overhand curve that
looked as if it were coming out of the sky. Part of the reason for this
was his huge hands and long fingers. He pulled down with the middle
finger and because of the strength in his hands and length of his fingers, had tremendous rotation on the curve. Add a forkball that he
threw in the 80-mile-per-hour range, a pitch that dipped down like
the splitter today but wasn't thrown as hard, and that gave him three
tremendous pitches, all thrown with the same arm speed.

On days that the curve and forkball weren't there, he could usually get by with his fastball. Sandy threw a fastball that made the hitter feel that it was rising. Physics tells us that it's impossible for a pitch to rise. But the rotation on the ball combined with its speed and the angle from which it's thrown can give the appearance of it jumping at the hitter. Sandy also always talked about throwing the ball out, not up or down. Throw it through the target, he said. He felt that some pitchers tend to stand straight up and try to throw on a downward angle. Doing that, they lose leverage provided by the legs. In Sandy's time, because of the slope of a fifteen-inch-high mound, by throwing through the target you got the ball down naturally.

Joey Amalfitano told me that he was the second to last hitter to bat during Sandy's perfect game against the Cubs in 1965. He went up there, took three swings, and headed back to the bench. On the way, he passed Harvey Kuenn, who was up next. "See you in a second, Harvey," Joey said to him. Harvey later said he didn't need to ask what kind of stuff Sandy had that night. He was unhittable.

In his last four seasons before his premature retirement at age thirty, his earned run averages were 1.88, 1.74, 2.04, and 1.73. He also fanned more than 300 hitters in three of those last four years (the other year he was injured and limited to 29 starts), and his record was an incredible 97–27. Despite only 163 career wins, Sandy was elected to the Hall of Fame in 1972, his first year of eligibility. Like I said, he was the best.

2. Bob Gibson. An intimidating pitcher with a mean streak, Bob Gibson had no fear. He simply hated hitters. Though he looked upon every start as a big game, he was especially tough in the postseason, compiling a World Series record of 7–2, with eight complete games in nine starts and 92 strikeouts in 81 innings. The only game he didn't finish went to extra innings. Even his own teammates rarely spoke with him on the day he was scheduled to pitch. Once they saw that game face on, they knew they had better leave him alone.

Gibby had great stuff, including a live fastball, a quick-breaking slider, a good curve, and pinpoint control. In the days when pitchers protected their own, Gibson wasn't shy about coming inside, and he hit more than his share of batters. He once said that he did it to protect teammate Lou Brock, who was stealing so many bases that pitchers would often knock him down.

In 1968, Gibson put together a season that will forever cement his greatness. His record was 22–9 and he compiled an earned run average of 1.12, third lowest in the post-1900 era, and threw 13 shutouts. He also fanned 268 in 304.2 innings while walking just 62 batters. Three of his losses were by 1–0 scores, and at one point in the season he won 15 games in a row, including five straight shutouts. Largely because of Gibson's dominance in 1968, the mound was lowered five inches before the start of the 1969 season, giving some advantage back to the hitter.

Gibson wound up with 251 victories in a career that produced five 20-win seasons and two others in which he won 19, and he also struck out more than 3,000 hitters. With his great stuff, big-game ability, great athleticism, and competitive fire he was the second greatest pitcher I ever saw.

3. Roger Clemens. For a guy who Dan Duquette said was in the twilight of his career in 1996, Roger Clemens may be having the longest and most successful twilight in the history of the game. Four Cy Young Awards (he also won three before leaving Boston for a record total of seven) and a couple of World Series rings later, he's still pitching, having come out of a brief retirement to throw for the Houston Astros in 2004 and continuing to be highly effective at the age of forty-two. After an 18–4 season with the Astros resulted in his latest Cy Young prize, Roger now has a career record of 328–164 with 4,317 strikeouts, second on the all-time list behind only Nolan Ryan.

When I think of Clemens, whom I managed at Boston in 1995 and 1996, I think of a guy who has always worked harder than anyone. He would run on his own in the morning, then run again with the rest of the team in the afternoon. There wasn't a time when he didn't try to help young pitchers, impart his work ethic, and advise them on how to become big winners.

A result of his tremendous work ethic is longevity, as he remains an effective power pitcher in his early forties. In addition to that, Roger is extremely smart on the mound. Part of his meticulous preparation includes knowing which umpire will be behind the plate. Some are low-ball umps, some high, and some have wider strike zones than others. Roger makes it his business to know this, as well as all the opposing hitters, the park in which he's pitching, and the elements on that particular day or night.

Roger is a guy who understands mechanics, and that the legs and trunk have to be strong. He's also a guy who has constantly made adjustments as he's aged, including the addition of a split-fingered fastball to his repertoire in the early 1990s. Before that, he had a fastball, slider, curve, and change. The splitter made him even tougher to hit.

A competitor who, like Koufax, often finds ways to win the big games, Roger has never been shy about pitching inside, but I don't believe he ever tried to intentionally hit someone in the head. Like other great ones, his feeling is, *If you're gonna take the plate away from me, I'm gonna straighten you up.* The Rocket has changed his mechanics somewhat over the years to be more compact in his delivery. Sometimes now he only goes to his chest instead of over his head on his windup. Great pitchers are always adjusting, and after more than 300 victories and 4,000 strikeouts, and those seven Cy Young Awards, I'll always rate Roger Clemens among the very best I've ever seen.

4. Tom Seaver. Not only did Tom Seaver help transform the New York Mets from a bunch of lovable losers into a team that could win, but he had a long and consistent career that resulted in more than 300 victories and 3,600 strikeouts. A classic drop-and-drive pitcher, Seaver used his legs extremely well, to the point that his back knee would hit the dirt as he drove toward the plate. Seaver's tremendous use of his lower body helped him generate arm speed and power.

Seaver was a fastball-slider pitcher with great control. A three-time Cy Young winner, he had that extra *feel* for working hitters and was extremely smart. A winner of 20 or more games on five occasions, Seaver was an intense competitor and so dominant on the mound that I'm picking him as the fourth best pitcher of my time.

5. Juan Marichal. Marichal was a unique stylist on the mound who came after hitters from all kinds of angles and with a variety of deliveries. He had the classic high kick, with his lead leg way up in the air and pitching arm nearly on the ground behind him, almost like a clock with its hands at 11 and 5. He used that windup to generate leverage and arm speed. But he could also drop down and come at hitters sidearm or three-quarters. By throwing from every angle he was extremely tough to hit. Juan was also the first pitcher I ever saw who sometimes used the double pump to upset the timing of the hitter. He used a fastball and slider primarily, but also had a screwball that could drive left-handed hitters nuts. Though he wasn't overpowering, his many different deliveries and arm angles made it difficult for hitters to pick the ball up.

Marichal's career lasted from 1960 to 1975, during which time he won 243 games, won 20 or more six times, and pitched 244 complete games. His .631 winning percentage and 2.89 career earned run average are further testaments to his Hall of Fame greatness.

6. Pedro Martinez. This may seem like a surprise pick for the sixth slot on the list, since Pedro is still active, but he has been such a dominant pitcher over the last decade that he simply cannot be ignored. Early in his career, Pedro had a great fastball with movement that clocked out at 97 miles per hour, a tremendous changeup that consistently fooled hitters, and a great overhand curve that would drop into the strike zone. Later he would add a cutter to help compensate for some loss of velocity on the fastball. With his great command and pitching aptitude, he can throw any one of his four pitches on any count at any time, and all of them are strikeout pitches. Because they're all thrown with the same arm speed and angle, the hitter cannot tell which pitch is coming until it's too late.

While Pedro is no longer a nine-inning pitcher, he continues to dominate after more than a decade, has been a Cy Young winner in both leagues, and has put together some great seasons in which he's rarely lost. He was 23–4 in 1999 and 20–4 in 2002, just to name two of his best years. At the end of the 2004 season Pedro had a 182–76 career mark, and his .705 winning percentage is third best all-time. In addition, he has 2,653 career strikeouts and a career earned run average of 2.71. His ERA is now seventy-seventh all-time, but in a changing baseball world he has the lowest ERA of all the modern-day starting pitchers over the last sixty years.

7. Randy Johnson. The Big Unit. What a great nickname for a six-ten left-hander who is as dominant as any pitcher who ever lived. Randy is one of the tallest pitchers in the history of the game and by far the most effective at that height. It wasn't easy getting those long arms and legs to work together, but once he got the mechanics down and began using his legs and lower half for more drive, his career took off.

Randy throws that big sidearm fastball, and with those long arms and legs, he looks as if he's only about forty-eight feet from home plate. The ball just explodes on hitters. He also has a devastating slider that dips down and in to right-handed hitters and down and away from southpaw swingers, a pitch that can be nearly unhittable. When he's on, he's totally dominant.

During his career he's had seasons of 19–8, 18–2, 20–4, 19–7, 21–6, and 24–5 that have led to five Cy Young Awards and a world championship with the Arizona Diamondbacks in 2001. He's also had six seasons of 300 strikeouts or more. In 2004, he became just the fourth pitcher in history to strike out more than 4,000 hitters in his career, joining greats Nolan Ryan, Roger Clemens, and Steve Carlton. Randy has continued to be dominant late into his career, and while a knee injury slowed him down in 2003, he began showing flashes of his old self early in 2004 at age forty, and prior to the All-Star break he threw a perfect game, the oldest pitcher ever to achieve that milestone. Though his final record was just 16–14, he played on a team that lost 111 games. His ERA was 2.60 and he fanned 290 hitters in just 245.2 innings. With a 246–128 lifetime mark through 2004, Randy Johnson is definitely one of the great ones.

8. Greg Maddux. Greg Maddux is something of an aberration in today's game, a dominant pitcher who doesn't throw a fastball in the mid- to upper nineties. He's living proof that a pitcher doesn't have to light up the radar gun to be successful. Although Maddux has an average fastball in the 85- to 89-mile-per-hour range, his ball moves. He also has perfect mechanics and pinpoint control, enabling him to paint the inside corner with the two-seam fastball to left-handed hitters.

Greg also has a good curve and a great changeup, and mixed with his control and the ball movement on those three pitches, he can dominate. His consistency is unparalleled. At the end of 2004, Maddux completed his seventeenth straight season of winning 15 or more games, a major-league record. He's won 20 twice, and 19 games five times, leading to four consecutive Cy Young Awards from 1992 to 1995. Greg is also one of the best fielding pitchers of his generation who is a thirteen-time Gold Glove winner.

Maddux was one of the Braves' big three for years, with Tom Glavine and John Smoltz, and helped them win eleven division titles and a World Series victory. He returned to his first team, the Cubs, in 2004 at the age of thirty-eight, and in early August won the 300th game of his career, the twenty-second pitcher to reach that milestone. He ended the season with a 305–174 record and is one of the ten best I've ever seen.

9. Jim Palmer. I had the opportunity to catch Jim during the Orioles' spring-training games in 1978 and 1979. He was easy to catch, as he had great control with a fluid over-the-top delivery, made easy by his tall, lean build and long, loose arms. You just put the target down and he would hit it. He used a high leg kick and had an outstanding overhand curve and a good changeup to go with his live fastball. That's the classic three pitches, and he threw them all with the same arm speed and angle. Jim wasn't a leg-drive guy like Tom Seaver, yet the ball exploded on the hitters. His pitches were sneaky fast, as his fluid delivery lulled hitters to sleep before the ball burst in on them.

Jim also threw a high fastball, often just high enough so a hitter couldn't get to it. He did this intentionally, often putting the ball just above the batter's hands and forcing him to chase it. The result was often a pop-up or a strikeout. Palmer was also known for going up and down the ladder on a hitter, which would change the hitter's eyesight. Some other guys who tried it would end up putting the ball where it could be hit out. The reason for this kind of pitching is simple. On high pitches, the hitter sees the whole ball (as opposed to just the top half on low pitches), and that's why he'll often chase the pitch. But Palmer was clever. He usually managed to keep it just high enough, just above the hitter's hands, and more often than not, the batter could not catch up with it.

Palmer had eight 20-win seasons on the way to 268 lifetime wins and three Cy Young Awards. As with other pitchers from his era, he was a workhorse because of the four-man rotations, making between 36 and 40 starts in nine different seasons. He also had an 8–2 record in the postseason, including a shutout against the Dodgers in the 1966 World Series.

10. Nolan Ryan and Steve Carlton. There's a tie for the tenth and final slot. No extra innings in this one. Both Nolan Ryan and Steve Carlton were great pitchers, and I felt I couldn't leave either of them off.

No one had better stuff than Nolan Ryan, and he maintained it while pitching in the majors for twenty-six years. At the age of forty-six, Nolan could still throw 90-plus-mile-per-hour fastballs. He had a classic leg-drive delivery, which, combined with his God-given ability, created arm speed. In the days before the speed gun, Nolan probably threw pitches in the range of 102 to 103 miles per hour. You almost anticipated a no-hitter every time he took the mound, and he threw a record seven, including his last on June 11, 1990, when he blanked Oakland, 5–0, at the age of forty-three. He is also the all-time strikeout leader by a country mile, having fanned 5,714 hitters during his long career. That includes the single-season record of 383 in 1973. All told, he had six 300-strikeout seasons, including a final one when he was forty-two years old in 1989.

Why, then, do some people question Nolan's overall greatness? It's usually because they look at the stats. Nolan had just two 20-win seasons and, while winning 324 games, also lost 292, the third most in history. He also walked more hitters than any other pitcher in baseball annals. Knowing the stuff he had as well as his competitiveness, I think that had he played on better teams and had just a little more control, his record would have been phenomenal.

No matter what his overall record, I would want Nolan Ryan on the mound because with his dominant fastball he was capable of shutting down any team.

Steve Carlton, "Lefty," was a superb pitcher, a guy who had one of the most devastating sliders ever. Batters would start to swing at it, and suddenly, it was gone, just dropping out of sight. It's no wonder he fanned more than 4,000 hitters, and was second on the all-time list until Roger Clemens moved past him in 2003. But nothing can diminish Lefty's accomplishments—329 victories, four Cy Young Awards, eighteen straight seasons with double-digit wins, and six 20-win seasons. Perhaps more than anything else, he'll be remembered for the season he produced in 1972, the first year he pitched for the Philadelphia Phillies after a trade from the St. Louis Cardinals.

The Phils finished in last place that season with an abysmal 59–97 record. Not one of their pitchers had a record over .500 . . . except Steve Carlton. Lefty went out and compiled a 27–10 record. He won an incredible 45.8 percent of his team's games. He also had a 1.97 earned run average in 41 starts, completing 30 of the those games. In 346.1 innings he struck out 310 hitters. He inspired so much confidence in his teammates that when he was on the mound they seemed like a different team. There's never been another pitcher in history who has performed like that under similar conditions. It was incredible.

Close, but Not Quite

There is another group of pitchers from the same era who have had great careers and, arguably, might well sit somewhere in the top ten. So let's take a quick look at this second group of outstanding starters, any one of whom I'd welcome onto the pitching staff of my team.

Gaylord Perry. Gaylord was a guy who got into hitters' heads. Did he or didn't he throw the spitter? He always went through all those antics on the mound, going to his face, his cap, reaching behind his head, wiping his brow, then wiping his hand on his uniform . . . or not wiping it. He did this on every pitch.

Spitter or not, Gaylord Perry was a great pitcher, winning 314 games in a twenty-two-year career with eight different teams. He won 20 or more games five times, fanned more than 3,500 hitters, and won a pair of Cy Young Awards, one in each league. A fastball/slider pitcher, Gaylord was a nasty competitor, another guy who hated to come out of the game and finished 303 of his 777 starts. Though Gaylord's name will always be associated with the spitball, he should be remembered more for what he really was, a great pitcher who earned his way into the Hall of Fame.

Bert Blyleven. A native of Zeist, Holland, Bert Blyleven came to the United States as a boy and began a long love affair with the game of baseball. Some 287 big-league wins later, Blyleven retired with the reputation of throwing one of the best curveballs the game has ever seen. It was a paralyzing curve, a ball that would just break off the table, and was so effective that it became a major strikeout pitch, enabling Blyleven to fan more than 3,700 big-league hitters. Though he won 20 or more games only once, he was a workhorse, often approaching 300 innings. Blyleven always gave up a lot of home runs, maybe because of those times when the curve would hang, but more often than not it was a devastating out pitch that was equally effective against both left- and right-handed batters.

Don Sutton. Don came up at the tail end of the Koufax-Drysdale era and was the Dodgers' number one starter for more than a decade, beginning in 1966. He was typical of the Dodger pitchers of the day, using a fastball, curve, and changeup. Don showed his stuff immediately, striking out 209 hitters as a rookie, the most for a National League first-year hurler since Grover Cleveland Alexander's 211 way back in 1911. He finished his career with 324 wins, 58 shutouts, and 3,574 strikeouts, yet he is the only pitcher in baseball history with more than 300 wins and just one 20-plus-win season. Don was elected to the Hall of Fame in 1998.

Catfish Hunter. Jim Hunter loved to talk pitching. I remember him saying that he might have given up 30 homers a year, but most of them were solo shots. He said, "I might give up three solo home runs, but I'll still win the game 4–3." He said he gave up so many because he threw strikes. Catfish was a great control pitcher. That was his game. He knew when a solo homer wouldn't hurt him, and he didn't let his ego get involved.

He was another guy who didn't light up the radar gun, but he was a big-game pitcher who rarely hurt his team when it needed a victory. The defense loved having him out there too because he wouldn't beat himself. Though he won only 224 games in a fifteen-year career, he was still a five-time 20-game winner who pitched in six World Series with the A's and Yankees. He was elected to the Hall of Fame in 1987. Catfish's death from ALS disease in 1999 was a tragedy for his family, friends, and all of baseball.

Ferguson Jenkins. Possessor of a good fastball and curve, as well as outstanding control, Fergie Jenkins was a competitor who rarely beat himself. A seven-time 20-game winner, he wound up his nineteen-year career with 284 victories and nearly 3,200 strikeouts. He often pitched in tough luck, losing 13 career 1–0 games, the third most in big-league history, and was on the losing end 45 times when his team was shut out. Only five other big-league pitchers lost more games when their teams didn't score. So it's obvious that with a few breaks Jenkins could have been a 300-game winner.

Most of his great years came with the Cubs, though he won 25 games with Texas in 1974. He was a remarkably consistent pitcher in a great era and was finally recognized for his achievements when he was named to the Hall of Fame in 1991.

Phil Niekro. Phil Niekro was a great knuckleball pitcher with an easy delivery that allowed him to eat innings—three times tossing more than 300 innings in a season. He started, and often finished, and usually took his team deep into the game. Like some other knuckleballers, Niekro could be hit if his pitch wasn't working that day, so he also lost his share, but when his knuckler was really dancing he was untouchable.

As with most knuckleballers, Phil was able to pitch well into his forties. He won 16 games for the Yankees in both 1984 and '85 when he was forty-five and forty-six years old, and finished his twenty-four-year career with 318 victories and 3,342 strikeouts. He won his last games with Cleveland in 1987 at the age of forty-eight, giving him 121 victories after the age of forty, a big-league record. Though he lost 274 games in his career, he was named to the Hall of Fame in 1997.

Tom Glavine. Tom Glavine is a self-made pitcher, a guy who understands the importance of being in command of himself and his ability. He's a lot like Greg Maddux in that he isn't a hard thrower, but he can sure paint the outside corner of the plate with his two-seam fastball. Tom also has a good overhand curve and a great changeup that fades away from right-handed hitters.

Tom was never a big strikeout guy, but he's a five-time 20-game winner and owns a pair of Cy Young Awards. He was fortunate to spend most of his career with great Atlanta Braves teams before coming to the Mets in 2003. He ended the 2004 season with 262 career victories.

Curt Schilling. Curt is the last of the group and, like Tom Glavine, was still active in 2005. A late bloomer and a real throwback, he's finishing his career in strong fashion, having come into his own as a workhorse and a winner in the late 1990s and early 2000s. Curt is a big-game pitcher and a strikeout artist who has fanned more than 300 hitters in three different seasons and has 2,745 Ks in his career. Curt has good mechanics and understands the importance of the lower half of the body in the delivery of the baseball. He has a great fastball, a great splitter, a cutter, a curve, and a slider. He's also a guy you want out there in a big game because he won't shy away from the challenge. He was great for the Diamondbacks in the 2001 World Series and equally great for the Red Sox in 2004, when he pitched and won key games against the Yankees in the ALCS and Cardinals in the World Series despite a severe ankle injury.

Because he's a late bloomer, he had just 184 wins at the end of 2004 and probably won't climb onto the top ten list. But right now, in a big game, you can't make a better choice than Curt Schilling.

The Closers

Today, thanks to an evolving game and the era of specialization, there are two kinds of pitching superstars—the starter and the closer. The closer has now become an indispensable part of the team, a guy who can come in and shut the door in the ninth inning. Closers not only make big bucks, but they're starting to make the Hall of Fame as well.

Today's closer usually pitches just one inning, the ninth. The terms "four-out save" and "five-out save" have evolved in recent years, meaning the closer comes in with one or two outs in the eighth. But that doesn't happen too often, especially if a team has a good setup man to get the team to the final inning. Closers in the 1970s and into the 1980s, however, used to pitch two or three innings quite often to get their save. It wasn't unusual for Bruce Sutter or Rich Gossage to come in to start the seventh, or even to get the last out in the sixth, and then finish the game. The hope was that if a closer went three, he wouldn't be needed at all in the next game or two.

Why is the closer viewed as being so special? First of all, not every pitcher can fill the role. The best closers all have a similar mental makeup. A closer has to be able to shake off a mistake, even a loss, and come back the next day ready to go again. He's got to have no fear, and he must want the ball with the bases loaded or with the winning run on third. You want a guy who throws strikes, not someone who puts men on base. A guy like Mitch Williams had a great arm, but he also had the potential to walk the bases loaded. When Dennis Eckersley closed for the A's, his first pitch to almost every hitter was a strike.

The great closers all have a dominant out pitch—whether it's an Eric Gagne fastball, a Mariano Rivera cutter, or a Trevor Hoffman changeup. In fact, both Gagne and John Smoltz have three great pitches that they can throw for strikes on any count. Rivera has the latest-breaking cutter I've ever seen. That late movement just eats up left-handed hitters. They start to swing, aiming to hit it on the sweet spot, and suddenly they're hitting it with the label and the bat splits.

Most closers, though, have two great pitches. Rich Gossage had a power fastball and a slider, just like Lee Smith. John Franco likes to set things up for his change, as does current closer Keith Foulke. John Wetteland had a power fastball and a great overhand curve. So closers come in all shapes and sizes, with a wide variety of pitches and styles. But they also have a great deal in common—ice water in their veins, an attitude that enables them to forget mistakes, a great out pitch, and a desire for the ball in the toughest of situations. Here, then, is my list of the ten best closers I've seen in my baseball life.

1. Mariano Rivera. I told you Mariano Rivera was good. Now you know how good. I remember seeing Mariano's potential when I managed against the Yanks in the mid-nineties when he first came up. The Yankees put him in the pen, first as a setup man for John Wetteland, where he began to flourish. We soon found out that if we didn't have a lead after the sixth inning the game was over. Mariano pitched the seventh and eighth, and Wetteland the ninth. Mariano was dominant even then. I remember him overpowering Mo Vaughn one day with a high cutter. Mo waved at it and went back to the bench. Mariano kind of laughed, looking at Jeter and covering his face with his glove. Jeter was laughing too, but in a way that said, *Man, I'm glad I'm not facing this guy tonight.*

As I said, Mariano's late-breaking cutter is the best I've ever seen, and because of it he eats up lefties like no other right-hander ever has. He has long fingers, which helps give the ball its late break and enables him to make the ball explode in on the bat. He also has the perfect closer's mentality. I think it was really evident in the seventh game of the 2003 ALCS, when Mariano closed out Boston and collapsed on the mound, emotionally drained. It's a job that brings tremendous pressure with it, and the closer has to keep that ice water flowing until it's finally over, as it was with Mariano in that hard-fought series with the Red Sox.

Pitching in the pressure-cooker of New York, Mariano Rivera has become the best closer in postseason history, a man who has had as much to do with all those Yankee championships as anyone. He is the best closer I've seen.

2. Eric Gagne. This might seem a strange choice because Gagne has not been closing for that long. But I've got to rank him second behind Rivera because nobody touches him! Gagne consistently overmatches great hitters. He wasn't a very good starter, but since 2002 he's become the most dominant closer in the game, including his record-breaking 2003 season in which he converted all 55 save attempts for the L.A. Dodgers. He ran his record-breaking streak to 84 straight before it ended in July of 2004.

Gagne has three great pitches, starting with a 98-mile-per-hour fastball. He then throws a changeup at about 86 miles per hour and a sharp overhand curve that comes in at about 75 miles per hour. What makes these pitches even more effective is that he throws each with the same mechanics, the same arm angle and arm speed, the same leg drive, and perfect alignment of his feet with home plate. And what makes him even more effective is that he throws them all for strikes. As a kid, he used to go to Montreal Expos games, watch guys like John Wetteland and Pedro Martinez when they warmed up in the bullpen, and try to copy their mechanics. Because of his superb technique, he doesn't tip any of his pitches, so hitters cannot pick them up, not even at the last second. All they can do is guess. If a hitter is looking fastball, Gagne might drop the change in. If a hitter is waiting for the change, he can throw that tantalizing curve or come back with that 98-mile-per-hour heater.

This will give you an even better idea what Eric Gagne is all about. Early in the 2004 season he was facing Barry Bonds. Because the Dodgers had a 3–0 lead and there was only one man on base, he decided to challenge the game's best hitter. He threw heat and Barry turned on it, hitting the ball a mile into McCovey Cove . . . but foul! Eric didn't try to fool him. He threw the heater again, and this time Bonds hit the ball over the center-field fence for a two-run homer. Gagne looked at Bonds in admiration, then went back to work and got the final two outs for yet another save. Had the game been on the line, he undoubtedly would have pitched Bonds differently. Barry won the battle, but Gagne and the Dodgers won the war, and Eric said later it was the most fun he had all year. That's the kind of closer he's become. He had fun challenging Bonds, but though he lost the challenge, he still had the confidence to get the final outs for the save.

3. Dennis Eckersley. "Eck" was a fastball/slider pitcher with uncanny control. He had a high leg kick, long arms, and a three-quarter delivery. It all worked in his favor, even his long hair, which may have distracted hitters just a little. He almost always threw a first-pitch strike, which gave him a huge advantage as a closer. Eckersley is an example of a player who was a very good big-league starter and then later in his career turned out to be a phenomenal closer. A former 20-game winner, he probably could have remained a starter with the potential to win 15 games or more, but he made the switch to closer in 1987, his thirteenth season, and wound up pitching for twenty-four years, retiring after the 1998 season at the age of forty-three with 390 saves, third most in history. In 1992, Eckersley had a 7–1 record to go along with 51 saves and became the only closer to win both the Cy Young Award and Most Valuable Player prize in the same year. It came as no surprise when, in 2004, he was elected into the Baseball Hall of Fame.

4. Rollie Fingers. Rollie Fingers was the stopper on those great Oakland teams that won three straight World Series from 1972 to 1974. Another fastball/slider pitcher with good control and nerves of steel, Fingers proved himself on the biggest stage of all with six World Series saves. At six four and with long arms and a three-quarter motion, he was extremely difficult to hit. He could also be tricky, as shown by the maneuver he made in the 1972 World Series against Cincinnati.

Fingers was pitching in the top of the eighth with runners on first and third, one out, and Johnny Bench at the plate. With the count at 2-2, the runner on first, Bobby Tolan, stole second as the pitch missed for ball three. A's manager Dick Williams then signaled for Fingers to walk Bench intentionally, loading the bases. Bench stood in, relaxed, expecting to take first. But as Fingers wound up, catcher Gene Tenace suddenly shifted to his left and Fingers fired a slider on the outside corner of the plate. Bench stood in amazement as the umpire called strike three. That's another thing a closer has to be . . . resourceful. When Rollie Fingers retired after the 1985 season he had 341 saves, and in 1992 he became the first closer ever voted into the Hall of Fame.

5. Rich Gossage. "Goose" was a huge man and an intimidating closer with an exploding fastball and an effective slider. He could easily come in with one or two outs in the sixth and finish the game. Gossage often dared hitters to make contact with his fastball and often took them "up the ladder," throwing each pitch a little higher and harder than the last. Because Gossage pitched more innings than closers today, he had more decisions, winning 115 games in his long career, most of them as a reliever. In many ways, it was a tougher era for closers because they had more responsibility. A reliever like Rich Gossage had in effect a dual role, serving as both setup man and closer. He had to be ready for those two- and three-inning stints, yet still be durable enough to pitch between 55 and 70 games a year. Gossage wound up with 310 saves to go with those 115 victories and appeared in more than 1,000 big-league games, before retiring at the age of forty-three.

6. Bruce Sutter. In a way, Bruce Sutter revolutionized baseball. Sutter was the first pitcher to use the split-fingered fastball as his out pitch, and it made him the dominant closer of the 1980s. Hitters weren't used to seeing a pitch that looked like a fastball until the last instant, when it suddenly fell off the table and they found themselves swinging at air. I remember catching Sutter in spring training with the Cards in 1982 and thinking then that I was glad I didn't have to hit against him.

In the 1982 World Series, Sutter showed the entire baseball world just how effective the splitter could be. He won the second game against the Milwaukee Brewers, then saved Games 3 and 7, fanning six batters in 7⅔ innings of work. In the seventh and final game, he retired all six hitters he faced, a two-inning save that gave the Cards the championship. A Cy Young Award winner in 1979, Sutter endured eleven surgeries, which ultimately shortened his career. He retired with 300 saves and the knowledge that the pitch he developed had become one of baseball's most prolific out pitches, thrown by starters and relievers alike.

7. John Smoltz. John Smoltz won more than 150 games and a Cy Young Award, in 1996, as a starter before arm injuries led the Braves to try him as a closer. And some closer he became. He assumed the role full-time in 2002 and by the end of the 2003 season had saved 100 games in those two seasons alone. His dominance is close to that of Eric Gagne's in that Smoltz has three out pitches—fastball, slider, and splitter—and he throws all three for strikes.

Once he discovered it was easier on his arm to pitch just an inning or so more frequently, he accepted the closer's role and excelled. Though he's only been a full-time closer for three years at this writing, he's still one of the best I've seen. Despite his great success as a closer, John decided to return to the starting rotation in 2005.

8. John Wetteland. John Wetteland didn't win a game his first two years in pro ball. He was a kid I managed in the minors in 1985 and stood behind when others in the Dodgers organization wanted to release him. I saw something in John then and watched him carefully. He always had good stuff but had the habit of using all his pitches with every hitter, something that isn't always necessary. As a starter he would go deep into the count and by the fifth inning would already have thrown about 110 pitches. So in 1991, at Albuquerque, Dave Wallace (the Dodgers pitching instructor at the time) and I decided to make him a closer. He promptly saved 20 of 21 games.

I was the farm director at Montreal in 1992 and was instrumental in the team making a trade for him because I knew both his stuff and his character. After the trade we made him our closer, and he excelled immediately. John simply had no fear. He always had confidence in himself to complement his very solid mechanics. His fastball got better as he got older, and he had a classic top-to-bottom overhand curve.

Later he developed a cutter, giving him a third out pitch. He was great on the New York stage for the Yankees and closed on their '96 championship team, finishing all four of their victories in the World Series that year, for which he earned the MVP. He continued as an outstanding closer with Texas until a back ailment caused his premature retirement. John was good enough to be named Closer of the Nineties, and finished his career with 330 saves.

9. John Franco. I caught John's first Triple-A start at Albuquerque in 1982. He had a fastball, change, curve, and slider then, but didn't have real good command of his fastball. I was calling all the pitches that night and John got roughed up pretty good. Sandy Koufax was in the dugout with our manager, Del Crandall, and told me after the game that once John got command of his fastball, he would be fine.

When John began closing for Cincinnati he showed everyone that the change was his out pitch although he also had pretty good breaking stuff. Though he's not a big guy, I really think his personality and confidence played a major role in his becoming a great closer. He simply projected an aura that told people he could get the job done. Part of the reason he has lasted well into his forties is because he doesn't rely on power and always has good mechanics. He's been able to accept a setup role in his final years, but his 424 saves, second on the all-time list, show just how great he has been.

10. Lee Smith. Ironically, the guy with the most career saves occupies tenth place on my list. I remember Doc Edwards, a former big-league catcher and my manager at Triple-A Rochester, telling me years ago that Lee Smith was going to be a great closer. Lee was a huge man with a power fastball and a power slider who also developed a splitter toward the end of his career. Early in his career he often had two- or three-inning saves; later, as the game changed, he would generally come in for only the ninth. Lee played for eight different teams and closed in both the National and American Leagues, though he's most remembered for his work with the Cubs and Cardinals.

So why am I placing a guy with 478 lifetime saves in tenth place?

Unlike the closers ranked at the top, Lee struggled with his control at times and walked too many batters. For a closer, he simply gave too many hitters a free pass. But Smith would always battle right until the final out and overpowered a lot of hitters during his time. His best season might have been 1991, when he had 47 saves in his first full year with the Cardinals.

CHAPTER ELEVEN

◆

The Most Complete Players I Have Seen

Besides having the requisite five tools, a complete player needs tremendous instincts, an aptitude and intelligence for the game. Willie Mays had it. He was always aware of game situations and thinking one step ahead. Cal Ripken Jr. had it too. He helped his catchers in Baltimore call the pitches, and used to call his own hit-and-runs. These were special players.

The complete player is a rare and valued commodity. There's always a rush when a scout comes upon a kid who can hit for average and power, as well as run, field, and throw. That's your classic five-tool player. Ultimate success, however, is not automatic, even for a five-tool player. I remember Al Campanis spreading his hands out one day and saying, "The five tools are only good if they all come together, if a guy has the ability to pull them all together." Then he would make a fist.

Campanis was right. A complete player has an aptitude for the game that complements his skills. I can recall going to a game at Dodger Stadium when I was just a kid. The Dodgers were playing the Giants. At one point Willie Mays drew a walk. I already knew Mays was a great player, but what happened next told me that he was more than great, that he was one of the special few. The next hitter slammed a base hit to right center. Willie rounded second, raced to third, and then rounded the bag again.

Dodger second baseman Jim Lefebvre went out to short right center as the cutoff man. He caught the ball about fifteen feet beyond the infield on the outfield grass. When he took the throw he turned with his arm cocked in the throwing position. Willie stopped and Lefebvre dropped his arm to run the ball back to the infield. But as soon as he dropped his arm, Willie took off again and scored. In fact, he scored easily. Years later, when I interviewed Willie and reminded him of the play, he remembered immediately.

"I rounded third and challenged him," he said. "I kept stutter-stepping, and as soon as he dropped his arm I took off. I knew once he dropped it that he wouldn't have time to get his arm back up and throw me out."

That's the instinct of a complete player. Jackie Robinson was a lot like that. I've seen films of Jackie dancing off the bases, always bluffing, threatening to run. Every time he was on third he'd bluff coming to the plate, and then, sooner or later, he'd run. He drove pitchers nuts, distracted them. A pitcher could never forget about Jackie when he was on the bases, and Willie had that same quality. Give him an inch and he'd make you pay. Those are the kinds of instincts you simply can't teach. The special ones have it; most of the others don't. The five tools are the starting point for most complete players.

Hitting for Average. The ability to hit for average on a regular basis takes a variety of skills, not just a good batting stroke. For openers, not too many players can consistently hit for a high average if all they do is try to pull the ball. The only exception I can think of is Ted Williams. Most high-average hitters use the whole field. Great hitters usually have a short, compact swing and great focus, picking up the ball early, right from the release point. Many of them actually say they can see the seams on the ball as it travels toward the plate. The greatest hitters also have the quickest pitch recognition. They pick things up, have great eyesight, and see things the pitcher does that the average hitter can't see. Sometimes they can tell which pitch is coming by the way the pitcher cocks his wrist, or they'll spot something else a pitcher does to tip a particular pitch.

The great hitters also have a presence at the plate. It's an aura they project—a confidence. Aaron had it, Mantle had it, Pete Rose had it. Barry Bonds, A-Rod, and Albert Pujols have it today. They just have a way about them that tells everyone they know what they can do, whether it's hitting behind the runner, going to the opposite field, or knowing when the situation calls for the power to be turned on.

Hitting for Power. In some cases, power can be taught. I've seen a number of players who didn't start their careers as power hitters, but ended up hitting a lot of home runs. Ken Boyer, the great third baseman of the Cardinals, is a good example. He was hitting maybe 8 or 9 homers a year in the minors, but he hit a lot more once he came to the bigs. My own experience in the minors is a perfect example. I didn't understand how you could use your legs to create bat speed, and although I was a big guy, I didn't hit for much power. A player like Don Mattingly wasn't big, and wasn't expected to hit many home runs, but he worked at it until he mastered the art of hitting the long ball. Mattingly uncoiled, much as Stan Musial did. He used his legs and hands, and had great balance. In other words, he used every ounce of his ability to become a good long-ball hitter.

A player who has the strength to hit for power but not the technique has to be taught to generate power from his lower body, namely his legs. I always use the analogy of having to push a refrigerator. If you stand up straight and push, you won't get much leverage, but if you get down and use the lower half of your body, you'll find it's much easier to push. A hitter can stand up straight when he's waiting for the pitch, but if he wants to drive it he's got to dip down and use his legs as he gets ready to swing. He also has to hit through the ball with a slight uppercut to his swing. Like I said, if some of the elements are already there, the final touches can be added.

The great ones don't have to be taught, but every once in a while they need some help in making minor adjustments. All of them have a way to get ready to pull the trigger, and all of them use their lower half to generate power and bat speed. If you look at films of Babe Ruth you can see that he had a beautiful swing and lowered his hands before uncoiling. Mantle hit the ball a country mile. It was natural strength, but he coiled and generated great bat speed. Aaron had the great wrists, Mays the incredible instincts and sense of timing that allowed him to stay back and really jump on the ball. Barry Bonds has great vision and bat speed, and tremendous technique. So when you have that great power guy who can also hit .300, then you know you've got a special hitter and an all-time great.

Running. Speed alone doesn't make a great base runner or great out-fielder. Running takes technique and instinct. But raw speed is the attribute that keeps the most players from having that five-tool ability, because it can't be taught. Mattingly, for example, made himself a four-tool player by acquiring power, but simply wasn't a fast runner.

Henry Aaron and Frank Robinson were two guys who could both run and knew how to use their speed. In their early years they both could steal when it was called for, and each finished his career with more than 200 stolen bases. Both could probably have stolen more bases if there had been more emphasis on the running game back then. But they rarely made mistakes on the base paths, knew when to take the extra base, and used their speed to advantage.

Throwing. When looking at a young player's throwing ability, scouts always look for arm strength first because accuracy can be taught. Players can develop better techniques for getting rid of the ball. Like a fastball pitcher, a position player with a great arm can bring the crowd to its feet. Watching Pudge Rodriguez throw from behind the plate, or back in the day Clemente firing from right field to third base, is simply a thing of beauty. Having a big arm at almost any position can help keep the score down by nipping runners at first, catching them stealing, or cutting them down at the plate.

Fielding. Besides having speed and throwing ability, great fielders have great instincts and anticipation, and almost never throw to the wrong base. When Ozzie Smith played shortstop it was hard to take your eyes off him because you knew the potential for a spectacular play existed every time a ball was hit in his direction.

Here are the fifteen most complete ballplayers I've seen since I began watching baseball in the 1960s. As with my picks in other chapters,

I'm not including players I didn't see either in person or on television, or see enough of in their prime to make an accurate judgment. There is also a secondary list of players who came close but couldn't crack the top fifteen.

1. Willie Mays. Let's make it official. Willie Mays was the most complete player I've seen since I began watching the game. Willie once told me about the great catch he made in the 1954 World Series off the bat of Vic Wertz at the Polo Grounds.

"I wasn't worried about the ball," he said. "I knew immediately that I would catch it with two men on base. I was more worried about getting it back into the infield quickly enough."

That was Willie, always acutely aware of the game situation and thinking one or two steps ahead.

His speed enabled him to cover huge amounts of ground in the outfield, and he always got a great jump on the ball. Not only did he catch everything remotely within his reach, but I don't think he ever threw to the wrong base. Once the team moved to San Francisco he learned to hit with power to right field because the prevailing winds there blew from left to right at Candlestick Park. Willie could adapt to any situation, and I really can't imagine a more complete player ever. The numbers speak for themselves. He finished with a .302 average, 660 homers, 3,283 hits, 1,903 RBIs, and 338 steals. Willie also did the little things that never appeared in the box score but contributed mightily to his teams winning many games.

2. Henry Aaron. Henry Aaron was Willie Mays without the charisma, flair, and flamboyance. Aaron was simply an incredibly consistent player who didn't have a weakness. Like Mays, he had great instincts for the game. Like Joe DiMaggio before him, Henry Aaron was a player who made everything look easy, but he was also a guy with a burning desire to win.

He was both a batting champ and a home run champ, and in a twenty-three-year career he hit more homers (755) and drove in more runs (2,297) than anyone in history. He was also outstanding defen-

sively, getting a great jump on the ball and often cutting down runners with his fine throwing arm.

3. Roberto Clemente. During the majority of his playing career, Roberto Clemente was unsung. Then in 1971, at the age of thirty-seven, he had that fantastic World Series when he batted .414 with a pair of homers, and showed the entire baseball world his five-tool talents up close. He would play only one more season, getting his 3,000th hit in his final game, before his tragic death. So his Series performance couldn't have come at a better time.

Clemente simply had the best arm I've ever seen, and at the plate he could jack the ball out to all fields and was a notorious bad ball hitter. He always gave 100 percent at the plate, on the bases, and in the field.

4. Barry Bonds. Ever since he erupted for a record 73 home runs in 2001, Barry Bonds has been viewed as a super slugger. Unfortunately, his home-run-hitting feats cause fans to forget that he's a terrific base runner and the only player in baseball history with more than 500 steals and 700 home runs. He was also an accomplished defensive player, as evidenced by his eight Gold Gloves.

Unfortunately his achievements over the past few years will now and forever probably be subject to question and suspicion due to baseball's steroid scandal. Bonds has admitted using a substance now identified as an anabolic steroid, though he says he didn't know that at the time. Because of his admission and all the home runs he has hit since the age of thirty-five, many now question whether the numbers he has generated over the last five years have been achieved legitimately.

Still, when all is said and done, Barry will always be remembered as one of the most complete players ever to step on the field—and one need only mention his seven MVP awards to support this claim.

5. Mickey Mantle. Mickey Mantle was a switch-hitter with power from both sides of the plate in addition to being baseball's fastest runner when he joined the Yankees in 1951. He wasn't quite the instinctive

outfielder that Mays was, but he could cover tremendous ground with his speed and had a strong arm. The young Mick was simply the epitome of the five-tool player.

Mickey was also a solid .300 hitter the first two-thirds of his career before repeated injuries began to rob him of his skills. He won the Triple Crown in 1956, hit a career best .365 the next year, and hit more than 50 homers twice, including a high of 54 in 1961 when a late-season injury took him out of the home run race with teammate Roger Maris. He ended his career with 536 home runs, more than any switch-hitter in history, and had it not been for the numerous injuries over the years, he might well have been right behind Mays on this list.

6. Alex Rodriguez. Though Alex Rodriguez is still in his prime he fully deserves his spot on the list of complete players. It's frightening to think he just turned thirty in July 2005. Obviously, he may rise even higher before his career is over. A-Rod is the youngest player ever to hit 350 home runs, finishing the 2004 season with 381 dingers. And his career average of .305 also confirms his skill at the plate. As a Gold Glove shortstop with the Rangers in 2003, A-Rod made just 8 errors. A year later, he signed with the Yankees and agreed to move to third base so he could play alongside Derek Jeter. In his first year at third, A-Rod made just 13 errors, a very smooth transition.

I'll tell you just how good I think Alex Rodriguez is: he has the potential for 700-plus career home runs and could well wind up among the top five players ever to play the game.

7. Frank Robinson. When a guy hit 586 lifetime homers, won the Most Valuable Player award in both leagues, and was known as one of the toughest guys ever to walk onto a baseball field, you know he was a complete player—and that's just what Frank Robinson was. Sometimes it seems that Robby is overlooked because he played in the same era as Mays, Mantle, Aaron, and Clemente, but he started his career by tying the then rookie record for homers with 38 in 1956, and his career took off from that point. When the Reds traded him to the Orioles after the 1965 season, claiming he was an "old thirty," they

made one of the worst trades in baseball history. Robinson would play another eleven years and only add to his legend as a Hall of Fame player.

Frank was another of the great sluggers who could steal a base when necessary (204 lifetime) and was a prototypical right fielder with a great throwing arm. He wound up his career with a .294 lifetime average and 2,943 hits.

His toughness and knowledge of the game allowed him to become the major leagues' first black manager, and as of 2004 he was still at it, managing at Montreal and continues to manage again in 2005 as the team moved to Washington, D.C.

8. Ken Griffey Jr. Junior is a player who has lived up to the hype from day one. Prior to the injuries that have robbed him of almost three and a half seasons, Junior was touted as the best overall player in the game, and for good reason.

A spectacular center fielder, he has taken away countless home runs and crashed into walls, and most of his injuries have been the result of playing hard. He has never been a guy who's dogged it. His instincts in the outfield are similar to Willie Mays's. I once saw him cut a double off in the left-center-field gap against Pudge Rodriguez at Arlington. He speared it with a slide in the outfield, got up, and threw a strike to second to nail Pudge. I had never seen anything quite like it. That kind of ability narrows the gaps in the outfield.

Despite losing major time to injury, his numbers remain impressive. His lifetime batting average is .294 with seven .300 seasons. He has four home run titles including two straight seasons with 56, 501 career homers, 2,156 career hits, a .294 batting average, 178 steals, and, not surprisingly, ten Gold Gloves.

9. Joe Morgan. Not a big man, but at five feet seven inches Joe Morgan certainly played big. Joe was a fine fielder with good range, quickness, a strong arm, and the know-how to turn a fast double play.

As a hitter, Joe is remembered for the way he flapped his left arm at the plate when waiting for the pitch. But like all great hitters, he did it for a reason, saying it helped him keep his arm down and get through the baseball when he swung. It was his way to load up and generate his power and bat speed. He also worked the count extremely well, and when he retired he had the third most walks in big-league history (1,865). He was a speed guy who set the tone for the offense both in Houston and Cincinnati, finishing with 689 steals. Yet he also had power, hitting 268 career homers.

Some will point to his lifetime .271 batting average as being below that of the so-called complete players, but in Joe's case all his walks offset the average and gave him a high on-base percentage. In addition to his skills, he was a leader and a winner with great baseball instincts.

10. Derek Jeter. I remember Derek as a rookie in 1996. I was managing the Red Sox; it was the bottom of the ninth at Yankee Stadium, there was a runner on second, and we walked Bernie Williams to pitch to Jeter. He promptly looped a base hit to left field to beat us. It's fitting that my first recollection of him is as a winner, a guy who came through in the clutch, because he's done that ever since. It's no wonder he's the captain of the Yankees.

At the plate he has a classic inside-out swing and can go to right and right center as well as anyone. He's also got surprising power to right and has hit as many as 24 homers in a season. As a shortstop, he's sure-handed and steady, has good range, and makes a classic jump throw from deep in the third-base hole. Derek has great instincts for the game, which he shows time and again.

A .315 lifetime hitter with a best of .349, Jeter also won his first Gold Glove after the 2004 season and upped his career stolen base total to 201. Derek has never lost his leadership ability and his passion to win, and has handled the pressure of playing in New York from day one.

11. Ivan "Pudge" Rodriguez. With his quick feet, quick glove, and power arm, Pudge could probably play any infield position well. As a catcher he's won ten straight Gold Gloves—eleven overall—and was the American League's Most Valuable Player in 1999. Even more impressive is the fact that he throws out runners at a 55–60 percent clip while the major-league average is in the low 30s.

Pudge has always had a quick bat. He knows how to go to right, and while he's not a huge power hitter, he now has 250 career home runs, with highs of 35 homers and 113 RBIs in a single season. He has hit .347, .334, and .332 to go with a lifetime .306 average, and he's even swiped 25 bases one year, just another testament to his all-around ability.

12. Cal Ripken Jr. I played with Cal during his one year in Triple-A back in 1981, and I still feel to this day that he was the best minor-league player I ever saw. I was always impressed by his size, how he held the bat back, and the way he could take the outside slider down and away and hook it over the left-field wall. He could also stay inside the ball and rifle it down the right-field line.

Cal was always a great fielder. His first-step instincts were tremendous, and he had a powerful arm with the ability to throw from different angles. His baseball IQ was also immense, as he always seemed to know where the hitters would put the ball based on what his pitcher was throwing.

His .276 lifetime average may not be as high as those of other players on this list, and he may not be the classic five-tool player, but he does have a pair of MVP awards and 431 lifetime home runs. Most of all it was his leadership and baseball intelligence, as well as his renowned durability, that made Cal a complete player and earned him a place on my list.

13. Al Kaline. I didn't see a great deal of Al Kaline, but I saw enough to know how good he was. He was the heart and soul of some great Detroit Tigers teams and a fine right fielder with a great arm. He was also enough of a power hitter to belt 399 lifetime homers, and he was the youngest American League batting champ since Ty Cobb when he hit .340 at the age of twenty in 1955. Kaline had perfect mechanics at the plate and in the field. He was simply a ballplayer who did everything right and represented the game at its highest level.

14. Dave Winfield. When Dave Winfield was selected by the San Diego Padres out of the University of Minnesota in 1973, not only were the Padres getting a six-foot six-inch, 220-pound outfielder, but also a tremendous athlete who was good enough to be drafted by teams in the National Football League and the National Basketball Association as well. Winfield went from the campus directly to the majors and quickly became a franchise player for the Padres.

He didn't have classic mechanics at the plate. His feet were moving all the time, and he had that big hitch in his swing, but his great athletic ability allowed him to have great timing. More of a line-drive hitter than a guy with a classic home run stroke, Winfield still cracked 465 over the course of his career. His lifetime batting average was .283, though he had a season high of .340. For a big man he had surprisingly good speed and stole more than 200 bases. Possessing a powerful throwing arm, he won seven Gold Gloves, two in the National League and five more in the American.

Dave came back from missing an entire season to back surgery in 1989 to have several more fine years, really cementing his greatness with Toronto in 1992 when he played in 156 games and hit .290, with 26 homers and 108 RBIs. He became the oldest player ever to drive in more than 100 runs that year as he approached his forty-first birthday. Dave retired with 3,110 hits, and was elected to the Hall of Fame in 2001.

15. Vladimir Guerrero. A classic five-tool player, Vladimir Guerrero is on his way to becoming an all-time great. He has an unorthodox swing with a lot of hand movement, but he can power the low ball, and for a big guy, he doesn't strike out that much. He was an outstanding hitter in Montreal, and continued his exploits with an MVP season in 2004 at Anaheim, where his clutch homers in the final weeks led the Angels to the American League West title. He wound up hitting .337 with 39 homers and 126 runs batted in. His lifetime batting mark through 2004 is .325, and he can also run, having swiped 40 bases in 2002 and coming within one homer of being a rare 40-40 man.

As a right fielder, Vladimir owns one of the great arms in baseball. He's simply an explosive, multitalented player with all the tools to achieve greatness, and he's on the road to becoming one of the greatest players ever to step on a baseball diamond.

Those are the fifteen most complete players I have seen. You'll find some of the same names among the best hitters, and also mentioned as great position players. That's why they are complete. They do it all. Naturally, it isn't always easy to compile such a list and it's always open for debate. So once again, I'm proposing a second group, players who were considered for the top group, but didn't quite make it.

Mike Schmidt. When Mike Schmidt retired in 1989 he had 548 homers. He was also a great defensive third baseman with a powerful throwing arm, good enough to win ten Gold Gloves, and is considered by some to be baseball's best all-time third sacker. His three Most Valuable Player awards and Hall of Fame induction are further testament to his being one of the dominant players of his era.

There are just two things that keep Mike out of the top fifteen. One is his .267 lifetime average with just a single .300 season; and he also struck out 1,883 times, which is sixth on the all-time list.

Reggie Smith. A switch-hitter with power from both sides of the plate, Reggie Smith was a .287 lifetime batter who was also an outstanding right fielder with a very strong arm. He had 314 lifetime homers with a high of 32, but knocked in 100 runs just once.

Reggie was a five-tool guy who was always an asset to his team, and it's no coincidence that he was on four World Series teams, playing a major role in the Dodgers' pennant-winning clubs of 1977 and 1978.

Kirby Puckett. I first saw Kirby playing at Visalia in the California League in 1983. He had that roly-poly body even back then, but he could run, hit, and throw. He was a gifted center fielder whose great speed and leaping ability allowed him to take more than one home run away from opposing hitters, and his six Gold Gloves are further evidence of his defensive prowess.

He had a .318 lifetime average with a season high of .356, and he also hit 207 homers in his twelve seasons, though he never hit more than 31 in a single year. He was the heart and soul of the Minnesota Twins throughout his career, and had he not been forced to retire prematurely when he was diagnosed with glaucoma in the spring of 1996, his statistics would be even more impressive. Regardless, his shortened career stands on its own merits, and he was elected to the Hall of Fame in 2001.

Andre Dawson. I can remember Mel Didier, who was the farm director for the Montreal Expos before becoming a major-league scout for the Dodgers, telling me that Andre Dawson would be a great five-tool player. I watched Andre quite a bit over his career and as a young player he had it all. Late in his career bad knees robbed him of his speed, but before that happened he was an accomplished base stealer, finishing his career with 314 thefts and with a high of 39 one year. He had one super season in 1987 when he belted 49 home runs with 137 RBIs and was named the National League's Most Valuable Player.

Andre finished with 2,774 career hits and 438 home runs, and had a cannon for an arm in right field. Only his lifetime batting mark of .279 prevents him from making a real challenge to the top fifteen.

Billy Williams. Sweet-swinging Billy Williams played from 1959 to 1976, all but two years with the Chicago Cubs, where he shared the stage with Ernie Banks and Ron Santo. He had a .290 lifetime average and won a batting title in 1972 with a .333 average. He also walloped 426 homers and had 2,711 career hits. In addition he was a solid outfielder, playing mostly in right, where he exhibited a better than average throwing arm. What's more, he did it day in and day out, once compiling a consecutive-game streak that reached 1,117, a National League record until it was broken by Steve Garvey. He was elected to the Hall of Fame in 1987.

Billy was a low-key guy, once saying, "I just go out there and catch the ball and hit the ball and play the game like it should be played." But while he did everything extremely well, he didn't do any one thing spectacularly, and I feel he is just a cut below the complete players who made it to the top list.

Robin Yount. Robin is an old friend. We were teammates at Taft High School in Woodland Hills, California, in the early 1970s. But friendship notwithstanding, he was a great ballplayer. Robin joined the Brewers as an eighteen-year-old in 1974 and, as a player, always had great instincts for the game. He started as a shortstop, won a Gold Glove, then later in his career became a center fielder. He could hit to all fields, had deceiving speed, and was a good base runner, and while he wasn't a classic power hitter, he still hit 251 career homers.

Robin won the MVP in 1982 and 1989; however, his lifetime batting average of .285 and his home run total are the two factors that keep him from cracking the top fifteen. Still, he played two demanding defensive positions very well and had 3,142 career hits, which is a big reason he was elected to the Hall of Fame in 1999.

Rafael Palmeiro. Raffy has always been highly underrated. When people talk about the great first basemen of the last fifteen years, his name rarely comes up. But having managed him, I know the kind of hitter he is and I loved having him in the lineup every day. Raffy is a guy who made himself into a power hitter, learning while still maintaining a high batting average. When I first saw him in Puerto Rico, playing winter ball in the mid-1980s, he was a line-drive hitter who often went to the opposite field. At the beginning of 2005, he had 551 homers and counting.

Palmeiro is also a great first baseman who used to joke that he would never win a Gold Glove until Don Mattingly retired. He was right. After Mattingly quit, Raffy won three straight. Steady as a rock, Raffy had a .289 lifetime batting average through 2004, six .300 seasons, and 2,922 lifetime hits in nineteen seasons on his résumé. He also had nine straight 100-RBI seasons, and it would probably have been eleven had it not been for the strike of 1994. While he doesn't have speed as a raw tool—the one thing that keeps him from serious top fifteen consideration—he knows how to run, and that makes him a complete player. I've heard Raffy called no more than a "numbers hanger," but those people are wrong. He's an outstanding player, a quiet leader, and a consistent winner who someday will surely have a plaque in the Hall of Fame.

Carl Yastrzemski. A legend in Boston, Yaz took over in left field for Ted Williams in 1961 and stayed for twenty-three years. Though not a real speed merchant in the outfield, Yaz played the Green Monster wall in Fenway as well as anyone, ultimately teaching the tricks to his successor, Jim Rice.

Yaz was also a great hitter. He was a Triple Crown winner who had 452 homers and 3,419 hits in his career. His lifetime average was .285, but he had six .300 seasons and was a clutch player who led the Bosox into the 1967 "Impossible Dream" World Series. Though they lost to the Cardinals and Bob Gibson's three complete-game wins, Yaz was outstanding, hitting .400 (10 for 25) with 3 home runs. The intangibles he brought to the game made him a complete player and a fully deserving Hall of Famer, but his lack of speed and his lifetime batting average prevent him from cracking the top fifteen.

Sammy Sosa. Sammy could flat-out fly when he was young and always had a very strong throwing arm and a powerful swing. Over the years Sammy has also learned to hit for both average and power. He's now had four .300 seasons to up his lifetime average to .277 through 2004. Of course, it's his power that has made his name. He's the only player to hit 60 or more home runs three times (66, 63, 64) and has 578 career homers through 2004. He's also knocked in 160 and 158 runs in two different seasons, yet was fast enough to steal 36 and 34 bases, en route to 233 lifetime steals. I think that because he has concentrated on his hitting, he's never reached his full potential as an outfielder, though he continues to show an explosive throwing arm. He should easily top 600 homers for his career and wind up in the top five and in the Hall of Fame. Sammy Sosa is a complete player, but because of his lifetime average and to a smaller degree his overall outfield play, he won't make the top fifteen.

Gary Sheffield. I managed against Gary his first year in the minors, in 1986, when he was playing for Helena and I was the skipper at Great Falls, Montana. When I saw him at seventeen there was no question in my mind why he was a number one draft pick in the country. He was a shortstop then, a great athlete with tremendous range and a great throwing arm.

Gary has a great batting eye and walks more than he strikes out (1,202 walks versus 879 strikeouts as of 2004), which is unusual for today's sluggers. A versatile player who has played short, third, left, and right in the big leagues, he volunteered to return to third for the Yanks when Aaron Boone was hurt and before the Bombers acquired Alex Rodriguez. That's the kind of unselfish team player he is. He's also a player who has improved with age. His lifetime batting average was up to .298 at the end of 2004, coming on the heels of six straight .300-plus seasons from 1998 to 2003. He now has 415 lifetime home runs with season highs of 43 and 42, along with 205 stolen bases. He's very close to that top fifteen, and with a few more great seasons in the twilight of his career, he just might get there.

Roberto Alomar. Roberto Alomar is the best defensive second baseman that I've ever seen. He's also a switch-hitter who was almost always above .300 in his prime years between 1989 and 2001. His lifetime average at the end of 2004 stood at an even .300, but he could also hit for more than average. His 210 career homers, great for a second baseman, 475 steals, 2,724 lifetime hits, and ten Gold Gloves, make him a complete player.

It's his late-career falloff that keeps him from being considered for the top fifteen. But there are some from this generation who say he's the best all-around at his position in baseball history. Robbie decided to retire just before the start of the 2005 season.

Nomar Garciaparra. Like his contemporaries Derek Jeter and Alex Rodriguez, Nomar Garciaparra is still in the prime of his career. I had the good fortune of being his first manager at Boston in 1996. He's a solid shortstop with great range and a good arm, maybe just a cut below

Jeter's and Rodriguez's. Nomar has always been a first-ball hitter, and that strategy has worked for him, seeing as he's a .322 lifetime hitter with 182 home runs.

Jeter, A-Rod, and Nomar were perhaps the three greatest short-stops ever to play at the same time in one league. Now playing for the Chicago Cubs in the National League, Nomar isn't quite the fielder that the other two are, and he doesn't have the power of A-Rod, nor has he produced in the clutch as well as Jeter has. He's also been slowed by injuries in several seasons. But he's still a tremendous player who can solidify his place in baseball history in the coming years.

Chipper Jones. Chipper Jones has been a consistent and stabilizing force for the Atlanta Braves since 1995. In 2004, he slammed his 300th career homer and already has one of the top home run totals (310) for switch-hitters in baseball history. In addition, he has also batted higher than .300 seven times and has driven in more than 100 runs eight times. Chipper has also proved his versatility in the field by playing both left field and third base. In addition to everything else he's a leader who plays hard day in and day out. At six feet four, 210 pounds, he's a big man, yet he has stolen 118 bases in his career, including a high of 25 in 1999. Though he has already proved to everyone that he is a complete player, Chipper had an off season in 2004, hitting just .248. He may still have a chance to make the top fifteen, but will have to rebound and continue to produce the kind of seasons he has had in the past. Repeated leg injuries after his switch to the outfield led to his return to third base during the second half of the 2004 season. Being back in the infield could help keep him healthy and should result in increased production at the plate.

◆

Chapter Twelve

The Greatest Games I've Ever Seen

I've seen many great games in my life, some as a fan, others as a player, more as a manager, and now from the perspective of a broadcaster. Each one is different, great in its own way. Greatness may come as a result of an individual player doing something extraordinary, or from an entire team rising to the occasion. A game can become great from sheer competitiveness, a game that suddenly produces an intensity level that quickly spreads to the players on both teams. All of these games are games I'll never forget.

A great game can happen at any time. There's no set formula for greatness, no way to tell when that first pitch is thrown what will happen over the next nine innings . . . or more. There are nights when a game can be routine for four or five innings and suddenly—boom— you're on the edge of your seat watching something special. If you're in the dugout when it happens—as a player, coach, or manager—all your senses are heightened as the excitement and intensity grow, and the competitive juices begin flowing. You're in a game you want to win so badly that it grips at your insides. When that happens, everyone wants to be the hero, and no one wants to be the goat. In games like this, players become so focused and intense that there is no telling what their bodies might do.

Heroes can come in all shapes and sizes. When a Sandy Koufax goes out and throws a perfect game, it's certainly special. But when a

Kenny Rogers takes the mound shortly before a players' strike is due and everybody is down, no one expects much. Then, suddenly, about the sixth or seventh inning, when you realize he is pitching a perfect game, everything changes. All the negative things—the pending strike, the animosity of the players—are forgotten and everyone concentrates on those last nine outs.

I have picked twelve games from my long association with baseball that, in my mind, are among the greatest I've ever seen. I'm not going to rank them in the order of greatness because the differences in the games themselves and my particular positions at the time just don't make that feasible. It's virtually impossible to say that a game I watched as a fan was greater than one I managed, or observed from the press box as a broadcaster. Instead, I'm going to put them in chronological order. The first one was played when I was just eleven years old, back in 1965, and the last was on July 1, 2004. And who can say that by the time you read this I won't have witnessed another game so exciting and compelling that it will make its way onto this list? As I said, a great game can happen at any time.

October 14, 1965—Koufax Shuts Out Twins in World Series Finale

I was just an eleven-year-old kid in 1965, but this one has always stuck in my mind as one of the greatest performances I've ever seen. Game 1 of the World Series that year fell on October 6, which was also Yom Kippur, the holiest day on the Jewish calendar, and the deeply religious Sandy Koufax didn't pitch, a choice he made throughout his career. Don Drysdale started in his place and was beaten by Jim "Mudcat" Grant and the Twins, 8–2. Sandy pitched the second game, matched goose eggs with Jim Kaat for five innings, then gave up two in the sixth and came out. Minnesota won, 5–1, and the Dodgers were in trouble. But my old buddy Claude Osteen shut out the Twins in Game 3, 4–0, and then Drysdale came back to win the fourth game, 7–2, going the distance. Sandy was next, and this time he shut down the Twins on four hits and struck out ten as L.A. won, 7–0. But when the Twins won the sixth game, 5–1, the stage was set for the seventh and decisive contest.

Ordinarily it would have been Drysdale's turn to go. In the days of the four-man rotation he'd had his usual three days' rest. But manager Walt Alston changed his mind and decided he wanted to go with Sandy on just two days' rest. All the players from that Dodger team I've spoken with over the years agreed with their skipper and said they wanted Sandy on the mound that day. I can understand now why Walt Alston made that decision. Of course, had Sandy not had his stuff, Alston would have been second-guessed to this day.

Anyway, I was camped in front of a television set to watch the game that day. Even at that young age I remember wondering just what Koufax would have left on two days' rest. What I saw once again was the most dominant pitcher of his era at the top of his game. The Twins couldn't touch him. The Dodgers got two runs in the fourth on a Lou Johnson home run, and that was all Sandy needed. He threw a three-hit shutout, striking out ten, and he did it on the road in Minnesota, bringing the Dodgers their second championship in three years.

What I learned years later made his performance all the greater. Sandy apparently didn't have control of his great curveball that day, so catcher John Roseboro decided early on just to let Sandy use his fastball. And that's basically all he threw that afternoon. When we became friends years later Sandy told me that pitchers have to learn how to pitch with just their fastball, not only moving it in and out, but up and down as well. He said there were many games when he used nothing but fastballs in the final few innings. But on this day in 1965, he used it the entire game and shut down one of the best-hitting teams in the majors. Even as an eleven-year-old, I knew it was one of the greatest games I'd ever see.

October 21, 1975—Carlton Fisk's Twelfth-Inning Homer Wins Game 6 of the World Series

This was another game I watched on television. I had just finished my junior year as a catcher at San Diego State and had led the league in hitting. So I was beginning to get attention from the scouts, and like most kids my age who were finding success in the game, I was looking toward a bright future as a player. When the Cincinnati Reds took on the Boston Red Sox in the World Series that year, I was even more interested because two of the best catchers in the game would be facing off—Cincinnati's Johnny Bench and Carlton Fisk of the Red Sox.

Boston won the first game, a shutout by Luis Tiant, but Cincy bounced back to win the next two. The Red Sox then tied the series with a victory in the fourth game behind Tiant again, and I began to feel it was going to be a seven-game Series. Then Cincy won the fifth, 6–2, with Don Gullett on the mound, and the teams traveled back to Fenway Park for the sixth game. Tiant would be pitching once more, this time facing Cincinnati right-hander Gary Nolan.

Fred Lynn hit a three-run homer in the first inning and it looked right away that it might be a Boston day, which would mean a seventh game. Tiant had already pitched two outstanding games, but because of rain delays, he was working on five days' rest—so he was ready. Then the flow of the game changed. True to his nickname, "Captain Hook," Reds manager Sparky Anderson began bringing in a parade of relievers in the third inning, and they held the Sox at bay. Cincy broke through to tie it with three in the fifth, then took the lead with two more in the seventh and one in the eighth. Going into the bottom of the eighth the Reds held a 6–3 lead and were just six outs from winning the Series. That's when, without warning, this turned into a great game.

In the bottom of the eighth the Sox mounted a rally. Finally, it came down to this. Two men on, two men out. One of Cincy's top relievers, righty Rawley Eastwick, was on the mound and pinch hitter Bernie Carbo was at the plate. Carbo had delivered a pinch homer in Game 3, but it seemed like wishful thinking to ask him to do it again. Yet that's exactly what happened. He took an Eastwick fastball into the center-field bleachers for a dramatic game-tying home run that had the Fenway faithful going nuts. (And it brought me to the edge of my seat as well.)

That's when I began to sense the drama, and in a very different way from when I watched Koufax spin his magic in 1965. Ten years after Sandy's gem I was a ballplayer, albeit still in college, but once the ninth inning began I felt the tension because the Series could now end at any moment and I could identify more with what the players were experiencing and began envisioning how I would feel if I were one of them down on the field. I also knew even then that games like this often end with one swing. One mistake and boom . . . home run. The tension continued to build in the ninth, tenth, and eleventh innings. Neither team scored, and Sparky kept marching in his relievers. He would wind up using eight pitchers before the game ended.

When Cincy didn't score in the top of the twelfth and sent right-hander Pat Darcy to the mound to start the bottom of the inning, Carlton Fisk was set to lead off. I learned in later years that Fisk had a feeling he was about to hit one off the Green Monster and turned to Fred Lynn, who was on deck, and said, "Drive me in."

Darcy's first pitch was a ball. The next pitch was a fastball and Fisk connected, hitting it high and deep down the left-field line. Every baseball fan has probably seen a film of the hit, with Fisk dancing sideways toward first, watching the ball, and then waving his arms several times to his right, as if trying to help the ball stay fair, which it did. His home run not only won the game, but tied the Series and gave the Red Sox a chance to win it the next day.

Watching Fisk hit that homer was special, as I envisioned myself doing something like that someday. Cincy won the Series on Joe Morgan's clutch base hit in the ninth inning of the seventh game, but Carlton Fisk's home run would always be special to me. It was one of those moments that would forever be frozen in time and one I would never forget.

October 18, 1977—Reggie Jackson Hits Three Home Runs in Game 6 of the World Series

Just two years after Carlton Fisk's dramatic home run I found myself in front of the television again, this time watching my beloved Dodgers facing their old archrival, the New York Yankees, in yet another World Series. By this time I had been drafted into the Baltimore Orioles organization and was on my way, I hoped, to the big leagues. Having just completed my second year in pro ball, the Orioles sent me to the Florida Instructional League when the Series was taking place. Several of us had rented a house in Madeira Beach, and we were all watching the game together.

The Yanks, managed by the volatile Billy Martin, battled each other and everyone else all year. They were a team full of individual personalities starting with their captain, Thurman Munson, who was joined by Reggie Jackson, Lou Piniella, Graig Nettles, Mickey Rivers, Mike Torrez, and Sparky Lyle. Any one of them could blow sky high at any time. The more laid-back players—Willie Randolph, Chris Chambliss, Ron Guidry, Catfish Hunter, Roy White, and Bucky Dent—were also talented, and despite a season-long series of internal clashes, they still won 100 games.

The Dodgers won 98 games behind manager Tommy Lasorda and had plenty of talent of their own with Steve Garvey, Ron Cey, Dusty Baker, Reggie Smith, Don Sutton, Tommy John, and others. But this looked to most people like the Yankees' year, and when they won three of the first four games, they were certainly in the driver's seat. The Dodgers managed to win Game 5 behind Don Sutton, but then the Series returned to Yankee Stadium for the sixth game with the Yanks' Mike Torrez opposing Burt Hooton. What I didn't know as Torrez threw the first pitch was that I was about to see one of the most amazing and dominant hitting performances in the history of the game.

The Dodgers touched up Torrez for a pair of runs in the first inning, and I immediately began thinking of a seventh game. The first time Reggie Jackson came up Hooton walked him on four pitches. Then the Yanks got a pair in the second to tie the game. When Reggie came up again in the fourth, the Dodgers had a 3–2 lead and Thurman Munson was on first. Reggie went after Hooton's first pitch and slammed it into the lower right-field stands for a home run that gave the Yanks a 4–3 lead. Little did I know that this was only the start of something special.

Another run in the inning raised the Yankees' lead to 5–3, and by the time Reggie came up again in the fifth reliever Elias Sosa was in the game for the Dodgers. Once again there was a runner on as Reggie got set in the batter's box. Sosa delivered and Reggie went after the first pitch once more. This time it was a laser shot that reached the lower stands in right in what seemed a milli-instant. The crowd began chanting, "Reggie! Reggie! Reggie!" as he made his familiar trot around the bases. Two homers and a 7–3 lead. It was beginning to look as if the Dodgers were done.

But if they were done, Reggie wasn't. When he came up again in the eighth the Yankees still had a 7–3 lead, only now knuckleballer Charlie Hough was pitching for L.A. I was wondering what Reggie might do for an encore, and it took only one pitch to find out. Hough threw his trademark knuckler and Reggie swung. This time he hit a long, high, majestic drive to straightaway center. It kept carrying and went over the fence for his third and longest home run of the game. Not only was he just the second player in history to hit three home runs in a World Series game, but Reggie had done it on three consecutive pitches and against three different pitchers. He had also homered in Games 4 and 5, making him the first player ever to hit five homers in the Fall Classic.

Though I wasn't happy when the Yanks won the game to close out the Series, I knew I had seen something special, something I might never see again. On that autumn day in 1977, Reggie Jackson became Mr. October forever.

April 18–June 23, 1981—the Longest Game in History, Thirty-three Innings

This one is totally unforgettable for a lot of reasons. It happened nearly a quarter century ago, but sometimes it still seems like last night. That's how vivid the memories continue to be. It was a cold, damp, foggy April 18 night in Pawtucket, Rhode Island, and early in the Triple-A season. I was catching for the Rochester Red Wings, Baltimore's Triple-A team, and we were going up against the Pawtucket Red Sox. Unfortunately, I wasn't playing that night because I was on the disabled list for the only time in my playing career, recovering from a badly pulled hamstring and waiting for a roster spot to open. But I was in uniform and on the bench that night. None of us, of course, expected anything out of the ordinary when the game began at

8:00 P.M. How could we have known that we were about to be involved in the longest game in professional baseball annals, a game that
would ultimately go thirty-three innings before there was a winner,
with the first thirty-two of those innings played on that cold, damp
night in Pawtucket?

It was a game that featured a number of future big leaguers, including Hall of Famers Cal Ripken for Rochester and Wade Boggs for
Pawtucket. Both played third base for their respective teams and
would play the entire game. Other guys who eventually played in the
majors included Dallas Williams, Floyd Rayford, and Jim Umbarger
for Rochester and Rich Gedman, Marty Barrett, Bruce Hurst, and
Bobby Ojeda for Pawtucket. I'm sure each and every one of them remembers this game. How could anyone forget?

The scoring was simple. We got a run in the seventh inning only
to have Pawtucket tie it in the bottom of the ninth. When it went to extras, no one scored until the twenty-first inning, when we pushed another across. Pawtucket tied it, though, in the bottom of the inning on
a double by Boggs. After that the goose eggs started to mount again,
and no one scored as the innings and the hours passed. I remember us
being told there was no curfew, but apparently there was a misunder-
standing about a 12:50 A.M. curfew rule, though I can't remember
what it was. And because no one could seem to locate the league president, we played on.

The cold and wind were the worst part. Guys on our team were
drinking coffee to stay warm and some even started a fire and began
burning broken bats. Everyone was tired, but in a game like this a
strange thing happens. Players get a kind of focus that takes them to a
different level, and because of that focus, they begin making plays they
might not normally make. You reach a point where you don't think
about the fatigue, just try to do things to stay alert and keep your head
in the game.

To make things even more difficult, a layer of fog covered the
ballpark the last nine innings or so. Finally, the umpire realized that
under these conditions no one could score. When it finally was called
after thirty-two innings, none of us could sleep. There was another
game the next afternoon and if you went to sleep you were done. We

got back to the hotel about 5:00 A.M. and soon after that went to break-fast, then got ready to go right back to the ballpark.

This was an amazing game for many different reasons. Our catcher, Dave Huppert, went thirty-one innings. I had caught double-headers before, but to catch more than thirty innings, to keep squat-ting down like that, what an accomplishment. The irony was that our other catcher, Ed Putnam, was going to pinch-hit, but it was so cold that he pulled a muscle while warming up on deck and couldn't hit or go behind the plate. The next afternoon Huppert was the only healthy catcher and had to go the distance again. Had I been healthy, who knows how far I would have gone if I had started that night, but I've got to think Huppert would have replaced me at some point.

I also remember Jim Umbarger, who had played for Billy Martin in Oakland, coming in for the twenty-second inning and pitching ten shutout innings until the game was suspended. He pitched the equiv-alent of a complete-game shutout, and it was less than a third of the game. I know there were almost 2,000 fans there when we started, and conflicting reports say there were either 17, 19, or 23 people left when it was suspended. Those few brave souls were all given season tickets for the remaining home games that year.

What else? I remember the Pawtucket DH, Russ Larribee, strik-ing out seven times in eleven plate appearances. He was a left-handed hitter, and I can still picture him swinging and missing, swinging and missing. With the weather conditions, I just don't think he could see the ball. Our centerfielder, Dallas Williams, went 0-13 and saw his batting average drop from .346 to .237. Remember, it was early in the season. All told, the game took more than eight hours and was finally suspended at 4:09 A.M.

It was resumed at McCoy Stadium on June 23, and this time there were more than 5,700 fans in attendance. Ironically, it took just an-other eighteen minutes for the game to be completed. After Rochester failed to scored in the top of the thirty-third inning, Pawtucket quickly got the winning run off Steve Grilli, who wasn't even with the team when the game started two months earlier. A hit batter, a single, and a walk loaded the bases, and Grilli was replaced by Cliff Speck, who promptly gave up the game-winning hit to Dave Koza. Pawtucket's Bob Ojeda got the victory, and the longest game in history was finally over.

The final irony was that I missed the thirty-third inning. By the time the game was resumed, I was back in Rochester getting ready to move from the Baltimore to the St. Louis organization. So I wasn't on the active roster. I listened to the end of the game on the radio and laughed at the way it ended so quickly. But who could ever forget those first thirty-two innings on a cold, damp, foggy night in Pawtucket? More than eight hours of baseball in a game so unusual that it had to be one of the greatest ever.

July 14, 1988—San Antonio Missions Versus Jackson (Mississippi) Mets, Twenty-seven Innings

Here we go again, another marathon extra-inning game, once again in the minor leagues. This was a Double-A Texas League game between the San Antonio Missions and the Jackson Mets. I was managing the Missions, who were part of the Dodger organization, and this was my first year at the Double-A level. I had no idea when we hosted the Jackson Mets on a beautiful Thursday night in San Antonio that the game would make history.

I had a nice team featuring future major leaguers John Wetteland, Mike Huff, Mike Muñoz, and Wayne Kirby, but on this night I probably could have had Ty Cobb, Babe Ruth, Barry Bonds, and Alex Rodriguez and it wouldn't have mattered. No one could score. At the end of nine it was a scoreless tie and we went into extras. Soon the innings were piling up, and I couldn't help thinking about that game in Pawtucket seven years earlier. Not again, I thought. As a manager, I was looking to try everything to manufacture a run, but I think the guys began trying so hard that they were swinging at bad pitches. Conversely, the pitchers on both sides were throwing very hard because they didn't want to lose.

At 1:00 A.M. I asked the umpires if there was a curfew. They laughed. No curfew in this league, they said. About the twenty-fourth inning I asked them again about stopping it, told them I had been through this before, that I was running out of players and didn't want to get anyone hurt. I asked them to call the league president, Carl Sawatski, a former big leaguer. Tucker Ashford, the Jackson manager, wanted the teams to continue to play. I guess the umps decided to let it go another inning or two and if no one scored, then they would suspend it.

It seems incredible to go all those innings without a run scoring, but strange things happen on the baseball field as the intensity level rises. I remember Mike Huff leading off one of the later innings by hitting one in the gap, a sure double. Only Mike tried to stretch it into a triple and was thrown out with a perfect relay and tag. In another inning Walt McConnell, my third baseman and a great, hard-nosed guy who had bad feet, dove headfirst and backhanded a ball down the line. He jumped up like a gazelle and threw the runner out at first. Had he not made the play, Jackson would have scored. I also remember using John Wetteland as a pinch hitter about the twentieth inning. He led off with a base hit and had to stay in because I didn't have a pinch runner for him. Next thing I know he took a big lead and got picked off.

When Jackson shortstop Craig Shipley opened the top of the twenty-sixth inning with a ground out, the game had set a record for the longest game in Texas League history, breaking the mark of twenty-five innings from a 1965 game between Austin and Fort Worth–Dallas. And when the twenty-sixth inning ended the game had set a record for the longest scoreless game in baseball history. Then, after some seven hours and ten minutes, the game was finally suspended. It had been played on a Thursday night into Friday morning, and was the beginning of a four-game series, so it was decided we would finish it on Saturday.

Just as had happened with the Rochester-Pawtucket game, this marathon ended quickly when it was resumed. It took more than seven hours on Thursday night to set things up for a thirteen-minute conclusion on Saturday. In the bottom of the twenty-seventh Mc-Connell singled. Luis Lopez followed with a double down the left-field line, sending McConnell to third. Then Mets pitcher Blaine Beatty, the only guy who didn't play Friday morning, walked Manny Benitez intentionally to load the bases. Switch-hitting Manny Francois was up next. He hit a soft liner that fell in front of the center fielder, and McConnell trotted home with the winning run, the game's only run! Just like that, the game that wouldn't end was over.

Looking back, it's hard to believe that I was involved in two of the longest games in baseball history, one as a player and the other as a manager. Both were special in many ways. And when I look back at the greatest games I've seen in my long career, I can't leave either of them off the list. Especially when the two games took a total of sixty innings to complete compared with the usual eighteen.

October 15, 1988—Kirk Gibson's Pinch Home Run off Dennis Eckersley

Almost three months to the day after our twenty-seven-inning game in San Antonio there was another game that I'll never forget, and one that produced one of baseball's most unexpected and dramatic moments. It happened in Game 1 of the 1988 World Series between the Dodgers and the powerful Oakland A's. By the time the Series rolled around I was back in Arizona working with our catchers in the Instructional League and getting ready to go to Puerto Rico to manage in winter ball. I watched the game with Tim Johnson, who would become my bench coach at Boston seven years later.

This one was supposed to be a mismatch. The A's were a powerhouse that had won 104 games during the regular season under Tony LaRussa. They were a team that featured the "Bash Brothers," Jose Canseco and Mark McGwire. Canseco was coming off a year in which he led the league with 42 homers and 124 RBIs. Dave Stewart and Bob Welch anchored a solid pitching staff, one that featured the game's best closer, Dennis Eckersley. As for the Dodgers, they weren't even supposed to be there. The New York Mets, with 100 victories, were considered the class of the National League. They had beaten the Dodgers eleven of twelve times during the regular season, but in the NLCS, the Dodgers upset the heavily favored Mets in seven games, with 23-game-winner Orel Hershiser pitching a shutout in the deciding contest.

The experts still figured the A's would win it all. To make matters worse, Kirk Gibson, who had been the Dodgers' spiritual leader as well as their best bat all season, was expected to miss the Series with a torn left hamstring and a stretched ligament in his right knee. Gibson had hit .290 with 25 homers and 76 RBIs during the regular season. That, combined with his leadership abilities, would make him the National League's Most Valuable Player that season. His absence in the Series was sure to make the Dodgers even more vulnerable.

I had been a Dodger since 1982 and knew many of the guys who were on the big club. So I had more than a fan's interest in this one. I still felt I was moving up through the system, and I also knew that if they got a ring, I got a ring. Peter O'Malley saw to it that all the managers in the entire organization, as well the scouts and everyone in player development, got a ring. His feeling was that anyone who had anything to do with the Dodger roster deserved it.

The A's were by far the more rested team, having swept the Red Sox in the ALCS. They seemed to have everything going for them as the Series opened at Dodger Stadium with Oakland ace Dave Stewart rested and ready to go against righty Tim Belcher. Surprisingly, the Dodgers touched up Stewart for a pair of runs in the first, but in the top of the second Oakland loaded the bases and Canseco hit one a ton, a mammoth shot to dead center that actually dented a television camera that was situated out there. It was a grand slam with a punctuation mark attached to it, and I felt right then and there that it was going to set the tone for the remainder of the Series, that the Dodger pitchers outside of Hershiser just wouldn't be able to hold the Oakland lineup and the Bash Brothers down.

But from that point on in Game 1, the pitchers took over. The Dodgers managed a run in the sixth to bring the score to 4–3, and it remained that way right into the ninth. Belcher had come out after two innings, but the L.A. relievers did the job, while Stewart continued to toil for the A's. After Oakland went down in the top of the ninth it began to look as if the game was over because the A's were bringing in Dennis Eckersley to close it out. In just his first year as a full-time closer, this former starter had become the most dependable late-inning reliever in the game, with a league-leading 45 saves on the season.

Sure enough, Eck came in throwing strikes and got the first two hitters easily. Then Mike Davis was sent up as a pinch hitter. Davis hadn't had a good year, hitting just .196, but because he had power, Eckersley pitched him carefully. Eck said later, "I knew he wasn't having a good year, but I had played with the guy who hit 22 home runs the season before." To the surprise of everyone, Davis drew a walk. Young Dave Anderson was already on deck, ready to be announced as the next pinch hitter.

No one knew until much later what was happening below the stands at that time. Kirk Gibson had been down there all game, getting treatment on his legs. There was no way anyone expected him to play. In fact, at some point during the inning, Dodger announcer Vin Scully told his audience, "The spearhead of the Dodger offense all throughout the year will see no action here tonight." Kirk heard this down in the training room and he got mad, took the ice off his legs, stood up, and began taking some practice swings off the batting tee. When Davis drew the walk, Gibson went into the tunnel leading to the dugout and called to Tommy Lasorda. He told his manager he wanted to hit.

Maybe Lasorda just had a hunch, or maybe it was the old baseball adage that if you go down, you go down with your best. He called Anderson back and gave the okay to Gibson. When Kirk came out the fans roared. But everyone also wondered what he could do, because he was operating on not one, but two bad legs. Eckersley and the A's knew the kind of competitor and hitter Gibby was, but they also knew how badly he was hurting, so Eck went right at him. Gibson swung at a fastball and missed, almost falling down. But he also took a couple of pitches that were just off the plate. Then he offered at another and didn't get it. Finally, the count had run out. It was 3-2 and Gibson stepped out of the box. When he did, he remembered something that Dodger advance scout Mel Didier had said before the Series began: "Pardner, if Dennis Eckersley goes 3-2 to power-hitting lefties, you can bet the bank you're gonna get a backdoor slider."

The backdoor slider looks as if it's going to be outside, then at the last moment breaks over the outside corner for a strike. Its purpose is to freeze a lefty so that he'll take the pitch for a called strike. That's exactly what Gibson looked for and just what Eck threw. Using his hands and arms to compensate for his legs, Gibby went out, got it, and hooked it into the right-field stands for a game-winning home run. Jack Buck, who was calling the game on national television, summed it all up for posterity when he said, "I don't believe what I just saw."

It was one of the most dramatic home runs in baseball history and has since been voted the greatest moment in Dodger history. Besides winning that first game, Gibby's homer set the tone for the rest of the Series, and the Dodgers won it in five games, despite the fact that Gibson didn't play again. Interestingly enough, Mel Didier, the scout who had told Gibby about the backdoor slider, was in the stands at Dodger Stadium that day. As soon as Kirk hit the homer his only thought was to reach the clubhouse before the media got in. He wanted to make sure Gibby didn't tell the media that he knew which pitch was coming. That's a veteran scout for you. They never want to give away any secrets because you may need them again in the future.

A couple of years later Gibby was in Albuquerque on a rehab assignment when I was managing there, and we became good friends. He told me then that the story about the backdoor slider was absolutely true. "If Eckersley had thrown anything but the backdoor slider I was done," he said. "That's the only pitch I was looking for and the only one under the circumstances that I could have hit."

Of course, it's one thing to look for it, another to hit it out, and still another to hit it out with two bad legs. It was just an incredible moment and a perfect example of why one dramatic moment can make a game great.

September, 1990—A Championship for Albuquerque, My First as a Manager

The 1990 season was my second managing at Albuquerque, the Dodgers Triple-A team in the Pacific Coast League. My team didn't have much power, but we just base-hit people to death, ran a lot, and were tough to strike out. We were also on a mission. The Dodgers had some top prospects that the farm director, Charley Blaney, wanted to keep together. I think he was envisioning another group that would be like the Garvey-Cey-Russell-Lopes era, guys that came up together and stayed together. So in 1990 he kept most of the top guys at Double-A, and I had players who were looked upon as being not quite as good.

But the team had some names that would later become recognizable. There were Carlos Hernandez and Darrin Fletcher behind the plate, and others like Jose Vizciano, Rafael Bournigal, Mike Christopher, Wayne Kirby, Mike Huff, Luis Lopez, Jose Offerman, Mike Hartley, Dave Hansen, Darren Holmes, and John Wetteland. I think eleven or twelve of the players on that team went to the big leagues, but other than Wetteland, no one really became a star.

In addition, we all knew that Albuquerque had been something of a Triple-A dynasty going back to the early 1980s, when Del Crandall was the manager. Now, managing the Dukes as he had, I felt it was important to continue that winning tradition, even though my team didn't have the same level of prospects that Del had back in 1982. And that's just what we did. In fact, once we started winning, we simply didn't stop. The team executed and knew how to play the game, and we blew the league away, winning 90-some games in a 140-game regular season.

In the playoffs, it finally came down to us and Edmonton for the title. They were an Angels affiliate, and the way the playoffs were set up the first two games would be played at Albuquerque, and the last three, if necessary, were scheduled for Edmonton. Five in a row with no days off. We won the first two, and I wanted to wrap it up in three. I had my best pitcher, John Wetteland, who was still a starter then, ready for the third game, and we sent him up to Edmonton one day early so he could get some rest. He told me later that he couldn't sleep that night, and I think we all experienced the same kind of anxiety.

The game itself was almost anticlimactic. If it had been a mid-August game you probably couldn't call it a great one, but when it can win a title for you it takes on a life of its own. Wetteland simply pitched great. We didn't have a lot of offense that day, but going into the bottom of the ninth we had a 2–0 lead and were three outs away from winning it all. Wetteland got the first out, but then one of their guys singled. I decided to make a change and brought in sinkerballer Mike Christopher to close it out. They sent Daryl Sconiers to the plate and he hit a sharp grounder to the left of Rafael Bournigal. He grabbed it, stepped on second, and fired to first for the double play. Game over. We had won it. Once again the Albuquerque Dukes were PCL champions.

I remember Claude Osteen jumping up and down like a kid who had won his first championship. Yet Claude had been part of a World Series winner in the bigs. When I asked him why he was going so crazy I'll never forget his answer. He said, "Kevin, the feeling is always the same when you win it all after a long season. I'm just as excited here as I was in the big leagues."

And I knew what he meant. The season was special for a lot of reasons. It was my first championship as a professional manager, and the team played my kind of baseball and had executed well all year, better than any other team in the league, so I got a lot of satisfaction from that victory. I'll never forget Darrin Fletcher coming up to me a few years ago when he was still playing for the Blue Jays and saying, "My favorite year in baseball, bar none, was playing for the Albuquerque team in 1990. It was the most fun I ever had."

Hearing something like that makes it special all over again.

July 28, 1994—Kenny Rogers Pitches Perfect Game

This game is one of the most memorable I ever experienced behind a major-league bench. It took place about two weeks before the disastrous strike, the one that wiped out the season and caused the cancellation of the playoffs and World Series. While we were a few games under .500, we were still in first place, but for the most part it was an ugly time. The players had voted and we knew the August 11 strike date was coming quickly.

On this night we were hosting the Angels. Despite the pending strike I still wanted the team to play hard so that we would remain in first when the season came to a halt, just in case they settled the dispute and came back for the playoffs. I had Kenny Rogers pitching that night. Kenny was 10–6 coming into the game that night and I remember also being told that the crowd of more than 46,500 fans was the largest ever to watch a regular-season game at the Ballpark at Arlington since it opened.

The Angels had some real good hitters in their lineup that night, guys like Chad Curtis, Jim Edmonds, Chili Davis, J. T. Snow, and the one and only Bo Jackson. So I knew Kenny would have his work cut out for him. There wasn't a whole lot to be happy about with the strike pending, but a ball game is a ball game, and once it begins you're totally locked into it. We scored a pair of runs in the first on back-to-back homers by Pudge and Jose Canseco, then two more in the third when Jose homered again and Dean Palmer drove home Juan Gonzalez. That gave us a 4–0 lead and Kenny hadn't given them anything, setting down the first nine hitters he faced. I could see he was sharp. He had great command in the early going, mixing his fastball, curve, and change, moving the ball around, and hitting the corners.

Then about the fifth inning, some of the guys started having fun. They got hold of a pair of Canseco's shoes and set them on fire in a trash can in the dugout while the game was going on. That loosened everyone up. Then, when Kenny set the Angels down again in the top of the sixth, Jackie Moore, one of my coaches, turned to me and said, "Hey, he's got a perfect game going, eighteen up and eighteen down." When everyone began realizing it, the dugout got quiet in hurry. Kenny was aware of it too. He began sitting at the end of the dugout by himself between innings. And I suddenly became more aware of positioning the defense, checking each guy and moving the fielders according to way Kenny was going to pitch the hitter.

In the seventh, we all began holding our breaths. Kenny went to a three-ball count on all three hitters. First was Chad Curtis, who finally grounded to third. Next came Spike Owen, and he wound up hitting a pop to short left field. Then came the dangerous Jim Edmonds. He worked the count full and then struck out. Seven innings in the book. Remember how tough I said the final nine outs are? They're even tougher when a guy is throwing a no-hitter, and even tougher than that when it's a potential perfect game. Two innings were left. I was in the dugout thinking that Kenny Rogers didn't have the kind of overpowering stuff that you associate with a perfect game. But now he was just six outs away.

In the ninth, pinch hitter Rex Hudler lead off and really clocked one. I thought it was going to be a gapper, but Rusty Greer, who was playing center, raced to his left and made a diving catch. It was the closest they came to getting a hit. Kenny got the second guy, and then the final out was a liner to center that Greer almost misjudged. It was one of those balls that took off as Rusty was coming in. He had to jump at the last second to snare it. Then we all went nuts and mobbed Kenny.

A perfect game is a rare commodity. And on this night Kenny became the first American League left-hander ever to throw one. I also felt justified because I was the first manager ever to give him an opportunity to start. When I looked up the stats I saw that he threw just 98 pitches, of which 64 were strikes—so he had total command. It was also special because we all knew it was our last home stand before the strike, and that the season would probably be killed. To be involved in a game of that magnitude under all the extenuating circumstances definitely makes it one of the greatest games I've ever seen.

October 3, 1995—Game 1, American League
Wild Card Versus Cleveland

The 1995 season was my first managing the Red Sox and we went wire to wire to win the American League East by seven full games over the Yankees. If you recall, 1994 was supposed to be the first year the wild card was used in the playoffs as both leagues split into three divisions, but the strike killed those plans. So in 1995 the wild-card round was officially introduced. It had been predetermined that the winner of the East would play the winner of the Central. Though we had the second best record in the American League, 86–58, we found ourselves playing the team with the best mark in baseball, the Cleveland Indians, who finished at 100–44, winning their division by thirty games. The way it's set up now, the team with the best record plays the wild-card team unless that team is in the same division. Had it been that way back then, we would have played the Seattle Mariners, who won the West, and the Indians would have played the Yankees.

The Indians had an all-star lineup with the likes of Kenny Lofton, Albert Belle, Carlos Baerga, Manny Ramirez, Jim Thome, Omar

Vizquel, Paul Sorrento, Eddie Murray, and Dave Winfield. They also had a good one-two at the top of their rotation with Dennis Martinez and Orel Hershiser, and a closer in Jose Mesa who was having an outstanding season. But we had played them very well all year, losing the season series by one game, 7–6. Even though the best-of-five was opening at Jacobs Field in Cleveland, technically we had home field advantage, since it was two on the road and three at home.

I had managed my first championship game at Albuquerque five years earlier and now I was the skipper in my first big-league playoff game. It was an intense experience, but not quite what you might think. I actually felt calm and cool.

Cleveland had right-hander Dennis Martinez going up against us that day and I had Roger Clemens on the hill. John Valentin got things started for us in the third when he slammed a two-run homer off Martinez to give us the early lead. It stayed that way until the sixth inning. Roger had been breezing along for the first five, and when he got the first two Cleveland hitters in the sixth it looked like more of the same. Then he walked their leadoff hitter, Omar Vizquel, on four pitches. Carlos Baerga was next, and with Vizquel running on his own, Baerga got around late on a 95-mile-per-hour fastball and hit a little chopper toward short. John Valentin had broken to cover second, and the ball rolled through as Vizquel raced around to third. Then up came Albert Belle, and he promptly hit one off the top of the wall in left for a two-run double. Tie game. But it wasn't tied for long. Belle went to third on an error and Eddie Murray followed with a single to right, giving Cleveland a 3–2 lead.

It stayed that way until the top of the eighth when Luis Alicea, my number nine hitter and a guy who had only a handful of homers in the regular season, hit a game-tying home run to right field. We were back in the game. But there was also a twenty-two-minute rain delay before we completed our half of the inning, and that's when I removed Clemens. He had thrown too many pitches to have to warm up all over again after that kind of delay. I used Rheal Cormier, Stan Belinda, and Mike Stanton to get us out of a jam in the eighth inning, and the score remained tied after nine. Now we went to extra innings.

Stanton held them at bay through the tenth and then in the top of the eleventh Tim Naehring, our third baseman, hit a home run down the left-field line to give us a 4–3 lead. All we needed now were three outs from our closer, Rick Aguilera, who had converted 20 of 21 saves since we got him in a midseason trade. Albert Belle led off for Cleveland. Aggie got him 0-2, a great pitcher's count, then threw his splitter. For one of the few times all year he hung it, and Belle crushed it way over the left-field wall to tie the game once more.

I remember Dan Duquette telling me that if Belle hit one to have the umpire check his bat because he had been caught corking one the year before. When I asked to have it checked, Belle just flexed his muscles at me and Indians manager Mike Hargrove began cursing me out. I really didn't want to win this way, but the GM had ordered it, so I complied. The umps would actually cut the bat open and find it was clean. It was raining when Aggie went back to work. Still, he got two outs, but also gave up a couple of base hits. The mound was wet, and he slipped on his last delivery, injuring a hamstring. I had to bring in Mike Maddux to get the third out.

We didn't score in our half of the twelfth, despite a leadoff double by Alicea, and then in the bottom of the inning the Indians quickly loaded the bases against Maddux with one out. With Eddie Murray coming up I went to a lefty, Zane Smith. Murray was something like 1-25 lifetime against Zane with a bunch of groundball outs. I told my infielders to go home on any grounder and to look to get two. Sure enough, he hit one to Tim Naehring at third. Tim made a nice play and got the force at home. Two outs. Smith then retired Jim Thome on a grounder to first to get us out of yet another inning. Now we moved into the thirteenth and I was hoping we could score, but we didn't. Once again the Tribe came up in a sudden-death situation.

After Smith got the first two hitters, catcher Tony Peña, who had replaced Sandy Alomar Jr. earlier in the game, was up. Smith ran the count to 3-0 and I was already thinking ahead to what I might do if he walked him. Tony would later tell me he had the take sign on, but when Smith threw a fastball down the middle Peña couldn't resist and hit a long home run over the left-field wall, giving them a 5–4, thirteen-inning victory and the all-important first game of the playoffs.

Sure, it was a devastating loss, but you try to get some sleep knowing that if you win the next day you tie it up and make it a two-of-three series. Unfortunately, it didn't happen. Orel Hershiser shut us out the next day and Charles Nagy nailed it down for them in the first game at Fenway, beating Tim Wakefield, 8–3, and we were done. But it was that first loss that set the tone for the series and led to a Tribe sweep. Still, the drama of that thirteen-inning loss, combined with the excitement of it being my first playoff game as a major-league manager, made it one of the greatest games I ever witnessed.

September 18, 1996—Roger Clemens Strikes Out 20 Detroit Tigers

This was simply a game where a great athlete did something very special. We were finishing the 1996 season and playing well, but while we still had a mathematical chance at making the wild card, it was a long shot at best. On this night, Roger Clemens took the mound against the Tigers in Detroit in a game we had to win.

Clemens had been Boston's ace for a decade, ever since his 24–4 breakout season of 1986. Among other things that year, he had fanned 20 Seattle Mariners to set a new one-game strikeout record. But as the 1996 season wore on, the perception in some circles was that Roger was no longer a dominant pitcher. GM Dan Duquette refused to speak with Roger, who was in his free-agent year, about a new contract until the season ended, and at this point a lot of us had an inkling that Roger wouldn't be back. In addition, when he took the mound against the Tigers that night, there were two pretty sacred Red Sox records within his reach. A victory would tie Roger with the legendary Cy Young with 192 career wins in Boston, and a shutout would pull him even with Young's Red Sox shutout mark of 38.

Before the game I told Roger the story about Koufax and Wills, where late in one game Maury took a ground ball and unexpectedly threw home to cut down a run when the Dodgers had a solid lead. When Sandy asked him why he had gone against sound baseball, which said to get the sure out at first, Maury told him that because the Dodgers rarely got Sandy many runs and that he always had to work so hard for his victories, he was determined to help him finish the shutout that night. I told Roger we would do the same thing for him if a similar circumstance arose.

Roger was throwing well and began putting zeroes up from the first inning on. He had exceptional command of the corners and his split was almost unhittable. Bill Haselman was catching Roger that night, and I remember when he came back after the seventh inning he said to me, "Hey, Skip. Do you realize that Rocket can break his own strikeout record? He's already got 16. If he fans five of the next six he'll wind up with 21." I was so involved with the game and admittedly thinking shutout that I had no idea he was striking out so many Tigers. But after Haselman informed us of the number, we all started counting.

By the eighth inning we had a 4–0 lead, so the game wasn't in doubt. Roger was still throwing hard, but you can't always get strike-outs at will, especially when some guys are just trying to put the bat on the ball. With two outs in the ninth, Roger had 19 strikeouts. When he faced Travis Fryman, who had already fanned three times, he was still throwing as hard as he had in the first inning. Then he got Fryman swinging for his twentieth strikeout of the game. He also got the win and the shutout, tying two long-standing Red Sox records and match-ing his 20-strikeout mark that he set against the Mariners in 1986.

What made this game even greater for me was that it was kind of a last hurrah for all of us. After the season Dan Duquette decided Roger was in "the twilight of his career" and let him go out on the free-agent market, effectively running him out of Boston. It was also my last season in Boston, and while I certainly have many great memories from my tenure there, that night in Detroit was like a last stand for both of us, and it will always be special.

November 4, 2001—Seventh Game of the World Series, Yankees and D-Backs

By 2001 I was working with Fox Sports and instead of managing base-ball games I was analyzing them. The World Series that year was be-tween the Arizona Diamondbacks and the New York Yankees. The Yanks had already won three World Series titles in a row and four of the last five. By contrast, the Diamondbacks were just in their fourth season of existence; but the new rules of the game made it easier for expansion teams to flourish, and the club had a tremendous one-two pitching tandem of Randy Johnson and Curt Schilling. With those two on top of their games, the D-Backs could beat anyone. It was a Series in which the D-Backs outplayed the Yankees and really should have wrapped it up in five games. But the New Yorkers kept coming back from the brink and then were themselves *this close* to winning it.

Arizona won Game 1 easily at Bank One Ballpark, riding a great performance by Schilling to a 9–1 victory. In Game 2, the Big Unit took the mound and was just as dominating. He threw a complete game shutout as the D-Backs won it, 4–0, to go up by two as the Series returned to Yankee Stadium. Then Joe Torre gave the ball to Roger Clemens, who was up against young Brian Anderson. Again the Yanks didn't hit much, but Clemens pitched brilliantly, and Mariano Rivera sealed the victory as the Yanks crept back with a 2–1 win.

In Game 4, D-Backs manager Bob Brenly decided to start Curt Schilling on three days' rest, and the big righty responded. He had his team leading 3–1 going into the last of the ninth when closer Byung-Hyun Kim came in for the final three outs—only he never got them. Paul O'Neill singled with one out. After Bernie Williams fanned, Tino Martinez drove Kim's first pitch over the right-center-field wall to tie the game. With Kim still pitching in the bottom of the tenth Derek Jeter came up with two outs and hit a walk-off homer into the right-field stands. The Yanks won it, 4–3, to even the Series.

Game 5 saw more of the same as Arizona started Miguel Batista and the Yanks couldn't hit him, either. Going to the bottom of the ninth Arizona held a 2–0 lead and Bob Brenly went back to Kim one more time. Jorge Posada opened the inning with a double, and then Kim retired the next two hitters before Scott Brosius took a Kim offering into the left-field seats for yet another two-out, game-tying ninth-inning homer. The Yanks then won it in the twelfth on a single by Alfonso Soriano. The Series was going back to Arizona with the Yanks on top, 3–2.

I'll never forget Curt Schilling grabbing hold of me on the field prior to Game 6 and saying, "I'm gonna pull a Namath. I'm going to guarantee that if we win Game 6 tonight, then we'll win Game 7 tomorrow."

He was, of course, referring to New York Jets quarterback Joe Namath guaranteeing a win over the heavily favored Baltimore Colts in Super Bowl III way back in 1969 . . . and then pulling it off. Game 6 was over before it began. By the end of three innings the D-Backs had a 12–0 lead, and Johnson cruised to a 15–2 victory, setting up a Game 7 with Schilling, on three days' rest, going up against Roger Clemens who, at age thirty-nine, was the oldest Game 7 starter in baseball history.

This one began as a classic pitchers' duel. Both veteran aces matched serves for five scoreless innings. Then in the bottom of the sixth the D-Backs broke through for a run, but the Yanks tied it quickly in the top of the seventh. In the eighth Alfonso Soriano led off and took an 0-2 pitch deep to give the Yankees a 2–1 lead. Schilling had pitched well, but didn't finish the inning. With one out, after David Justice singled, Miguel Batista came in. He got the second out, and then Brenly surprised everyone. He brought Game 6 starter Randy Johnson in to close out the inning, which he did.

Before the bottom of the eighth there was a debate in the Yankee dugout between Joe Torre and bench coach Don Zimmer over whether to bring closer Mariano Rivera in to pitch the eighth inning. Torre finally agreed with Zimmer, and Mariano rewarded his manager by striking out the side in the eighth.

Then veteran Mark Grace gave Diamondback fans some hope when he opened the ninth with a single to center. Next, Damian Miller laid down a bunt and the athletic, sure-fielding Rivera pounced on it. He whirled and fired toward second, but his throw was wide and pulled Jeter off the bag. It was an error as both runners were safe. This would prove the key play in the game. The next hitter, Jay Bell, also bunted, but this time Rivera made a fine play, throwing out pinch runner David Dellucci at third. From my spot alongside the dugout I could see the tension in all the Yankee players. They were so close to celebrating, had the guy they wanted on the mound, but it wasn't over yet.

Moments later the air was suddenly out of them as Tony Womack lined a double down the right-field line to tie the score. Rivera then hit

Craig Counsell with a pitch to load the bases, which brought Luis Gonzalez to the plate. On an 0-1 pitch Rivera threw his devastating cutter, but the southpaw-swinging Gonzalez got enough of it to bloop a soft fly over the drawn-in infield. Bell scored and the D-Backs began to celebrate. They had won it.

This was a great game in an unforgettable World Series that featured late-inning home runs and one heart-stopping finish after another. It was simply great theater filled with high drama.

July 1, 2004—Yankees and Red Sox Go Thirteen Wild Innings

Whenever the Yankees meet the Red Sox, a great game can happen. No matter when these old rivals clash the atmosphere is intense, and even a meaningless game during August can feel like the playoffs. It doesn't matter if they're playing at Yankee Stadium or Fenway Park. The names and players may change, but these two teams now have arguably the most intense rivalry in all sports. I always loved high-intensity matchups and thus totally enjoyed managing games against the Yankees because they always kept you focused.

The Sox had swept the Yankees in April of 2004, jumping out to an early lead in the American League East. But, as so often happens, the roles reversed and by the time the Sox traveled to New York to play the Yanks at the outset of July, the Bombers were firmly entrenched in first with the Red Sox chasing them once more. Boston had Pedro Martinez on the mound and it didn't take long for emotions to rise. In the Yankee first, Gary Sheffield suddenly backed out of the box just as Pedro began his windup. That didn't sit well with the volatile right-hander and his next pitch hit Sheffield squarely in the left arm. The two had words as Sheffield went to first. But the inning ended quietly as the Yanks failed to score. The Yankees had rookie left-hander Brad Halsey starting, and he kept the Red Sox at bay for five-plus innings. The Yanks had scored three runs on homers by Tony Clark and Jorge Posada, while the Sox got two on a Manny Ramirez blast. So the Yanks had a 3–2 lead when Boston tied the game in the sixth as Pokey Reese hit into a double play, allowing a run to score.

From that point the game remained scoreless as the Yanks failed to capitalize on several golden opportunities in the ninth and tenth innings. Then two defensive plays suddenly elevated the game to the realm of greatness. The first came in the top of the eleventh.

Mariano Rivera was struggling in his second inning of work and the Sox loaded the bases with none out. Kevin Millar slammed one down the third-base line. If it got through and went into the corner it could clear the bases. But A-Rod made a quick move to his right, backhanded the ball, stepped on third for the force. Then, with one knee on the ground and pinch runner Gabe Kapler between him and catcher Jorge Posada, A-Rod made the only throw he could, looping the ball over Kapler's right shoulder. Posada grabbed it and made the tag to complete the double play and prevent the go-ahead run from scoring. Rivera got the next hitter and the game continued tied.

In the top of the twelfth the Red Sox were threatening again. With two out and two on, pinch hitter Trot Nixon lofted a pop behind third. Left fielder Ruben Sierra couldn't reach it, nor could A-Rod. But Derek Jeter came racing over from short, caught the ball going full speed about a foot inside the foul line, then crossed the line and flew headfirst into the stands . . . still clutching the ball. The Yankee captain emerged with a cut high on his cheekbone and another on his chin, and was helped from the field as the crowd went wild. Now this was a game of unbelievable intensity. As I said before, players rise to the occasion in games like this, often doing things by instinct and not worrying about the consequences.

Then in the thirteenth it looked as if it was over. Manny Ramirez hit his second homer of the game, this one off reliever Tanyon Sturtze, and the Red Sox took a 4–3 lead. But the Yanks still had one more at bat. With Curtis Leskanic on the mound, Ruben Sierra kept the game alive with a two-out single. Miguel Cairo then drove him home with a clutch double, tying the game, as the large crowd went wild once more. Now backup catcher John Flaherty came up as a pinch hitter, and he took Leskanic's pitch toward the left-field corner, out of the reach of Manny Ramirez. It bounced into the stands for a ground-rule double and Cairo came home with the winning run.

This one was an instant classic, the kind of game that defines the beauty of baseball. It was a midseason game that became great not only because of the evolving circumstances on the field, but also because of the way individuals rose to the occasion time and again, making it every bit as compelling as a playoff or World Series contest. Even the managers were totally into it, making strategic moves as if it were a chess game, trying to stay one step ahead of the guy in the other dugout. Taking all these factors into consideration, this was simply one of the very best I've ever seen.

All these games (and the greatest players chronicled in the book) are evidence of why the sport captures the imagination of so many fans. Heck, there's a reason they call it the national pastime. But that's the beauty of baseball; once the umpire shouts, "Play ball!" it's still the greatest game in the world, a game that has survived for more than a hundred years and, despite a few bumps in the road, will never be ruined, because the players, coaches, and managers still love it and will always make it come alive in the place where it belongs—on the field.

Epilogue

Like all sports, baseball is constantly changing and evolving, and there have always been problems or controversies that needed to be dealt with in one way or another. The Black Sox Scandal will never be forgotten despite the fact that it happened more than eighty years ago. I lived through the marijuana and cocaine eras in the late 1970s and early 1980s, and felt strongly back then that users of these so-called recreational drugs didn't belong in baseball and needed to be eliminated at both the major- and minor-league levels. But I never dreamed that another illegal substance—anabolic steroids—would result in a handful of baseball's biggest stars and top executives being subpoenaed to testify before the House Government Reform Committee. But that's exactly what happened in March 2005, bringing baseball's now-exposed steroid problem squarely in front of Congress as well as the American public. It was certainly not one of the game's finest hours.

Steroids, of course, have been an open secret ever since the BALCO investigation, which is mentioned in the opening chapter of the book. What I think prompted Congress to become involved was the publication of Jose Canseco's tell-all book, *Juiced*. Canseco, of course, has now admitted his own steroid use, but in the book he said that the problem was widespread and he also implicated others, most notably Mark McGwire.

McGwire, Sammy Sosa, Rafael Palmeiro, Frank Thomas, and Curt Schilling joined Canseco to answer questions from the committee. Schilling and Thomas were called because they have long been outspoken in their desire to rid steroids from the game. Both Sosa and

Palmeiro, implicated indirectly by Canseco, denied having ever used performance-enhancing drugs, while McGwire didn't help his reputation by, in effect, taking the Fifth and refusing to answer questions or comment on anything from the past.

Baseball officials, including commissioner Bud Selig and players union head Donald Fehr, were subject to even more intense grilling. Members of the congressional committee seemed to think the new testing guidelines and the ensuing penalties weren't severe enough. The committee adjourned the one-day hearings and baseball and performance-enhancing drugs again made the front pages everywhere—not exactly the place the national pastime should be, at least not for these reasons.

Because the hearings and resulting fallout occurred after the main text for this book had been completed, I thought I would use these final pages to summarize my thoughts about this difficult time in baseball. People will undoubtedly ask why I didn't suspect some of my players of using performance-enhancing drugs when I took over the Texas Rangers in 1993. After all, Jose Canseco played for me in Texas, and then again in Boston, and I've spoken of him often in the book. But you've got to remember that there wasn't much known about steroid use back then. In fact, steroids weren't deemed illegal until 1991 and by that time players on the whole were already growing bigger and stronger. In addition, there was very little information being shared about other possible signs of steroid use and when you're not on the lookout for tell-tale signs, odds are you simply won't see them. Someone abusing alcohol, marijuana, or cocaine will tip their hand because their performance will eventually suffer. But steroids are considered performance enhancers, so it's hard to be suspicious of someone who's performing at a higher level. As you can see, one and one doesn't always equal two. Look at it this way, even when Mark McGwire and Sammy Sosa blew away Roger Maris's home run record in 1998, it was portrayed everywhere as two sluggers going blow for blow. It was a totally feel-good story and a real positive time for baseball. It was not a story that played out under the suspicious cloak of possible steroid use. In effect, it took years for the full story to emerge.

Now the time has come to clean up this mess. More clean players must continue to speak out and push for the total elimination of these substances. And the Players' Association, which has always gone the extra mile to protect the player from any intrusion into his privacy, must cooperate fully. Education about the dangers of these substances has to be widespread and intense, right down through the college and high school levels. Perhaps we even need signs in every big-league clubhouse similar to the ones now warning against baseball's oldest and biggest taboo—gambling. The two signs should be posted side by side and the threat of punishment a daily reminder. Baseball should also launch its own marketing program warning young players against using steroids, maybe even coming up with a catch phrase similar to the Just Say No campaign on drugs during the 1980s.

Along these same lines, there's something else that must be addressed. The steroid story has pushed the use of another popular substance into the background, and baseball has never fully addressed it. That's the use of amphetamines by players at all levels of the game. I talked about players using "greenies" when I was in the minors in the late 1970s and early 1980s, and the use of such pills has never fully gone away. In their own way, greenies are also a performance enhancer and can be dangerously addictive. They, too, should be part of a new testing program. Perhaps the penalties for their use shouldn't be quite as severe as for steroids, but players should be prohibited from using them as well.

One of the gripes the congressional committee had was with the proposed penalties for steroid use, saying that the penalties were too lenient and not fully defined. As of this writing, a first offender will miss just ten days without pay. That bothered committee members. So did the five-strikes-and-you're-out policy that the congressmen also felt was not severe enough. The player is simply given too many chances and I tend to agree. The message baseball sends must be loud and clear. I would prefer to see a three-strikes-and-you're-out policy, closer to the one mentioned by Senator Jim Bunning, a Hall of Fame pitcher. I don't think too many players would be willing to risk violating the policy if first-time offenders were suspended for thirty days, second-time offenders for one full year, and third-time offenders were treated the same way as those caught gambling on the game—gone for life.

As for the home run records that have been set since the mid-1990s, I think they have to stand. It wouldn't be right to strike records set four, five, six, or seven years ago because no one can prove definitively that these records might have been accomplished with the help of performance-enhancing drugs. As a result of the recent revelations that have come to light, some people want to give the single-season home run record back to Roger Maris. Individual fans will have to draw their own conclusions, but right or wrong the official record books won't change.

Baseball, however, now has the responsibility to make sure the integrity of the game is maintained. The use of performance-enhancing substances has to end now. It's no longer a secret. Congress has threatened to do the job if baseball won't, and that should be the final wake-up call.

Anyone who has read the book to this point will appreciate my passion for the game, so it should not come as a surprise that I feel the way I do. I have always loved baseball in its purest form. That's how I played and, as a manager, that's always how I expected my teams to play. And now, as a broadcaster, that's the kind of game I want to see on the field.

Major leaguers are the best players in the world. They have been for more than a hundred years. The top players have always been special, and that is why people remember Cobb, Mathewson, Ruth, Williams, Musial, DiMaggio, Feller, Mays, Koufax, Clemente, Aaron, Gibson, and the rest. Those who have admitted, or are strongly suspected of, steroid use won't be remembered in quite the same way. As I said in the opening pages of this book, ballplayers are always looking for an edge. Steroids, however, are simply not the kind of edge anyone needs. Hopefully, the problem will now be eradicated and baseball can stay out on the field where it belongs and not have to appear in the halls of Congress ever again.